The
Accidental
Landlord

The
Accidental
Landlord

Danielle Babb, Ph.D., MBA

ALPHA

A member of Penguin Group (USA) Inc.

This book is dedicated to my nephew, Zachary, who reminds me every time I see him that life is so much more important than work will ever deem it.

ALPHA BOOKS

Published by the Penguin Group

Penguin Group (USA) Inc., 375 Hudson Street, New York, New York 10014, USA

Penguin Group (Canada), 90 Eglinton Avenue East, Suite 700, Toronto, Ontario M4P 2Y3, Canada (a division of Pearson Penguin Canada Inc.)

Penguin Books Ltd., 80 Strand, London WC2R 0RL, England

Penguin Ireland, 25 St. Stephen's Green, Dublin 2, Ireland (a division of Penguin Books Ltd.)

Penguin Group (Australia), 250 Camberwell Road, Camberwell, Victoria 3124, Australia (a division of Pearson Australia Group Pty. Ltd.)

Penguin Books India Pvt. Ltd., 11 Community Centre, Panchsheel Park, New Delhi—110 017, India

Penguin Group (NZ), 67 Apollo Drive, Rosedale, North Shore, Auckland 1311, New Zealand (a division of Pearson New Zealand Ltd.)

Penguin Books (South Africa) (Pty.) Ltd., 24 Sturdee Avenue, Rosebank, Johannesburg 2196, South Africa

Penguin Books Ltd., Registered Offices: 80 Strand, London WC2R 0RL, England

Copyright © 2008 by Danielle Babb

International Standard Book Number: 978-1-59257-807-8
Library of Congress Catalog Card Number: 2008924721

10 09 08   8 7 6 5 4 3 2 1

Interpretation of the printing code: The rightmost number of the first series of numbers is the year of the book's printing; the rightmost number of the second series of numbers is the number of the book's printing. For example, a printing code of 08-1 shows that the first printing occurred in 2008.

Printed in the United States of America

Most Alpha books are available at special quantity discounts for bulk purchases for sales promotions, premiums, fund-raising, or educational use. Special books, or book excerpts, can also be created to fit specific needs.

For details, write: Special Markets, Alpha Books, 375 Hudson Street, New York, NY 10014.

Contents

Appendixes

Dear Potential Landlord,

Chances are you're browsing through this book because you're finding yourself in a peculiar situation due to the tightening of the housing market over the past couple of years and you need to rent your home. I have been in this position myself and have had many good and bad experiences that I will share with you throughout this book. I have also partnered with a fantastic company, The Landlord Protection Agency, which you can find out more about by visiting my website at www.accidentallandlordbook.com. Here you will also find other tools to support your efforts!

I know this can be an intimidating and difficult time, but the rewards of "landlording" can be exhilarating and financially beneficial. I do my best in this book to walk you through not only the steps, but also the potential pitfalls you might face.

As a California-licensed real estate professional with a Ph.D. in technology, my goal is to leverage technology in every way possible to make our lives easier, particularly as investors and real estate experts. I talk a lot about ways you can leverage the Internet to save yourself headaches and hassles. I'm also a professor and the author of other books on real estate, including *Commissions at Risk*, *Finding Foreclosures*, and *Real Estate v2.0*. I have a professional website you can browse to get to know me as an author at www.drdaniellebabb.com. I look forward to this journey with you and welcome any comments, feedback, or questions anytime!

Best to you,

Dani Babb, Ph.D., MBA

Foreword

Have you ever heard of anyone becoming a landlord by "accident"? In the past, most people became landlords on purpose, by purchasing investment property to rent for profit and appreciation. Market conditions are now turning more and more would-be sellers into landlords. In most cases, these are people who aren't prepared to be landlords and haven't the slightest idea of how to properly manage a rental property. Without knowledge of landlord protection, you as a landlord are in big trouble!

The book you are holding is an excellent guide on how to make managing a rental property as easy as possible, whether you are an "accidental landlord" or an experienced real estate professional. In it, Danielle Babb presents to you in simple terms some of the finest proven techniques and forms used by professional landlords across the United States and Canada. In addition, *The Accidental Landlord* is full of timesaving and moneymaking ideas. She provides you with helpful Internet sources to make your experience as a landlord easy and even fun.

Danielle is a real estate investor and landlord herself who understands firsthand what it takes to manage tenants. After only a few conversations, I soon realized that she and I share much of the same philosophy concerning real estate investing and landlording. She has thoroughly impressed me with her knowledge and advice in real estate analysis and technology. She's also a published author of five excellent books *(this one included)* on real estate and cutting-edge business-enhancing technology. Her credentials as a Ph.D. and national TV real estate expert make her an excellent source of reliable information and advice.

As a real estate broker and investor for more than 25 years, I've always been involved with residential rentals. I used to think that to be a successful real estate investor, I had to buy as many properties as possible. Sounds good, right? Well, at first I was not an educated landlord, so I learned about tenants the hard way. Tenants can destroy not only your home, but your life as well if you let them! My hard-learned lessons and successes as a landlord led me to create the popular website The Landlord Protection Agency© (www.theLPA.com).

I've found the best lessons are usually the most painful ones, but with Danielle Babb pointing you in the right direction, you can save a lot of time, money, and pain by taking the easy steps of managing your investment correctly and more efficiently.

You are about to read a very special book by a very special person. If you are a landlord or expect to be one, you should own this book. Enjoy it!

John Nuzzolese

President of The Landlord Protection Agency©

Introduction

A strange phenomenon has bewildered economists and changed the way home-owners look at the places they call home. It used to be a widely held belief that our homes were a solid investment, one that would appreciate at a modest pace of 8 percent to 12 percent per year in good markets and slightly lower in less-than-stellar economies, but ultimately when we retired we'd have a nest egg in our homes. Even better, we'd get to create a life in this place called home—the center of our family life, a refuge from our hectic work lives.

All sorts of unexpected and reality-changing things have happened in the home real estate market. Throughout the late 1990s and early 2000s, real estate was *the* golden investment—the one thing that was a "sure bet" because it was tangible with limited land and could provide greater and faster returns than a flailing and unstable stock market. Everyday investors were troubled by what they saw after the "tech bubble burst" on the NASDAQ after the '90s and began looking for more surefire and stable investments. Having forgotten the trouble of the early 1990s, they chose real estate.

Some people moved their families to better neighborhoods with better schools. Some who were less risk adverse took out the sudden instant equity and purchased other homes with the money—I am one of those myself. Many of us moved up into bigger, better homes, living the American dream. Some of us used our homes to finance other houses, either getting caught up in the buying frenzy ourselves or becoming an unintended victim of others' speculating.

Some of us took out the money in our homes and invested it in Dow stocks that were severely off of record highs after the terrorist attacks of 9/11. Others looked at their dwindling 401(k) dollars and instead invested in homes that appreciated in the double-digits year after year in several markets—most notably, Arizona, Nevada, the Northeast, South Florida, and the West Coast. "There's only so much land" was a common mantra I consistently heard—I preached this to my family and friends myself and bought up houses like penny stocks with low down payments, adjustable or pay option adjustable-rate mortgages (ARMs), and even negative amortization loans. A feeling of invincibility that now reminds me of my tech-boom-era day-trading days in the mid-90s soon came to bite many of us.

Another fuel to this greatly changed market? As hedge funds looked for better investments than those of the stock market, they were willing to take on riskier securities—primarily those mortgage-backed securities we hear so much of today that combined A-rated paper (mortgages given to those with good credit and a history of paying their bills) with lower-rated credit (even D-rated paper, the rating assigned to those most likely to default). Due to this incredible demand for all things mortgage-backed, lenders began to practice creative lending, requiring low down payments, allowing those with poor credit to obtain financing, and allowing individuals to just simply "state their income" (the so-called stated income loans), which in turn led to little personal investment in the home.

For most, this was a welcome blessing and homes are now occupied by families who are prosperously thriving in them. For many others, they need to move but can't afford to pay the bank; they find themselves owing more than their home is worth after the "market bubble burst."

In the past, when we bought a home with 15 percent or 20 percent down, we had a very serious stake in the home; the lender wasn't the only one at risk. In the 2000s, lenders took on far more risk. Appraisers weren't able to appraise property fast enough to keep up with prices that in some markets literally went up thousands each week.

Banks began offering loans to those who'd never had the option of homeownership before—individuals with bankruptcies, numerous foreclosures, and a history of not paying bills. One of my own family members was able to secure three mortgages during the early 2000s, despite a history of bankruptcy and foreclosure—all with no money down. Many Americans jumped at the chance, and the home boom grew bigger. Creative loan options allowed homeowners to add what they weren't qualified to pay to the principal balance of their home loans (as the previously stated negative amortization loans), but many were unaware (though it was thoroughly documented on the loan papers) that at some point, a loan-to-value cap would require them to pay the full payment. Nor did many realize that their "introductory rate" would actually increase, in some cases doubling or tripling their payments by 2007 or 2009. This led to a desperate attempt by many to move into more affordable housing or make more money by moving (again requiring a home sale), and logically following, a steep increase in home inventory occurred. By the summer of 2007, inventory for resale homes was at ten months' worth and new-home inventory was at eight months'—historic levels since organizations began tracking them.

How Did We Get Here?

Let's take a step back to understand another important fundamental. In late 2004, the Federal Reserve, responsible for monetary policy in the United States, began doing something no one believed could happen during the post-9/11 recovery (though most of us admit we had no clue how long the recovery would take, so we therefore had no clue when the Fed would begin raising interest rates). It raised the federal reserve funds rate, and interest rates on mortgages therefore began to climb. Suddenly rates were resetting on homeowners, and for many (yours truly included)— the only thing that allowed us to make our mortgage payments was the payment cap of 5 percent to 9 percent per year, which expires after 1 to 7 years, depending on your loan. Writing this book in the winter of 2007, I can tell you that the worst is yet to come. Many millions of homeowners who are in the default stage are yet to hit foreclosure; without intervention, they will lose their homes.

So, what happens when homeowners see their homes worth $500,000 one year and their neighbors selling theirs for $400,000 the next? This may well have happened to you. If you still have equity, you might choose to leave and buy a bigger home for fewer dollars—essentially upgrading while the getting is still good. This is a buyer's market if there has ever been one in my lifetime—or in my parents'. Foreclosures are at an all-time high, offering good deals for those who need to get into this market. However, many homeowners need to move and either still believe they can get $500,000 or don't have the equity left to sell for $400,000 and still pay their debts and obligations, much less put a down payment on a new home. Some just simply cannot afford the mortgage and need to rent to someone who can pay until they are back on their feet or interest rates allow for a refinance that makes their home affordable again.

Still yet, you might be facing other concerns or issues. Job changes are a common reason people move. This can be a relatively short move within the same state or a major move to another state. Unfortunately, many of you might have taken home equity lines of credit (HELOCs) and second mortgages on your homes to pay off debt, take lavish vacations, or even purchase additional property with a euphoric ignorance that the "market could never go down." A sudden job change for you at the same time your home value drops 20 percent or more in 1 year can leave you with a sense of disbelief and unwillingness to let your home "go" for such a "cheap price" (not considering the 5-straight-year price increase!). This is mostly a psychological phenomenon, but for many of you, you might have taken equity up to 95 percent or 100 percent of the value, and when the value disappeared, you were forced to move but literally were unable to because you couldn't pay off your primary and secondary debt obligations on the home. Many of you perhaps even have third mortgages that have to be paid.

Retirement is another reason people are forced to move. Some of you might have retired and suddenly found yourselves living on nest eggs that are netting you less monthly income than you had hoped or planned for, or you want to move closer to family or retire in a warmer climate. The Sun Belt states are common places to move—Nevada, Arizona, California, and Florida. Many retiring boomers have suddenly found themselves with hundreds of thousands of dollars less than they'd expected, and many have chosen to rent their homes and wait for the market to rebound. You may well be in this category.

Be careful using real estate for retirement income if your retirement date is less than ten years away. So far since we have been tracking stats, real estate has never lost value over a ten-year period, but you don't want to wage your retirement on it if you're looking to start fishing within a few years!

Health issues are listed among the top three reasons for bankruptcy in this country, and they certainly are cause for financial distress—including the inability to pay for a mortgage. Treatments for some diseases are very costly and might not be covered by insurance, and homeowners are forced to borrow money until there is nothing left. You might have been forced to decide between doctors and mortgages—first borrowing against equity in your homes, cars, and even your "fallback savings" or retirement and 401(k)s. This is understandable but dangerous, as the fall of the market left many people with health issues needing to move to be closer to better doctors or to reduce their expenses but incapable of selling their homes.

Yet still others see the rental market increasing and the demand growing and feel that renting their homes will be profitable. There has been an increase in rental demands in our nation—the higher home prices climbed, the less affordable purchasing a home became. A lot of people turned to renting as an alternative to home buying for a variety of reasons: lower costs, the ability to move easily, and the number of great rentals on the market as speculators and investors bought brand-new properties only to put them on the rental market within days of taking ownership! There continues to be an increase in demands for rentals due to high foreclosure rates and a tightening of the credit market, so if you do choose to rent your home, you should have no shortage of potential renters! It's always tough to decide when to buy or rent, and many websites and online calculators (and plenty of lenders) will try to help you make that decision. Be as unbiased as you can when looking at the numbers, and try to make a rational decision that works best for you.

Any one of these situations could be the one you are in, and the reason you picked up this book. You're already contemplating the potential of renting your home. You have a few options. You might decide to take the remaining equity out of your home and move anyway, using this equity as your down payment while keeping your home on the market and not renting it. This is possible if you can live on the extra equity in the home for at least the average inventory period (as noted earlier, ten months for resale homes) and still pay your bills at the same time you are paying two mortgages. This leaves your resale home vacant but allows you to move. This might even entice some buyers because the home appears move-in ready (and it is). This might not be an option for many of you.

Many individuals needing to move have simply chosen to put their homes up for rent and ride out the market. You might be contemplating this yourself. This is a tactic investors have been using since the initial decline in prices, and it is now becoming common practice for everyday homeowners. In my small community of roughly 80 houses, I've seen 10 for sale in the past six months and 4 for rent. That ratio was unheard of six months ago, particularly in this community that has regularly sustained high sale prices and low inventory (not the case today).

So, what happens if you need to rent your home and ride out the market? What if you need to move to another part of the state or country or even retire, yet you cannot afford to sell your home in this market? What if you don't want to sell your house for less than you paid for it despite the real estate loss on your taxes? I was in that exact predicament in 2004 and again in 2007. As a real estate investor, I knew what to do to keep myself out of foreclosure, but for millions of Americans facing the same decision, the options are unclear or confusing. This book will fill that gap—within the first two chapters you will know whether it's financially feasible to rent your home and, if it is, whether you have the stomach for it.

Another option is to take the equity out of the house you own (assuming there is any and it's sufficient as a down payment for the other home you're trying to buy), buy the other house to take advantage of the buyer's market we see today and will see for awhile to come, and rent the other house to wait for the market to rebound. For many, including myself, this is the best solution. You essentially get two fantastic investments—one that was purchased at what I believe is the bottom of the market (the new home) and one you can wait it out with (your rented home). You might even decide to rent your home and take advantage of investors offering tremendous rental incentives and rent for awhile, particularly if your goal is to cut back on expenses (be mindful of tax advantages you are foregoing, however!). In the future, I firmly believe renting your home and buying others in this incredible market is the road to wealth.

How This Book Can Help

In this book I will show you step-by-step how to find and keep a good renter, what to do when questions come up, which options to offer to those leasing your property, and what to do in case you run into issues. It will help you use technology to fill in the gaps and allow you to become an *accidental landlord*. I'm offering support for this book on my website at www.drdaniellebabb.com and look forward to working with you! You can also find a special deal in the appendixes from the Landlord Protection Agency!

I have also conducted a firsthand survey of landlords across the nation and have included numerous sidebars throughout the book called "Talk from the Trenches." This information is quoted or analyzed directly from the survey, to give you a glimpse into what many landlords had to say from the survey. The survey numbered in the hundreds of responses and provides great insight into what is happening out there in the world of landlording.

In addition, boxed sidebars throughout the book provide you with beneficial information or a further explanation of the topic at hand and survey results.

In my survey of landlords, 58 percent of individuals who responded wanted to use their home as an investment. The remaining 42 percent had various intentions; they needed to move fast due to job changes, had to handle retirement concerns, or were just flat out unable to sell and saw this as a viable alternative.

In addition, I found that 17 percent of landlords were waiting for the market to rebound in price, 8 percent needed to move quickly and weren't able to move fast enough, 4 percent wanted to avoid capital gains taxes, 21 percent felt their property would net good cash flow, 20 percent felt rentals were strong in their area, and 7 percent owed more on their houses than they were worth.

Still yet, about 25 percent of respondents rented one house at some point due to a military move. This total of 102 percent reflects at least one individual that selected more than one category.

Acknowledgments

My husband and the love of my life, Matt. Thanks for your sacrifices.

My friends Alex, Arlene, Cheryl Ann, and Shane for love, support, and acceptance.

To my family for their encouragement.

My absolutely wonderful, terrific agent, Bob Diforio.

To Peg and Julia at Booth Media Group for the hard work they put in on my behalf.

To Post Modern and Jay Antonos, for their coaching, direction, and friendship.

Last but most definitely not least, to John at the LPA—his expertise, generosity, kindness, and thoroughness make for a terrific partner and a highly recommended business model!

1

The Costs Associated with Renting Your Home

In the book's introduction I talked about many of the reasons the real estate market changed and the impact it has had—and continues to have—on homeowners. You may have a couple reasons for trying to determine whether renting your home makes sense. Perhaps you cannot afford your newly reset mortgage, you need to move and don't want to settle for less than you paid for your home (or than you owe, which might be more than you paid), you aren't sure you'll like your new home, or you need to move to reduce your costs in general. Regardless the reason, you face the tough decision of whether to rent your home.

A lot of costs are involved with owning a property that you rent. Some are obvious; some aren't—it's important to recognize them all.

Homeowner's Associations and Condo/Co-op Boards

Even before you start to consider the costs of renting your home, you need to find out whether you are allowed to rent. Yes, *allowed!* I know, it is your property—but sometimes homeowner's associations (HOAs) highly discourage you from having renters. They may make it very difficult for you and send in numerous complaints about your tenants. They might have other restrictions, too, such as renting is allowed, but displaying a sign is not. These are referred to as Covenants, Conditions, and Restrictions (CC&Rs). HOAs have a lot of power in many states, so it's vital that you check with your HOA about the rules of renting your home. They can also put liens on your home if you break the rules and don't pay their sometimes hefty fines.

Most co-ops and condos allow you to freely rent or sublease your place. But, some have more significant restrictions that you need to be aware of. Older buildings or those that tend to fall in rent control ordinances often have a maximum percentage of units that can be rented out. If you try to rent when the place is technically "maxed out," you may be out of luck. Some have other rules, for example, there is a building in San Francisco famous for only allowing the home to be rented out for one year during the entire time you own it!

So what is the reason for these caps? Well co-ops often think they're doing their fellow owners a favor by capping the number of rentals in a unit. High percentages of rentals, in general, can make it difficult to sell a unit or refinance. They can also make it difficult for the co-op to refinance or take out loans against the property. But, unfortunately, if you own one of these and need to rent it out, it can really wreak havoc on you in the future. Some co-op boards have created opportunities for those owners facing financially difficult times to be able to rent, while others have just loosened the rules altogether. New York City has about 8,000 co-op buildings; half of them are in Manhattan; and about 15 percent of those are rented out. So it is possible, but it can be difficult. Some owners have gotten around the rules by subletting rather than leasing; but many boards have responded, concerned about overall appeal of the building, by disallowing subletting altogether. Overall it is a stern warning! Be careful!

If you live in an area with an association, you may expect that the new tenant will begin paying the association fee. The standard rule is that anything that can have a lien placed on your home should be and generally is paid by the homeowner. This includes taxes, insurance, and association fees. If you have association fees, expect to continue paying them. This is not a cost the tenant generally incurs, and even if he agrees to pay them, do you really want to run the risk of the tenant not paying and having a lien put on your home or accruing hefty fines?

In the forms section of the book, you will note in any lease agreement what you will pay and what the tenant will pay. You should not include HOA fees as part of the tenant's responsibility. One thing you can do though is add it to the price, in general. You may be unable to do that because of competitiveness in the area, but if your HOA dues are $75 per quarter, you could increase rent by $25 per month to offset your costs. Just be sure you pay the bill yourself! Provide your tenants with copies of the CC&Rs, too, so they are aware of the rules. I recently was fined $50 because my tenant left cooking oil on the top of the fence after a barbeque. If the tenant causes you to be fined, you can add it to their rent the next month in the form of a notice of additional rent due letter, which is due the next month.

I've been fined when my tenants have left their trash cans out too long—certainly an unwelcome surprise in the mail. Also keep in mind that many associations don't allow "for rent" signs in the yard, so check with your association because this can change how difficult it is for you to rent your home.

Homeowner's and Renter's Insurance

As a homeowner, you know you have to buy insurance. When you make the decision to rent your home, the type of policy you must carry on the home changes. I explain this in more thorough detail in Chapter 10 about managing your money, but for now, know that your insurance will require changes. You go from needing a homeowner's policy to a landlord policy. In some areas, this actually lowers your payments, but in many cases it raises them. Run estimates with your insurance expert before you make the decision.

Keep in mind that the insurance you obtain as a landlord no longer covers the personal contents of the home. To cover the tenant's belongings, the tenant will need to obtain her own renter's insurance. Some tenants might refuse to pay for rental insurance, which is their choice. If you make having renter's insurance a stipulation in the rental agreement (and you should), you also might find yourself with a great tenant who wants you to cover her rental insurance costs. I personally would never do this, but if the rental market is tight, you might consider it.

Umbrella Policies

Although it's rare, an occasional tenant will want to sue you, thinking you are Mr. or Ms. Big Bucks and that you can "afford to pay them" if they burned themselves on that hot water because your water heater was set too high. For this reason, I always recommend an umbrella policy.

Umbrella policies are for large amounts; usually $1 million dollars or more. Say you have a $2 million umbrella policy in your name. You list with the insurance company all of the properties you own. If you were to be sued for more than the amount your landlord property insurance covers (or for a reason other than what your landlord insurance would generally cover), the umbrella policy will usually kick in. This provides you general protection and helps ensure that an unhappy tenant doesn't get their hands on the equity in another home you own. This helps insure you against personal loss, and is something I recommend for anyone with two or more properties.

> You can get an umbrella policy that covers multiple properties that you own. This can cost anywhere from $500 to $5,000 per year depending on your risk level and insurance amounts, the number of properties you own, and a variety of other factors that make up your insurance risk level. Check out PersonalUmbrella.com or consult your insurance agent.

Property Tax

You've been paying property taxes all along whether through an impound account with your lender or on your own. Many landlords don't realize, though, that these costs will continue and instead assume that the renter will take on many of the costs they have been paying. This is not the case. The tenant is paying for the use of your dwelling and nothing more.

Property taxes fall into that "can put a lien on the home" category! You—not the tenant—are required to pay property taxes. Again, even if the tenant agrees, the serious consequences that can result if the tenant doesn't pay those taxes are so severe that it isn't worth the risk. You must plan to continue paying your property taxes yourself and plan for any potential increase if that has been the trend in your area or if your county is considering a tax increase. Also falling into the lien category are mechanics liens. Promptly pay any contractors; the tenants should not be paying this directly because this might cause problems later down the road.

Property Depreciation

As you know by now, you always run the risk of your property being worth less in three, five, or ten years (whatever your goal time is) than it is today. While it's unlikely given the market history, markets are also unpredictable and a changing economy makes even the savviest economists worry.

You run the risk of your property being worth less due to supply and demand, but you might in fact cause depreciation simply by renting your home. In communities where most of the homes are owned by individuals and families who live in the homes, your neighbors might not be happy that you're choosing to rent your home.

In general, tenants don't take care of a property as well as a homeowner does; this stigma associated with renters is well-founded and tends to create a downward cycle of prices. In areas where lots of homeowners have had to rent, it can lead to an overall depreciation in prices for the entire neighborhood, which could ultimately mean your property is worth less, too. (It can also make your neighbors very angry.)

Factor this into the equation. Know ahead of time that you will have to fix up the property before you resell it, and if a neighborhood that was once primarily owner-occupied becomes a popular rental spot, it is likely the neighborhood will see price depreciation as a result.

Utilities

Believe it or not, you might still be paying for utilities you aren't using! The utilities paid by the tenant and those paid by the homeowner can vary by state and also, thankfully, by negotiation. On most of my properties I require the tenant to pay the electricity bills, cable/Internet bills, phone bills, and gas bills. As the landlord, I generally pay the water/sewer bill and trash bill (it's often part of the property tax bill).

You may negotiate this with your tenant, but check local laws first. You should plan on paying sewer and water at a minimum; so figure this into your costs. Remember that your tenant might not be as frugal with utilities as you are, especially if you are paying for their use.

Repairs

When you are living in your home and a towel bar breaks or a garbage disposal doesn't work and you can't afford to pay for it, you can budget to have it fixed in the future. Not so if you are renting your home. You have an obligation to fix and repair the home right away—either by doing it yourself or by hiring someone to fix it for you.

Those repairs you've been putting off? You must plan on taking care of any repair right away, particularly those that detrimentally impact the tenant's quality of life. Set aside a reserve fund (I use $100 as my monthly benchmark per property) for repairs. If a larger repair needs to be made (such as an air-conditioning fix, which gets expensive quickly), then I can fall back on this account for repairs. When you think of repairs, it's easy to think, "Well, when I lived there, I rarely needed to do anything." Remember, though, that your tenants might even call for a plugged toilet that they caused; you never know what will come up. Prepare for the worst and be happy when it doesn't happen.

Also remember that if you are going to move back into the home or sell it later, you will want to keep it in tip-top condition, not just for the tenant, but for your own resale value!

Damages

It is the tenant's obligation to pay for damages to the property if they were caused by the tenant, but this is often a very gray area. For example, I sent a repairman to one of my rentals because the tenant said the toilet was broken. As it turned out, the toilet wasn't just broken—the sewer system was entirely plugged by a kid's toy.

How will you know in advance? You won't, and don't assume you can recover the costs of these items from tenants because they often won't fess up. Sometimes you risk alienating the tenant, which is worse than asking him to cover the $100 repair bill.

It's very difficult to know ahead of time whether a property simply needs repair due to normal wear and tear or whether the tenant created the damage. Unfortunately, most landlords have to assume that if the tenant tells them he didn't cause the damage, he didn't. Don't naively believe that your tenants will tell you when their two-year-old really caused that problem you are now paying to fix!

In general, if the tenant causes damage (which you often don't find until the tenant has moved out, so pay careful attention to Chapter 12, in particular, the section on inspecting the property after move-out before giving back the deposit!), the tenant has to pay for it. You would take this out of the rental deposit that the tenant paid (one reason we charge a higher deposit for pets and so forth is because they tend to cause more damage).

Another really big problem is tenants that blame issues on "someone after them." A personal example reared its ugly head for me in March of 2008. Upon inspecting a rental, I found everything in the home completely destroyed—the ceilings had been punched by someone's fist, bottle caps had been pushed into decorative foam, beer bottles left in the A/C unit, the carpeting completely destroyed, urine and feces in the unit, everything taken from the house, and not one appliance working. The house was literally disgusting. Upon investigation, the tenant blamed everything on "someone must have gone in there after I left the place. I didn't leave it like that." The property manager (who has since been fired and the property is being managed by me, now) never did a walk-out inspection, and has made it very difficult for me to sue the tenant for damages and garnish her wages. While I'm going to do my best in court, these walk-through's are absolutely crucial. The renter lost her deposit, but hasn't yet paid for the $5000 in damage she's done to the house.

There are loopholes, though, if the tenant informs you of a potential problem and you don't act on it, so it's important that your tenant has a solid means of communicating with you (discussed in Chapter 10). Sometimes you will miss something though even upon the most critical inspections. I've had tenants do everything they can to make a problem they created less visible (duct-taping parts together, taping up plumbing, closing the lid on plugged toilets, even painting around furniture so the house seemed like it was freshly painted and so on) or to try to cover up pet odors from the dog they weren't supposed to have in your house. This brings up another point—if you let pets in, expect to let all that goes with them in, too.

Another important thing for you to know though is that you are responsible for making the home livable. This includes taking proper care in responding to requests. If a maintenance request is made, for instance, on an air-conditioning unit in the desert and you don't act right away, you may be found negligent and you can be legally sued. You have a responsibility and obligation to provide safe living conditions for the tenant.

Landscaping

Similar to repair issues, if you own your home and the lawn needs a bit of a trim, it's your discretion and option to wait a week until after it has grown another two inches! If you have a tenant, though, you have an obligation to keep the property in good condition, including landscaping. Not doing so can lead to tenant complaints, neighbor complaints, and (if you live in an association area) fines. Budget a set amount (I use $75–$100 per month) for a gardener for each home you rent, depending on how maintenance-free the yard is. Most of the time, tenants don't want to do yard work—even if they say they will, you can't count on it.

If you are going to keep the home rented for many years, you might even wish to replace high-maintenance shrubs or lawns with low-maintenance foliage to keep your costs lower. Sometimes making an initial investment if you intend to rent the property for awhile can save you money in the long run. However, if you're going to sell it later or return to live in it when you can afford it again after perhaps a refinance or a job change, you might want to even enhance the property with nicer landscaping than you had before, or at the very least maintain what you had.

Vacancies

You have done everything right when renting your house, so what is the worry? Well, tenants do leave! Sometimes we get so caught up in the satisfaction and financial relief of finding a tenant that we forget that the tenant will move out at some point. You might get lucky and have ten- or twenty-year tenants if that is in fact what you want, but you should plan for what is far more common—a $\frac{1}{12}$ vacancy rate.

The single biggest financial mistake I see accidental landlords make is not figuring in a vacancy factor. Banks assume $\frac{1}{12}$ vacancy—that is, one twelfth of the year, or one month every year, the home will be left vacant and you won't have any income. When banks calculate income streams, they assume this level of occupancy, and you should, too (unless you know for sure that the property will be vacant even longer; I've had properties vacant for over one year despite lowering the rent to ridiculously low payments). Don't rest assured on a one- or two-year lease, either, because it isn't unheard of for a tenant to break a lease!

How will you pay for the mortgage this month on top of your other obligations? This is a serious issue to consider. If you can get a tenant to sign a two- or three-year lease, it may be worth lowering the rent for that vacancy factor to be eliminated.

Another important element to the financial component is the lease period. While you may have a two-year lease, some states only allow you to enforce leases for up to one year at a time. Even if the tenant signs a five-year lease you may not be able to retain them for that long. Leases, in general, mean that any damages or losses you incur as a result of the tenant breaking the lease become the tenant's responsibility to pay. But, some state laws override that. If you have a five-year lease for instance you may only be able to enforce one year of it. Also, if you re-rent it immediately, you technically have no damages so you cannot bill the tenant for your losses.

However, if a tenant breaks a lease in a state that doesn't cap lease terms, then you can show damages equal to lost rent for the amount of time you didn't have a renter. This is why many landlords offer breaks on the rental price for a longer lease. You are guaranteed rent (assuming the renter can pay or be found when they leave), and the tenant is taking on more financial risk.

Property Management Fees

You might choose to rent your home but have a property management company take care of it for you. Although it can cost less due to the company having its own maintenance or landscaping crew and saving you money on forms or evictions/ real estate attorney fees, there are hidden costs here, too.

Property managers sometimes own their own maintenance companies, and some will up-charge maintenance, although it is considered an unethical practice. Also, you will pay a 6- to 10-percent commission on your rent each month and will pay a finder's fee that usually ranges from 50 percent of one month's rent to 100 percent of one month's rent. Additionally, some property managers still make you pay for advertising. They might also keep some of your bounced check fees or late payments that you'd normally collect and keep for yourself. These are all things to look out for in your property management contract.

We have covered many of the obvious—and the not so obvious—costs thus far. Now we'll move onto the pros and cons of landlording, to help you make the most informed decisions.

Pros and Cons of Becoming a Landlord

2

There can be many reasons you're contemplating renting your home. You might find your logic fighting your feelings, and vice versa. This is a crucial time to make a decision that is right for you, and you need to have enough information so you can make a good decision. I've run through the reasons you may be facing this decision in the book's introduction, so let's talk about some of the realistic plusses and minuses to help you make your decision.

Benefits of Renting Your Home

Despite the potential for unforeseen costs that are both long-term and short-term (which are hopefully in the foreseen category after reading Chapter 1), there are benefits, too. Some are obvious; others are less so. If there were not benefits, you wouldn't be contemplating it, so let's run through them so you can get a firm grip on how they relate to your situation.

Riding Out the Market

Obviously, you might be able to ride out a temporary decrease in home prices while waiting for an upswing in price before selling. If you are emotionally attached to your home, you can make the transition slowly—by first letting someone else live in the home and then eventually selling it. I did this, and it did ease my sadness a bit. I "visited" the home to check on it while it was rented, and soon I began appreciating the spaciousness and central location of my new home. Major builders in 2007 decided to hold fire sales—deemed the "Deal of the Century" by K. Hovnanian and "Mission: Possible" by Standard Pacific (which I worked for, by the way)—which dropped prices in some neighborhoods by hundreds of thousands of dollars literally overnight and offered free upgrades, making neighbors' homes harder to sell.

> Some of you might be in a difficult predicament—you have an interest in living in another area yet are not quite sure you'll like the new neighborhood. You may use this as a test-bed, renting in the new area and reserving the right to move back if things don't work out.

In some of these once-overheated areas or those areas where there is a large resale inventory level, many of you might have chosen to ride out the market and move—waiting for the market to rebound or at least allow you to break even before selling. This is an obvious and very big benefit to renting your home and, in today's market, probably the most common one that I see.

Taxes

Remember that any taxes on the home, even if it is rented, are still your responsibility. Not paying taxes can create all kinds of problems for you. You could set up an escrow or impound account with your mortgage company to make paying taxes a part of your payment and less burdensome, particularly in high tax areas or on homes that are valued high. Impounds can also cover insurance. Worse yet, although it varies by state, your property can be put up for sale by "tax sale" for not paying taxes! This can lead to a tax foreclosure or forced sale of the home. Don't ever rely on a tenant to pay the taxes. Not only is it not his responsibility, but you'd be taking a big gamble on something very important.

And now for the tax "benefit" portion of this section …. Taxes are expenses and go to cash flow. If you aren't a real estate professional according to the Internal Revenue Service, the losses, if you incur any monthly, come off of the appreciation at the end when you sell the home. Sometimes, though, landlords actually do meet the real estate professional requirement (check with your tax accountant or tax attorney to see if you qualify), which makes your taxes part of your monthly or yearly costs and go against income. This can be a huge benefit.

Leverage Equity

Some of you might be in an excellent position—you have equity in your home! You might want to take it out and leverage it, investing it in other opportunities such as stocks, bonds, CDs, or (my personal favorite) other real estate—especially in this market where deals abound! Good for you. If you can make this decision and can hold for at least ten years (no real estate market after any ten years in history has ever lost value), you can worry less as your risk is diversified due to time. When the market rebounds, you will have even more equity!

Positive Cash Flow

You also have the potential for positive cash flow! I know it sounds crazy, but it's true. I'll discuss this in the next section, but you can actually make money each month depending on what you owe and what comparable rentals are showing in your area. This is particularly true if you have paid down your mortgage, bought your home for a low price and don't have a high payment on it, or were fortunate enough to lock in a 5 percent fixed 30-year rate in the early 2000s.

Downsides to Renting Your Home

I've explained some of the long-term and short-term upsides, but there are some downsides, too.

Trashed Properties

It is not likely, but it is possible that you will end up with a property so destroyed that the deposit doesn't cover the costs or it takes weeks or months to repair it for rerental, moving back in, or selling. You might also have a situation in which the renter skips town or never pays you for repairs. Later in Chapter 10 I explain what you need to do to avoid this, including properly screening tenants and frequently checking up on the property.

Emotional Toll

I go into this more in Chapter 3, but there is an emotional toll to renting your home. Some tenants are flat-out tiring—they complain frequently, they don't pay and you find yourself without enough money to cover the mortgage, they do things to make the neighbors complain, they perform illegal activities in your home, they make it hard to collect rent (they use the notorious "the check is in the mail" excuse), or they end up doing something that causes you to have to evict them. If you do choose to rent your home, you need to minimize all these risks, which I begin covering in Chapter 4.

Tax Drawbacks

If the IRS does not classify you as a real estate professional, you may well have tax drawbacks. For instance, if you earn more than $250,000 in appreciation when you do sell the home, you might need to pay tax on that appreciation, which can make up for any gains you would have had if you'd just sold the home instead of choosing to rent it.

> It is very important that you consult tax authorities or your tax preparer on any tax-related issues. Experts have insight on your particular circumstances that may make a "general rule" inapplicable to you, or they might be able to advise you of a rule that does apply to you because of your particular situation.

If you haven't lived in your home at least two out of the last five years, then when you sell it, you will be paying capital gains on any profit exceeding $250,000 for a single person and $500,000 for a married couple. You should consult a tax authority on this issue before making decisions.

Cash Flow Problems and Financial Stress

Sometimes cash flow is an issue, particularly if you have negative cash flow on the property each month and cannot afford the difference. This can cause tremendous financial burden, sometimes more than paying off the rest of a loan during a sale in which you sell for less than you owe and charging the difference to your credit card. Cash flow has to be taken very seriously because living month-to-month is hard enough, and living month-to-month on two homes doubles the stress.

Doing the Math

So, how do you calculate whether renting is a good idea for you financially? Here is a good guide to go by. Fill in the table that follows, and you will find your monthly cash flow—you don't need to use advanced math to figure this out unless you want to calculate net present value and value streams, which you should do if you're going to buy multiple properties with your equity. If you do want to buy multiple properties, you can use a variety of online tools that calculate net present value and the value of income streams.

Monthly Cash Flow		
Monthly Rent (Income)	**Sample**	**Your Property**
Insurance	$80	_____
Association	$25	_____
Taxes	$500	_____
Landscaping	$100	_____
Damage Fund	$100	_____
Maintenance Fund	$100	_____
Vacancy Pro-Rated	$100 ($1,200/12)	_____
Mortgage Payments	$700 (interest at a min)	_____
Utilities	$50	_____
Costs:	$1,755	_____
Income from Rent:	$1,200	_____
Cash Flow:	–$455 (negative)	_____

If the cash flow is in the deficit category (this is a negative cash-flowing property), consult your tax advisor as to whether this could be a write-off for you. In some cases, you have to be considered a real estate professional to take this as a write-off, so your appreciation would need to be greater than your cash flow loss.

Even if it isn't, it might still be worth it if your data shows the market should rebound in your area or your area took a hard hit in the downturn. If your home is in the high-priced category (above the jumbo loan cut-off of $417,000), your home sale price will be more sensitive to interest rate cuts. If your home can be backed by Federal Housing Authority (FHA) insurance, you will have an easier time selling it when you decide to. If your home is priced lower than $417,000, your home price will be sensitive to the ability for subprime borrowers to get loans. Consider these factors when making your decisions.

> I recommend creating your own spreadsheet using a tool like Microsoft Excel and updating it regularly as you find out what having a tenant is actually costing you. Your estimates are a good place to start, but it needs constant updating so there are no surprises.

So, as a homeowner who already has trouble affording your mortgage or as a person renting your home to leverage equity, when might you use my previous example?

Well, I have often. When I believe the vacancy rate will be lower than antici-pated, when the home is newer so repairs will probably be less frequent and/or less expensive, when the home is still covered by a new home warranty, or when I believe that I will earn more than $455 in appreciation each month and can afford the deficit by cutting into my monthly income from my day job. Herein lies the key—appreciation and tax benefits must offset the negative cash flow!

In most cases, homeowners underestimate as opposed to overestimating their ex-penses and many can be in for a big shock when they are not even breaking even. So, where do you get the monthly rental income figure? I discuss that more in chapters to come, as well as how to use technology (and your neighbors) to find out. For now, here is a simple equation to follow if you have negative cash flow:

> Determine your property appreciation monthly (you can look at comparables)—value X
>
> Determine your negative cash flow each month—value Y

If X is greater than Y, you will have a yearly net gain assuming no unanticipated expenses, rising property taxes, or unexpected insurance changes.

Remember opportunity cost, too. Let's say you will run $500 per month upside-down in cash flow, but you will earn $1,000 per month in equity. Your positive return is $6,000 per year. You must weigh this against other investment opportunities. If you could sell and get $20,000 out of the home now, you must weigh the risk versus the return. Perhaps that $20,000 at a 5 percent return in a certificate of deposit (CD) will earn $1,000 per year in interest, and perhaps that is sufficient for you to decide to sell given the stress some homeowners feel renting their properties. These are all important considerations.

Let's take the previous example from our table and estimate costs using a property management company. Because you are using a property manager, you are likely to reduce your Damage Fund and Maintenance Fund by half for $50 each ($100 total). This is assuming the property manager has her own employees doing the work. Find out whether this is the case because, as you can see, the impact to the bottom line is very minimal ($4) when you use a property manager with her own team. If this isn't the case, you might find it costs even more. If you decide to use a property manager, the decision over the long term to rent and hold or sell is the same—yearly appreciation minus yearly negative cash flow will determine your positive net gain. Theoretically, if that number in the form of a percentage is greater than what you would get on other investment types such as stocks or CDs, it is a good investment.

Your insurance will stay the same, and your association will stay the same. Management fees though will now be a part of your equation; usually 8 to 10 percent. Utilities stay the same. This means that your overall cash flow may go down. However, there is one thing to consider here. In hard-to-rent areas, property managers will have pools of potential tenants that you don't have access to. If the area has a lot of vacancies or a lot of open properties, you may find that having the property rented out more quickly is worth the cost. Also, if you cannot visit the property often, you may want someone to do the drive-by's. I discussed a personal example in Chapter 1 (an extreme example of a renter trashing a home). This was despite having a property manager—so they aren't always worth it. When they are helpful though, they save you an incredible amount of time, money, and headache and earn their management fee many times over. My experience in Austin, Texas with Austin Real Pros property management has been so fantastic I would pay a higher management fee if I had to. It is very property-manager dependent; one of many reasons to ask for referrals before you sign that management agreement!

Be wary of any property manager who marks up her own repairs or has a separate company that handles repairs and up-charges her homeowners. I learned this lesson the hard way. In some states this isn't even legal! Don't always look at the least cost, but the way to do it right and save yourself money in the long run. Figure the best possible method within reason in your cash flow sheet.

Be sure you add in anything specific to your property. Do you have co-op fees? Additional management fees? Pool cleaning fees? A particularly large yard that may cost more in maintenance? Do you live in a drought area and need a lot of water? If your costs are high, consider ways you can reduce them.

Now that we have looked at the potential pros and cons of renting out your property with a property manager and the cash flow basics of rentals, you may well have decided to rent it out on your own. I applaud your work because it can be incredibly rewarding! It can also take an emotional toll so you need to be prepared. In Chapter 3, we will get into some of the details of what is involved, and what you need to be prepared for to be successful.

3

Are You Cut Out to Be a Landlord?

Being a landlord takes an incredible amount of dedication, care, concern, loyalty, time, and sometimes a strong stomach! If you don't have these qualities or aren't willing to invest in them, consider not renting your property or perhaps use a property manager to do the dirty work. Though, even with a property manager, you will still go through some of the ups and downs of finding tenants—you just won't necessarily have to see all the damage done to the home.

Emotional Toll

Many investors don't understand the emotional attachment we feel for our homes because they trade properties like any other commodity. Even investors like me feel a special attachment to our primary residence that we don't feel for our rental properties—we look at them much like stocks.

We start and possibly raise our families in the place we hang our hats; the home is tied to a variety of memories, good and bad—of children growing up, spouses growing old, and families expanding. It serves as a refuge from work. A part of us seems to be left behind when we move, and acclimation to new environments can be time-consuming and draining.

The emotional toll does dissipate, but it does feel like a loss, particularly if you're concerned about children, schools, and change. Right now emotions are quite possibly influencing your decision, so you need to try to compartmentalize them from the financial basis of your choices. This isn't to be taken lightly, but it also shouldn't influence your decision so much that you find yourself in bankruptcy court in a year or losing your home anyway due to foreclosure. You might find yourself feeling a lot of different emotions as you make this decision—that is completely normal.

Disassociating Yourself from Your Home

One of the things you'll have to do if you plan to be a landlord, particularly if you've lived in your home, is to disassociate yourself from it. This can be tough to do alone and even tougher with children who are attached to friends, neighbors, schools, and the special murals painted on their bedroom walls. You will have to emotionally disassociate yourself from your home, at least for awhile. Even if you plan on moving back in, you'll find common landlord issues more bothersome than usual if you are still highly attached to your house as a home. You need to be prepared for kids asking tough questions and missing their friends and backyard.

> **TALK FROM THE TRENCHES**
>
> Of the 100 landlords surveyed, more than 20 percent of those who rented their own homes found it difficult to make an emotional disconnect between the house and their home.

Do You Have a Plan?

You need a plan before moving forward. If you're just "thinking of renting until … well … I'm not sure when," reconsider landlording and sell instead, or come up with a plan. Here are some questions you need to ask yourself when coming up with your plan:

- When will you reevaluate whether renting the home is still a good decision for you?
- How long do you intend to have the home rented?
- What if the market doesn't rebound as you planned?

- What will your one-, two-, three-, four-, and five-year plans of action be?
- What if you are ready and willing to move back in, but you can't afford it?
- Do you need a savings plan to be able to pay off any potential monies owed to the bank not covered by a sale if you need to quickly?
- Are you emotionally prepared for someone else to live in your home and to live in your space if you plan on returning to the home?

In general, you need to be sure that you understand the repercussions of renting out your home. You can no longer just walk in—the right of use isn't yours anymore. You need to disassociate from the home, which is part of the emotional toll that renting takes. You need to be financially ready to make the move; have a backup plan, have savings, and know what your short- and long-term goals are. When you have those tightly nailed down, you're ready to move onto renting it out.

Acknowledging the Likelihood of Bad Tenants

Bad tenants are everywhere. Nearly all of us who have been landlording for awhile have had bad tenants! I have one right now who has so much trash on her lawn (and other awful things) that as of the date of publication of this book, nine neighbors (yes, nine) as far as one-half mile away have called the city to complain about the stench, yet she's nearly impossible to kick out due to rules, regulations, and laws. The city is threatening me with lawsuits if she doesn't clean up her act, and the property manager has been useless in resolving the problem.

I have had tenants check in one month and leave the next; I've had them pay their deposit, move in, and then not pay the first month's rent while waiting for eviction. I have had tenants trash homes, allow people to live in the home that weren't authorized, and use every excuse in the book not to pay rent. You name it, and most landlords have experienced it.

Recently I had a tenant illegally subleasing my home to twelve people—yes twelve—in a 1200 square foot home. She was earning $80 per person on rent per month, and was making money while she paid me the $795 she owed in rent.

The following are some comments concerning bad tenants from other landlords:

"Tenants left right after moving in due to eloping."

"Had a tenant with an incredible sense of entitlement."

"Trashing property, noisy, uncooperative, delayed paying rent."

"Two deadbeat tenants in a row."

"Nonpayment of rent, junk outside all over the yard."

"Plumbing issues with an apartment dweller flushing rags down the toilet twice."

"Tenant had a fire in the house."

"Neighbors kept calling about the tenant."

TALK FROM THE TRENCHES

Sixty-nine percent of landlords surveyed said that a good, qualified renter was hard or very hard to find. Twenty-seven percent said maintenance was difficult.

Don't let this scare you—let this make you take action! The more prepared you are and the more screening you do, the more likely you are to get a good tenant. Remember that most of the survey respondents still enjoy landlording, and you will not make the same mistakes because you've picked up this book and are reviewing the Landlord Protection Agency to help you out!

Even though bad tenants are the minority and you will learn to screen them out, they do exist. And if you get one, you will not have a pleasant experience. Are you ready for this? Can you stomach a tenant who does the worst possible things to your home? What plan of action will you take? Will you be strong enough to confront your tenant or even evict him if necessary? Can you disassociate yourself from your tenant enough that you don't let him take advantage of you?

Throughout this book, I share various stories, both personal and from a survey I've been conducting for months with both experienced and new landlords. Many of them will turn even the strongest person's stomach—tenants who smear feces all over walls, destroy closets and windows, damage all the appliances before they move, and create hidden damages that you discover later? These are rare, but they exist. Will you be able to handle it if they do?

Time Commitment and Financial Stress

One of the caveats of renting your home can be incredible financial stress. You might have months without a tenant or your vacancy rate might hit or exceed the $\frac{1}{12}$ rule that we generally plan for. Do you have the savings to accommodate this? Are you running your bank accounts on empty and cannot risk even one month's late rent, much less an absent tenant? Can you build your savings if you don't have any so that you are prepared in the event of a worst-case scenario?

You may also run into the same issues I have—tenants who are so consistently late on paying their rent that it makes it difficult for you to pay the mortgage. Remember this: Plan for the worst, and hope for the best.

Unforeseen Costs

Can you plan for unforeseen costs? Such as tenants disappearing and leaving you with a deposit that doesn't cover damages? A roof that suddenly needs replacement—to the tune of $20,000? Foundations that crack or earthquakes that cause tremendous structural damage not covered by insurance? I've had tenants tell me a roof was leaking right after I bought a place and then had a $10,000 repair bill afterward. Worse yet? I built a new home, only to find that the builder never included an association-required fence, requiring $13,000 in out-of-pocket expenses when the tenant moved in. Talk about sticker shock— very difficult on the wallet!

Tax Burdens

When you sell your home, you get special tax benefits in the amount of $250,000 ($500,000 maximum for a married couple) to offset some appreciation, but only if you've lived in the home for two of the last five years. If you rent for three or four years and end up making $100,000 in appreciation, can you handle the stress of a sudden and large tax payment? Taxes and money in general can lead to bankruptcy and divorce. Can you emotionally handle this?

I have also had properties increase in value and therefore increase in taxes when the assessor reassessed the property; this is another thing to watch out for. Keep tabs on the value of your property. And remember that anytime you add square footage, be prepared to add to your tax bill, too.

What if Your Property Goes Down in Value?

You might be renting your property to wait for values to rebound. But what if they don't and you still need to sell? Can you handle selling your home after two years of landlording for the same sale price or even less than you could today? If you can't fathom this risk, landlording may not be for you. This goes beyond a financial liability and can be a source of depression and regret.

Troublesome Tenants

Most tenants are good people looking to pay honest rent for a nice place to live. But what if your tenant calls at all hours of the night asking for ridiculous repairs? Asks for upgrades to your home? Refuses to leave, or leaves early, thereby breaking the lease? These were discussed in Chapter 1 as they relate to finances, but they are an emotional issue as well. Troublesome tenants can take an incredible amount of your time and lead to extreme stress. They can guilt you into feeling like a bad landlord or a bad person, and they may try to take advantage of your kindness. Will you be able to make the mental switch to treat these scam artists as they have asked to be treated, or will you have a hard time thinking of them as income liabilities?

Your Conclusion—To Rent or Not to Rent?

Ultimately, the decision to rent or not to rent lies within your heart and head. It needs to make financial sense for you—that is, even if you have negative cash flow, the overall benefit within your own time constraints (whether they be one or ten years) needs to make sense. If it doesn't, renting might not make sense for you. If it does and you're willing to go on a landlording adventure, consider this book and other resources a fantastic guide to learning all you need to know about how to become an Accidental Landlord.

> Being a landlord can be incredibly rewarding and can be a great investment. It can also give you time to make tough financial decisions that are best made after some time has passed, particularly if you are needing to rent your own home. Take some time to decide if you have the emotional and financial stamina it takes to be a landlord.

Yes!

So, you decided yes! Okay, let's get rolling! The remainder of the book tells you everything you need to know from finding tenants, to screening tenants, to managing the property, to ultimately selling or moving back in. You'll find fast forms to use and lots of resources.

No!

You might have read these first few chapters and decided the financial risk or the emotional toll isn't for you. Consider renting anyway but perhaps using a property manager, which is covered in this book. But if it still doesn't feel right for you, you know the answer—sell and take whatever loss you have to so you can live the life you want.

4

You've Decided to Rent, Now What?

First, welcome to the world of landlording! It can be rewarding both financially and in knowing you are offering a home to an individual or to a family, but it can also be stressful and intimidating. That is where this book comes in—to alleviate the stress and make it as rewarding as possible, both financially and otherwise. Deana Nuzzolese, the LPA's President's daughter, wisely said, "If you're too busy to help someone, you're too busy." Why is this so true? Because landlording can be extremely rewarding; you are helping other people by providing a home! But, if you're too busy to do it right, perhaps you shouldn't be a landlord—or should hire someone to do it for you.

So you've decided to rent—what are you going to do now? Well, first you need to prepare the home for rental. This means you need to go through it and repair or replace anything that is broken, install blinds in any windows that don't have them, install fresh shower curtains, give the home a detailed cleaning, fix up the landscaping, and get any routine maintenance contracts under way for landscaping and so forth. You should also paint the home in neutral colors and clean the carpets or floors—make this a home you would want to live in.

Homes without blinds rent far more slowly than homes with blinds! A sense of privacy and security is provided with window coverings, so if you took your prized handmade heirlooms with you, be sure to replace them with something for your tenants.

You might even want to hire a monthly housecleaner and include that in the price of the rent to ensure the house is kept up (and to provide feedback to you while offering another benefit to the renter).

Your Rental Options

You might want to consider offering various options to your potential tenants. Among these are month-to-month rentals for a higher price, short-term or long-term leases with benefits for whichever is in your best interest given your specific requirements, and even lease-to-own options (which I cover in the next section). Offering options lets the tenant feel more in control over the process and over his place of residence, and you'll start off your landlord experience with your new tenant on the right foot.

Another dilemma you as a potential landlord will face is whether to accept tenants who want a month-to-month rental agreement or hold out for a longer-term lease. No matter what you decide, remember that if you have a lease, you will need a lease agreement. If you do a month-to-month arrangement, a rental agreement usually suffices.

Also, consider your goals. Do you know you want to sell after at least two years? If so, a longer-term lease will be far less stressful on you. If you have a good tenant, consider offering him the option of a longer lease (even after signing a shorter contract) and applying a reduced rental rate effective immediately. Sometimes even existing tenants will modify their leases because they know they want to stay (here is where providing responsiveness and good communication helps keep tenants in your home), and if you're happy with the condition of the home (this is a good trial period!), then it can be a win-win.

Month-to-Month

If you intend to sell the house in six months or if there's a good chance you might be moving back in, a monthly arrangement might be better for you. Also consider the potential for market recovery.

It's fairly easy to find tenants when their obligation to you doesn't exceed thirty days! Of course, with a month-to-month contract, you also have the benefit of letting the renter go more easily, too; thirty days' notice is required in most states and counties. So, you get a benefit if you choose to accept renters on a monthly basis. I have had tenants rent my properties for years on a monthly basis. Some just feel more comfortable knowing they can quickly move if they need to. It doesn't necessarily make them bad renters, but it does raise red flags for me. I tend to collect heftier deposits (one and one-half times the rent) or make them pay more per month if they want month-to-month arrangements.

> Take a look also at www.buyincomeproperties. com. This site has some fantastic tips for people who are buying, renting, or selling a home and has excellent free forms available.

There are obvious downsides to this, too—downsides I have experienced myself. For instance, if the tenant wants out of the contract, she need only provide a month's notice, if that. I had a renter who was fantastic for four months; she took good care of the home, made payments on time, and even upgraded the home on her own dime! But, one day she emailed me that her husband lost his job and she was leaving—in two weeks. Because she'd done so much to the property, I let her go with only two weeks' notice instead of the required thirty days. Unfortunately, it took two months to find another tenant.

If I would have had a lease agreement, it would have required payment from her to break the lease, offsetting my costs. (Of course, tenants have been known to disappear, too!) It is harder to find tenants who will commit to a one- to two-year lease, and sometimes it requires lowering your monthly rent or offering half-a-month or one-month free rent. You might also choose to disincentive month-to-month renters by charging them more per month or requiring a bigger deposit, trying to encourage them to sign a lease agreement instead. Remember that leases become month-to-month if they're not renewed; so you need to send out the proper forms. These are all in Appendix B for you to readily use!

Lease

Another caveat for consideration in all of this is that sometimes investors prefer to buy property that already has a tenant in it! It's one less thing to worry about. So, you might be able to get an investor to buy if the new owner knows he doesn't have to find a renter. This is where having a lease with some months remaining can be another good benefit.

If you choose to lease for a particular period of time over renting, which is often month-to-month, be sure to state that in your advertising. You can get leasing forms online to make your life much easier! You might want to have a real estate attorney read over the agreements before the tenant signs them. There are some great resources online for leasing or renting your home.

Check out the Landlord Protection Agency at www.thelpa.com. I will refer to them throughout the book and you will notice the forms are from their great company. They will offer you many tools to rent out your home that I cannot put a price tag on. You can seek advice here, although they do recommend that you still contact a real estate attorney because the laws in each state and even different cities in some areas are so different. This site is outstanding. It provides forms, laws by state, question/answer forms for landlords, and a link to Megan's Law, and it even allows you to report tenants to the credit bureau from their site. You can also use their bad tenant registry to register problematic tenants and help other landlords stay away from the bad guys!

Another great resource is the Housing and Urban Development (HUD) at hud.gov. This is a government organization, and there are some other sites that give you additional HUD information, including fair housing and opportunity notices, which you might need to furnish your tenants with.

Lease-to-Own

Leasing to own sounds quite complicated, but really it's fairly straightforward. This is often referred to as a *lease-option*. Both of these are lease-with-option-to-purchase contracts. This is a form of a real estate purchase that combines a traditional rental agreement with an exclusive option of right of first refusal to purchase the home. This is a good option for those who love your home but, due to credit issues or other problems, cannot qualify now but expect to in the future.

Traditionally, the tenant/buyer agrees to a lease period, and when the lease period is over the tenant has a right to buy the home for a previously agreed upon price. The tenant or buyer pays the landlord a nonrefundable option deposit applied to the purchase price of the home, usually on a monthly basis.

The benefit for you, the landlord, is that you have a person who will lose a lot of money if she doesn't buy the house, so your chances of selling it at the end of the lease period are pretty good. You also can rest a little easier knowing that a person who intends to buy the house is more likely to take care of the house, so you probably won't end up with a trashed piece of property at the end of the deal.

The downside of course is that you're prearranging a price, and the home could have appreciated and you could be selling your home for less than it is worth. If the tenant cannot purchase the home or doesn't choose to at the end of the option period, the tenant and landlord together can do one of several things:

- Extend the option period—be careful if the house is worth more than the prearranged option amount!
- Convert the lease purchase into a traditional rental agreement—generally you keep the extra money paid.
- End the contract with the tenant moving out.

Appendix B has many examples of these contracts, but you should run yours by a real estate attorney before you sign it. The Landlord Protection Agency has a lease-to-own, by-state site that is very helpful when determining how to structure these leases! It's available at www.thelpa.com/lpa/forms/state-lease.html.

Lease Extensions

Lease extensions are addendums to leases that allow tenants to stay in the home for a specified period of time without creating a new tenancy or a new lease. Say, for instance, your tenant is scheduled to have his lease end in March. You may choose to extend the lease with existing conditions by one month, three months, or years; although if it's going to be awhile, you might want to consider a new lease and a rental increase.

Deciding on a Price

You need to decide on a fair price, but one that will also make tenants come to your property over others. To do that, you need to make sure you are pricing your property appropriately. To do this, you need comparables; in real estate, these are referred to as *comps*. They are usually an estimate as to what a homeowner can get if she sells—or rents. Most people don't realize that the rental market also has real estate rental comps!

So, what comps do you need to make good decisions? The rental comps and the sales comps. These used to be widely regarded as private information that only real estate and leasing agents could get, but thanks to technology (which I discuss thoroughly in my book *Commissions at Risk: A Real Estate Professionals Guide to Beating Online Competition*, Kaplan, 2006), this has all changed.

Rental Comps

Rental comps are the comparative analyses for similar properties and what they're renting for. There are several ways you can do this online, or you can scour newspaper ads and brochures to see what others are renting for. In addition, if you see "for rent" signs, feel free to call and inquire on the property.

> Real estate agents are usually equated with real estate sales; but some do know about rentals and rental comps, too. You might be wise to check with your local neighborhood agent and ask what rentals are going for; this will give you a good basis.

Rental comps are like sales comps, but they tell you the value of your property in terms of what it can rent for. Take a look at these two sites, or check your local newspapers. You might also want to call a property manager, but if you aren't using them to list and manage your home, they might not be very cooperative in valuing your rental. Check out these sites:

- www.rent-o-meter.com—This site is pure genius. It is based on user-entered information rather than professionally entered information. Renters use it to tell others what they are paying and what their accommodations are like: bedrooms, bathrooms, quality, ZIP code, amenities, and so on. Potential renters can look here to see if they're getting a good deal. But, better yet for you as a potential landlord, is the fact that you can see what others are pricing their rentals at. So, rather than guessing at a rental price, you can see what other properties are going for.

- www.craigslist.org—Craigslist, widely known as a large online garage sale, is available only in limited areas but is rapidly growing. Do searches in your state and community and see what others are renting homes for. This will give you an idea as to what you can get in a rental market and for a sale market, too! Many homeowners are opting to list their homes on craigslist in addition to more traditional means.

You can also do a search in Google for "rent <zip code>" and see what rentals are going for in that ZIP code. Check out HUD's Fair Market Rent System also. This is a good link to use: www.huduser.org/datasets/fmr/fmrs/index. asp?data=fmr08. It shows the standard rent and then a multiplier by state and county, as well as consumer price index updates and information by the number of bedrooms, and compares it to other surrounding areas.

Sales Comps

Sales comps are a way to summarize what the value of your home is by looking at homes within a two-mile radius (preferably the same subdivision) that are similar in size and features (upgrades, lot, curb appeal, and so on) and then estimating the value of the home based on what others sell for.

You can always hire your own independent appraiser, which is perfectly fine. Expect to pay between $200 and $500 depending on your area, the home size, the demand, the appraiser, and how comprehensive you want the analysis to be. Appraisers just pull comparative analyses though anyway, so you really can do this yourself and come up with an accurate number. The number the appraiser comes up with doesn't mean you'll be able to sell for that. Sometimes it's substantially higher or lower—it is highly market dependent, and of course dependent on the situation with mortgages as we have seen throughout 2007 and so far in 2008.

There are some fantastic sites you can use to find out what others have paid for homes similar to yours. Be sure to look for homes sold in the last three months.

Comps older than three months often aren't valid. If you decide to do this your-self, here are some sites you can use:

- www.zillow.com—Zillow should come with a label warning about over-inflated prices known as "Zestimates" (Zillow's comparative analysis system based on—well—we aren't entirely sure!), but nonetheless it offers good information if you look up the "what's sold" in your neighborhood feature. You can also list your house for sale here or enter a "Make Me Move" price that you might want to keep up during the duration of the rental. Best yet? They won't send you unsolicited ads and it's free!

- www.domania.com—Domania is a great site for checking the price of a home based on what others around it have sold for. Although its search criteria are picky and sometimes you have to try several search options to get a valid hit, when you do the data is extraordinary. Domania requires registration, but I haven't received unsolicited email or snail mail from them after registering.

- Realestate.yahoo.com/Homevalues—This is another newer site that is completely free and shows an excellent comparative analysis history!

Whatever site you use, don't pay for this information because it is easily obtain-able for free. Some sites offer teaser information and then ask for a credit card. Move onto a free one.

Covering Your Costs

When you list your home for rent, you might find you're not covering all your costs to own the home. This is what we call *negative cash flow*. If your negative cash flow on a yearly basis is still less than the appreciation from holding the property, it's still considered a good investment in the long term. Consider ways to boost your income, or find ways to cut your costs.

Have tenants pick up more of the utilities (you cannot really do this in a soft rental market, though), add an association or a maintenance fee (to cover house cleaning for instance), or do the work yourself (such as landscaping and house cleaning). Find a win-win; if your yearly costs exceed any appreciation you will get from the property, consider selling it as soon as possible or try raising the rent substantially if the property is in excellent condition and highly upgraded.

Consider offering the place furnished, and then use some of your furniture or buy some less-expensive furniture and put it in the home. Emphasize safety in your listing if your house is in a kid-friendly place, and emphasize the school districts if they are excellent. Consider anything that will get you more dollars for your home.

If Your Home Is Furnished

If your home is furnished, you should increase the price of the rental. You are after all offsetting the tenant's need for furniture. At the same time, you might run into a tenant who doesn't want it furnished, and you'll incur storage fees for your goods. Often, though, furnished apartments, particularly if your area is near a local college, go very quickly and are a great way to entice people to rent from you.

You will want to charge more for a furnished home, though, so check rental comps for what furnished units are going for in your area. Compare that to what unfurnished units in the same neighborhoods of similar size are going for, and then add the amount accordingly. However, do consider that if you get a good tenant who doesn't want to use your furniture, you might need to remove it.

I've been asked what to do when a tenant wants to rent everything—linens and dishes included! That is tough because your stuff will be worn and used and you'll need to charge for that. Some tenants won't like paying, but hold your ground. This can be a very costly mistake due to theft, misuse, broken items, and just general wear and tear.

Renting out a home that is fully furnished, in general, does net you more rental income. It also nets you more risk! Each of the items that could be stolen, broken, or damaged must be accounted for at the walk-through in both the move-in and move-out phases.

However, if you live in an area where the rental market for furnished homes is strong, you might consider leasing furniture. Now, the return on investment has to be there; and in most cases it might not be—still it is worth considering. Rental companies though do have very strict guidelines about use and the condition furniture (and appliances, too) must be in when returned, so you want to cover yourself.

Pets or kids are often a bad combination with furniture. If you have furniture you can easily leave behind and rent out a furnished house, you can charge more per-item in your deposit, and get a bit more rent, too. This is all something to consider and the decision to pursue or not will be very local to your own market. If you use a property manager, expect them to charge you a higher percentage finder's fee and monthly fee because counting forks is expensive and time consuming!

You should require a much steeper deposit if the home is furnished. I recommend 50 percent higher deposits, but again you are limited by state laws. Some states allow for a full month's additional deposit for furnishings. No doubt, though, the potential risk and damage or loss to you personally is much greater with a furnished home, so take this into consideration when you determine the deposit amount.

Pets

Pets can make a mess, and perhaps more importantly, an unruly household pet can wreak havoc on your house. Smells might make the home more difficult to rent or sell in the future, too. If you decide to allow pets, it's reasonable to put a cap on it or require the pets be outdoors only.

I generally charge $300 per pet as a pet deposit, but you might want to increase or decrease this by looking at other ads and what others in your area are doing. If having pets is the norm, you might want to have a slightly higher deposit and just list "pets welcome, no extra deposit required" because it's expected in the neighborhood.

Here is another thing to consider: Many associations disallow pets beyond a certain number. I have a personal story to share here. Renters on a home in Mohave Valley claimed two pets and paid their $300 deposit. Upon visiting the property (and receiving a $100 fine from the association), they had four dogs and two cats, and it looked like they hadn't cleaned up after them in years. The house was disgusting and the smell was finding its way to other homeowners' properties. You should seriously consider not renting to people with just too many pets, and be sure to call their former landlords to see how they kept up the house. When you do inspections be sure to look for signs that more pets may be hiding in the garage, as was the case with my tenant. Some landlords like to charge a monthly "pet rent" fee—while it's legal, many people will be turned off by this. (Then again, that might be your goal and it might keep people with pets away!)

Section 8 Housing

Section 8 housing rentals makes some landlords cringe, but many of us love this! Section 8 housing, as it's commonly known, is the housing choice voucher program which provides federal assistance through the U.S. Department of Housing and Urban Development (HUD) to help sponsor subsidized housing for low-income families and individuals. This is known as Section 8, referring to the portion of the U.S. Housing Act of 1937.

So what does this mean to you, and why do you care? Currently, HUD Section 8 programs allow either project-based (limited to specific apartment complexes for instance) or tenant-based vouchers, where the tenant is free to choose a unit in the private sector—and that may include yours!

Families or individuals who are eligible find a unit and lease it, and then pay a portion of the rent based on their income. Generally this doesn't exceed 30 percent of the family's income. The Public Housing Authority (PHA) pays the remainder of the rent, subject to a cap determined by the Fair Market Rent (FMR), which is determined by the Housing and Urban Development (HUD) department. So how is the cap determined? The county or city plays a role; whether the home is in a metropolitan area plays a role (if it is, it has a higher FMR), the size of the home, and whether the tenant pays the utilities (when owners pay, it has a higher FMR in general).

Now as a landlord, you may not charge a Section 8 tenant more than you'd charge any other tenant. You also must meet fair housing laws. You are not required to accept Section 8 tenants, but sometimes doing so in a tight rental market can mean your home gets rented before others.

There is a risk of course—we tend to associate lower incomes with not being able to take care of the property. You will need to decide for yourself whether the comfort of knowing you will get at least a portion of your rent is worth the perceived or real risk with these tenants. Some landlords don't want the government involved in their affairs, or fear that they won't be able to increase rent due to FMR caps. They may also be unable to collect for damages caused by the tenant or collect from tenants when they don't pay their share. Under HUD rules, you cannot change a lock or cut off utilities as a way of evicting a tenant even if the state law allows it. Also, HUD provides the tenant a lawyer at no cost if any claims go to court. Take this decision seriously, but look at the possibilities. The potential upside is the large pool of potential tenants, prompt payments from the PHA, and the restrictions that the PHA places on tenants—if a tenant doesn't pay his or her share, they can be removed from the program.

I have had one Section 8 tenant that lived in the home for one year, took good care of the place, and left without incident.

How You Will Handle Deposits

Deposits are sometimes the stumbling blocks for otherwise good tenants because they require savings, something some renters don't have. As more people are displaced due to the rising foreclosure rate, though, you will find a higher quantity and better quality of tenants, such as those who owned their own home and have gotten themselves in over their heads and need a fresh start. Remember that deposits are your insurance against damages or breaking the lease.

It's vital to know that some states restrict the amount of the deposit you can collect. Check local laws at the State Specific Lease Clause Index on LPA at www.thelpa.com/lpa/forms/state-lease.

How Much to Ask For

After you determine the amount that you will rent your place out for, it is common to make that amount the deposit, then add first and last month's rent. You may make the tenant a deal for a longer lease. For example, I recently waived first month's rent on a home in Bullhead City because the tenant signed a two-year lease. After looking at the home he had been renting, he put in his own landscaping and kept the home up nicely; so I felt confident allowing him to sign a two-year lease with no first month's rent and a lower deposit. This often helps the tenant move in with less financial stress.

I highly recommend you do not take a personal check for the deposit, unless you will wait fourteen days for it to clear. Request a money order, a cashier's check, or cash only. In some circumstances, you may wish to allow a tenant to spread his or her deposit out over a couple of months, but I would not go beyond that. If they can't afford the deposit, they may not be able to afford the rent. This is where checking credit and rental history is vital. If they have great credit and previous landlords say they've always paid on time, you might be more lenient. Perform your due diligence here.

Holding Deposits

I keep deposits in a separate account so they're always available if or when the tenant moves out. Remember that you have to return the deposit after you do the final walk-through on the property and you've assessed for and charged for all damages and cleaning. You must return deposits within thirty days unless otherwise stipulated in the rental or lease agreement or unless the state law in the state you're renting the home in dictates otherwise. For instance, in Arizona this time is two weeks! Again, deposits have specific rules, so check the LPA for rules for your specific state. When you download a lease file, you will be given an option to select a state, and it will tell you which sections of the lease agreement must be modified to meet that state's rules. Talk about pain-free renting.

> Keep deposits in an account separate from other funds so if you need to return them quickly, you have them. This is your legal obligation. Also, you will always know what your deposit account looks like and what the financial repercussion would be if a renter leaves. If you are having a bad month when a tenant decides to leave, you'll still be able to meet your financial demands.

Planning Tools

As a landlord, you might be entitled to special tax benefits, such as deducting any losses monthly against the appreciation in the home. Or if you are classified as a real estate professional (consult a tax professional please!), you may be able to take a business loss on a Real Estate Schedule. To do this, you need good planning tools. You can buy a real estate/property management version of QuickBooks, which is a great tool (go to Intuit online and download it for a small fee).

You might also use an Excel spreadsheet. Keep track of everything, including:

- Repairs
- Maintenance
- Advertising costs
- Vacancies
- Private mortgage insurance (PMI) that is often tacked onto mortgages where the loan-to-value ratio exceeds 80 percent
- Utilities
- Land cost versus building cost (this will be on your property tax statement)
- Property taxes
- Insurance costs
- Lost deposits
- Damages if applicable
- Rental income

In short, you need to begin tracking and planning for anything pertaining to your rental. In Chapter 10, we will dive into each of these specifically so you know what to record and how to record it!

> LTV, or Loan-To-Value, is the ratio of the value of the home compared to what you owe. When you go to refinance and when you begin to plan and decide what to do with the home you are renting out, you should know your equity position, LTV and combined LTV, or CLTV. For instance, if you owe $100,000 on your first mortgage and $50,000 on your second mortgage and the home is worth $200,000, then you owe $150,000—and your combined loan-to-value ratio (CLTV) is 75 percent. This is very favorable to banks. Keep the CLTV at 90 percent or below if possible; 80 percent is preferred for refinancing and getting the best deal, and being able to work around lower credit scores.

The most comprehensive resource I can find on the Web is on a site called the Landlord Protection Agency, which includes many resources to finding tenants who are looking for homes, forms, credit checks—you name it, they have it. You can access it from my website at www.drdaniellebabb.com or directly at www.thelpa.com. You can get a deal by using the coupons at the back of the book and using my site to access them! Use code REBOOK08 for the discount offered for readers of this book only!

Legal Homework

Sometimes you will need to turn to someone else for legal counsel. It can be worth a few hundred dollars for expertise if it saves you in time and worry. There are sites you can use for sound legal advice. Some of them are:

- Tenant Rights from HUD at www.hud.gov/renting/tenantrights.cfm
- Landlords Info at www.landlordsinfo.com
- Landlord Protection Agency at www.thelpa.com

In general, I recommend getting to know a real estate attorney, particularly one who specializes in landlord/tenant issues. Should you need to evict a tenant, she will come in handy. Be sure you read over HUD's rules for landlording, though; this is extremely important. You must be sure you are not violating any laws. Here is a list of laws by state: www.hud.gov/renting/tenantrights.cfm. Read through the legal assistance area, the landlord/tenant law, the Fair Employment and Housing rules, and the Housing Rights Center.

John at the LPA wisely says this, "One of my biggest fears is having a tenant with more landlord/tenant knowledge and expertise than I have." He sums up the requirement of knowing the law better than anyone I know.

D.I.Y. Legal Work

Sometimes you'll have to make very quick decisions or will not be able to afford to work with an attorney—or both. In that case, I recommend that you get onto the boards at the LPA—*boards* are a techie term for forums. The forums on this site will really help you work with others who are also professional landlords and might help get you out of trouble or teach you how to deal with a problem. Also, don't be afraid to call HUD—they are there to protect tenants' and landlords' rights. They go by the letter of the law, so you can get some good information. Also, be prepared with your slew of forms—the forms provided in this book and on the LPA's site might just save you from significant stress.

Have a plan for what you will do with common problems, such as a tenant who doesn't pay, an eviction, a tenant who is causing a disturbance, and so on. Having a plan makes it easier to take action and to logically make choices rather than making them emotionally when you are caught up in the moment and might not make the best, most sound legal choice for yourself.

How to Get Sound Legal Advice

When web sites don't cut it, you should talk with a real estate attorney. Real estate attorneys are specially trained to deal with real-estate–specific issues. These include how to evict, how to proceed with a lawsuit against a tenant, or other more severe concerns or issues. You probably won't run into problems severe enough to warranty this, but you should know of a real estate attorney before engaging in contracts.

One area to check out is again on the HUD website. The link is www.hud.gov/renting/. This site provides ways to offer subsidized or insured housing to tenants, voucher programs, overviews of your rights and responsibilities, information on how to handle security deposits, and counseling info for your state. The Public Housing Agency, a component of HUD, offers many resources if you want to offer public housing assistance, which my husband has offered in Tucson. We had excellent renters and guaranteed rent. Check out www.hud.gov/offices/pih/pha/contacts/index.cfm.

What to Ask to Find a Good Attorney

As with any professional in this business or others, you should know what type of experience the individual has and what his specialization is. Find out what the rate is and if a retainer is required to ask questions or if you can pay as you go for occasional questions. Find out whether the individual will work with your tax accountant if issues come up. Find out if they have experience with evictions, and ask to speak to references. If you get any uncomfortable feeling or the cost of the attorney is more than a month's rent, I suggest you look elsewhere for legal representation. Sometimes, depending on your county, all it takes is getting the local law authorities involved.

A bad attorney can make a bad situation into an utter nightmare. Check references, and then check again! The LPA is a great resource for looking up potential partners, including real estate attorneys who specialize in what your needs are.

Lease Agreements 101

5

The rental or lease agreement is your legally binding contract with the tenant. There are several types of rental agreements. You can have a month-to-month rental agreement, a lease agreement for a period of time (periodic tenancy), a lease-to-own agreement sometimes referred to as a *lease option agreement*, or a lease agreement with provisions and/or addendums (for example, if the home is furnished or you allow subletting). Month-to-month renters are obviously far less stable, and usually there is a reason they want month-to-month rental contracts. Some people allow this but charge a premium for the rent, such as 10 percent or more per month extra for the month-to-month rental. Remember that every time you lose a renter, you're losing at least a month's worth of rent.

The goal is to keep good tenants as long as possible. Tenants know it's more difficult to get a landlord to rent month-to-month. Leases are generally agreements for at least six months, although one-year leases (or longer with benefits) are more common. If the rental market is soft, consider a month-to-month rental option, but make sure you get a good deposit.

Ultimately, the option you choose should be based on your long-term goals (if you intend to sell the house in six months, month-to-month may be the best option for you, whereas if you intend to hold the property, you might want a long lease). This decision should also be based on how easy or difficult it is to rent homes in the area and the type of competition that exists in the neighborhood. Also, the level of stability in income you need is a factor in determining whether month-to-month renters will be acceptable.

> Remember that month-to-month tenancies can be terminated. If you want to increase the rent, a lease locks the rent for the period of the lease. Without a lease, the landlord can increase the tenant's rent with ten days' notice before rent is due if rent is paid monthly or three days' notice if it's paid weekly or semimonthly. The rules change for mobile homes, so be sure to look these up.

While the LPA also provides a lease agreement, you can download one at www.buyincomeproperties.com/freeforms/lease_agreement_for_furnished_house.html. Please note that it doesn't contain the same verbiage as the one at the LPA, and only an attorney can advise you as to which one would be best for you to use.

I provide this one here as an example of some of the differences between lease agreements for furnished and unfurnished homes. Furnished homes generally require greater deposits and more protection for you, the landlord/homeowner. I recommend you join the LPA and use their lease agreement, but this website will give you an example of one.

Standard Rental Agreement

Often this is just a rental contract that stipulates X dollars for Y usage. This is the most basic of agreements and is often used for month-to-month or very short-term rentals, including vacation rentals. Month-to-month or short-term rentals make the renter responsible for lost rent incurred if he or she breaks the lease, which is a benefit to you (provided the renter has the means to pay up, and you can find them!). In general it discourages tenants from moving out early, and helps you maintain a nice steady cash flow.

A rental agreement provides the following information:

- Renter's name—legal name of the renter or renters.
- Property address—address of the rented property.
- Term of the lease (how long)—Six months? One year? Two years?
- Late fees charged (timing of and the amount)—check state laws!
- Who's responsible for utilities—again check state laws.
- Who's responsible for appliances—the tenant is generally responsible for maintaining them, you are responsible for repairing them if the tenant didn't break it.
- Security deposit amount—this is to cover damages, not rent!
- Insurance coverage—you will stipulate that they must have renters insurance.
- Notice deadlines—for example, when is rent late? When do late fees apply? When will they be evicted?
- Real estate commissions to be paid (if applicable)—Are you paying a commission to anyone for finding the tenant? Is the tenant paying this?
- Acknowledgment and understanding of the lease.
- Signatures necessary—be sure to get everyone on the lease to sign, including (perhaps especially) cosigners.

What follows is a sample rental agreement; lease agreements tend to be more extensive. You might choose to use a lease agreement instead; you can download these from the LPA at www.thelpa.com/lpa/forms.html.

Standard Lease Agreements

A standard lease agreement is used for most tenancies that are in place for a specific period of time. For instance, if your tenant wants to rent for six months, one year, two years, and so on, you will create a lease agreement that stipulates everything from the deposit, to the process if the tenant doesn't pay her rent. Remember that lease agreements are contracts that spell out who is responsible for what, what your obligations as a landlord are, and what the tenant's obligations are. They also spell out the rights of both the landlord and the tenant.

RENTAL AGREEMENT

The Tenant(s) known as _____, hereby agree to rent the dwelling located at
_____.
The premises are to be occupied by the above named tenants only. Tenant may not sublet premises.

TERM The term shall commence on _____, at $_____ per month payable on the _____ of each month in full.

LATE FEES In the event rent is not paid by the _____( ) day after due date, Tenant agrees to pay a late charge of $_____

UTILITIES Tenant shall be responsible for the payment of the following utilities: water, electric, gas, heating fuel, Telephone.

APPLIANCES Appliances provided in this rental are: stove, refrigerator, dishwasher, ____air conditioner(s), _____.
Repairs will be born by said Tenants if damage is due to negligence of Tenants.

SECURITY Amount of security deposit is $_____. Security shall be held by Landlord until the time said Tenants have vacated the premises and Landlord has inspected it for damages. Tenant shall <u>not</u> have the right to apply Security Deposit in payment of any rent. Security deposits must be raised proportionately with rent increases.

INSURANCE Tenant is responsible for liability/fire insurance coverage on premises. Tenant agrees to obtain a "Renter's Insurance" policy and to provide Owner or agent with a copy of policy within seven (7) days of lease execution.

NOTICES Should tenant decide to vacate the premises, a _30_ day written notice to the landlord is required. Should landlord decide to have tenants vacated, a _30_ day written notice is required. Tenant agrees to allow premises to be shown at any and all reasonable times for re-rental.

REAL ESTATE COMMISSION (If applicable) In the event a commission was earned by a real estate broker, Tenant shall not take possession of the premises unless all fees due broker are paid in full as agreed. Commission is payable when this lease is signed by the Tenant(s). It is solely for locating the rental for the Tenant and is not refundable under any circumstances regardless of any disputes or conditions between the Landlord and Tenant before or after occupancy is taken.

ACKNOWLEDGMENT Tenants hereby acknowledge that they have read, understand and agree to all parts of this document, and have received a copy.

	AMOUNT RECEIVED	BALANCE DUE
RENT:	_____	_____
SECURITY:	_____	_____
BROKER'S FEE:	_____	_____

_____
_____
_____
_____

THE UNDERSIGNED TENANT(S) ACKNOWLEDGES RECEIPT OF A COPY HEREOF.

DATE: _____

OWNER/AGENT_____   TENANT_____

ADDRESS_____   TENANT_____

PHONE_____   PHONE_____

So, what goes into the lease agreement? Just about anything and everything. A lease agreement cannot be too long if you need it to cover an aspect of your tenancy relationship. The LPA lease agreement is by far the most comprehensive I've found, so you should check it out. Here are some basics to look for in whatever rental or lease agreement you decide on.

Property Address

You need to state the full legal property address and, if known, the lot and/or parcel number of the home. If you don't know it, it's usually listed on your tax bill and you can get it from there. This establishes a legal foundation for identifying the home.

Rental Amount

The rental amount will be the amount paid in rent each month. If you created a lease with an option to buy, you will need to stipulate how much in addition to regular rent will be going toward closing costs or toward a reduction in the price of the home. You also should indicate when rents can be increased and how many days' notice the tenant will be given.

Late Penalties

The tenant has a right to know what he will pay for paying rent late, for sending in checks that bounce for insufficient funds or other reasons, and how the fees will compound and be assessed. The tenant also needs to be aware how payments will be processed—first to pay fees, then to pay toward rent. Be very clear in spelling this out for your tenant.

Process for Eviction

The tenant must know the process you will go through if eviction should become necessary, including your requirement that both the tenant and you, the landlord, abide by federal, state, and local laws if eviction should become necessary. This process needs to be very clear and the tenant must know you mean business and that you cannot be taken advantage of.

Deposit Amount and Deposit Return

The amount the tenant must deposit before move-in and when the deposit will be returned must both be stipulated in the agreement. You should note when you will conduct the walk-through inspection and provide a list of fees that will be charged ahead of time for various items like cleaning or broken items. Note that the amount of time you have to return the deposit varies greatly by state. When you use the LPA to download your lease agreement, you will also be asked to select the state. You will then be given specific rules you must include in your lease (or exclude!) for that state.

Lease Agreement with Provisions

A lease agreement with provisions is a standard lease agreement that restricts leasing under certain conditions. For instance, the individual might have bad credit and you're conditioning her continued lease on the provision that she is not late one time and that you will carry out eviction proceedings immediately if she is. You might want to periodically monitor your tenant's credit or provision your right to remove the tenant under certain conditions. This type of lease is far rarer, and you should use one only under the advice of a real estate attorney.

Lease-to-Own Agreement

A lease-to-own agreement adds dollars to the tenant's rent in exchange for the option to buy the property later. In this lease agreement, you need to indicate exactly how much goes into the savings for the home to reduce the price or cover closing costs and what the option price is for buying the home.

Be very careful, and consider paying $300–$500 for a real estate attorney to review this particular type of lease. This can be very beneficial and help the tenant feel a sense of ownership that creates a great partnership (and a well-cared-for home), but it can backfire if not properly worded. Be sure to meet all legal requirements with a legal review. Take a look at the following option-to-buy agreement.

PF 58 Purchase Option Addendum   © 2008 By The Landlord Protection Agency, Inc.

Lease Addendum
Purchase Option Agreement

This addendum is made this _____ day of _____, 20____, and is added to and amends that certain agreement by and between _____ as Tenant(s) and _____ as Landlord(s), which agreement is dated _____ day of _____, 20____.

Said agreement is amended as follows:

PURCHASE OPTION   The Tenant shall be granted the exclusive right and privilege of purchasing the above described real property.

- **PURCHASE PRICE**   The total purchase price for said property is
  $_____
  ($_____) payable in lawful money of the United States, strictly within the following times, to-wit. All sums paid for this option and any extension thereof as herein provided, shall be first applied on the purchase price, and the balance shall be paid as follows:
  _____
  _____
  _____
  _____

- **DEPOSIT / DOWNPAYMENT**   Tenants agree to post a down payment/option deposit in the amount of $_____ to be applied towards the purchase price to secure the option. The parties agree that the option deposit shall be forfeit if the Tenant fails to purchase and close title on premises before the option period ending on
  _____.

- **EXTENSION OF OPTION**   The tenant / purchaser will be granted the option, providing the terms and conditions of this agreement have been complied with and satisfied, to extend this Option Agreement for a period of _____, upon payment from buyer to seller an additional sum of $_____ ($_____) Dollars *payable by cash or cashier's check*, prior to the expiration of the first option period subject to Owner's approval.

- **EXERCISE OF OPTION**   This option shall be exercised by written notice to seller on or before the expiration of the option period, or if extended, the expiration of the extended option period. Notice to exercise this option must be delivered personally or mailed via registered or certified mail to the owner at his address on or before such date of expiration, shall be timely and shall be deemed actual notice to seller.

- **REAL ESTATE COMMISSION**   It is further agreed that in the event Tenant exercises the option to purchase, _____, is the sole selling broker and shall be entitled to a real estate sales commission of _____% of the purchase price payable at closing.

Signed:

_____   _____

_____   _____

LPA 02099- Sub-Lease, plain English format,
simple, 11-04

© 2004 BY The Landlord Protection Agency, Inc.
Publisher, E. Meadow, NY 11554

SUBLEASE AGREEMENT

Made between _____, Lessor and

_____ Lessee, now

occupying _____ under a lease

dated _____, 20_____.

Lessor hereby agrees and consents to the subletting of the above specified premises with the understanding that the Sub-tenant

accepts the premises subject to all conditions as set forth in the said lease of _____, 20 _____, and which he

agrees to perform and fulfill as if he were the Lessee and that any breach of the lease made by the Sub-tenant shall constitute a

breach as if made by the Lessee.

It is further understood and agreed that in granting this privilege to the Lessee, the Lessor does not waive any of his rights under

the existing lease nor does he abrogate any of his rights for the recovery of the premises or for distress or otherwise, for rent, or for

other charges which may become due.

Unless otherwise approved, the Lessee shall sublet the above listed premises specifically to

_____
for the period commencing on the _____ day of _____, 20____, and monthly thereafter until
the last day of _____, 20_____, at which time this agreement is terminated.

_____
_____
_____
_____
_____
_____

THE UNDERSIGNED PARTIES ACKNOWLEDGES RECEIPT OF A COPY HEREOF.

DATE: _____

OWNER/LESSOR _____   LESSEE _____

ADDRESS_____   SUB-TENANT _____

PHONE_____   PHONE _____

Subleases

You might also need a real estate sublease if you intend to let the individual lease the place to yet another individual. While in general I don't recommend you allow subleases, if you do, you might want to provide your tenant with a binding form that will help him protect himself, and your property! A sample form is found on the previous page.

Lease Addendums

Addendums are additions to existing agreements. You might have an addendum for pets, for subleasing, for not smoking (or smoking with a fee), for just about anything that changes the lease.

Pet Addendum

One of the most common addendums is the pet addendum. This form is used to make any changes to the status of the allowance (or not) of pets on the property. Anytime a tenant is considering adding a pet, she needs to notify you. On the following page is a sample of the form you can use.

Utility Addendum

You may also need a utility addendum. You can download the form at the LPA. This is designed to reimburse the landlord or homeowner for the cost of utilities. You can download a quick, free utility addendum at www.totalrealestatesolutions. com/realestateforms/html/RentalUtilityAddendum.html.

Waterbed Addendum

It might sound silly, but waterbeds can be a source of problems in homes. If they leak, they can cause unruly damage to your home! Although some landlords refuse to allow them, you can use this form if it's okay with you that the tenant has a waterbed. Download the file at www.thelpa.com/free/waterbed.doc or look at the example that follows.

PET AGREEMENT

Premises: _____

This Pet Agreement addendum is made this _____ day of _____,
20_____, and is added to and amends that certain agreement by and between
_____ as Tenant(s) and
_____ as Landlord(s), which
agreement is dated _____ day of _____, 20_____. This is a conditional
privilege granted to the tenant in exchange for guaranteeing that the rules in this Pet Agreement
are strictly followed. This privilege may be terminated if any of the Pet Agreement rules are
violated. This privilege may also be terminated if tenant should violate or place Lease Rental
Agreement for the premises in default.

Tenants shall be permitted to keep a pet _____ named _____.

# of pets _____ Breed _____ Color_____ Weight _____
Breed _____ Color_____ Weight _____

The Pet Agreement Rules are as follows:
- Only a pet described and named in this Pet Agreement shall be permitted on the premises. Any others shall be a violation of the agreement.
- Tenants agree to be fully responsible and liable, and pay for any damages or injury caused by, or as a result of their pet. Pet damages can apply to floors, carpeting, walls, windows, screens, moldings, furniture and landscaping, etc.
- Tenants agree that they will not allow their pet to disturb or annoy neighbors in any way, whether the pet is inside the dwelling or outside.
- Tenant will keep control over the pet at all times, whether inside the dwelling or outside.
- Tenants agree that pet will not be left unattended over any unreasonable periods of time.
- Tenants agree that no pets offspring are allowed on premises.
- Tenants promise not to leave food for the pet outside the dwelling, which can attract other animals and bugs.
- Tenants agree to keep their pet clean at all times, and keep the premises in a clean and sanitary manner, properly disposing of pet droppings as quickly as possible.
- Tenant shall post a Pet Security deposit in the amount of $_____ which is to be held by owner until such time the premises are returned. The deposit will then be refunded to tenant as long as the premises are returned as agreed.
- Tenant shall pay a one time only Pet Fee in the amount of $_____.

The parties have entered into this Agreement on the date first above stated, and acknowledge
receipt of a copy hereof.

LANDLORD: **TENANT:**

_____   _____

_____   _____

WATERBED ADDENDUM

This addendum is made this _____ day of _____, 20____, and is added to and amends that certain agreement by and between _____ as Tenant(s) and _____ as Landlord(s), which agreement is dated _____ day of _____, 20____.

It is the tenant's intention to keep a waterbed in the residence named in the attached Lease/Rental Agreement. This shall be a conditional privilege granted to the tenant in exchange for guaranteeing that the rules in this waterbed addendum are strictly followed. The Owner/Agent reserves the right to revoke this privilege if the tenant violates any of the agreements herein.

The permission is granted to keep a waterbed under the following terms and conditions:

1) Tenant agrees to keep a waterbed located on the _____ floor of the dwelling.

2) Tenant agrees to be responsible for any defects or damages concerning the premises in relation to the waterbed during or as a result of having the waterbed in the dwelling.

3) Tenant agrees to obtain liability insurance to include coverage concerning the waterbed.

4) Tenant agrees to post $_____additional security deposit which will be returned after tenant vacates, providing the premises are returned as agreed.

5) In the event the Tenant gets rid of the waterbed, it is agreed that it will not be replaced with another waterbed without the owner/agent's expressed written permission. It is also agreed that removal will be done in a proper professional manner, not to cause any hardship on the dwelling or landlord.

Owner/Agent _____   Tenant _____ Date _____

Tenant _____ Date _____

Mold Addendum

Another example you should provide is a mold addendum, shown on the next page. The mold addendum makes the tenant responsible for keeping the property free of mold and mildew through proper maintenance and makes him responsible for cleaning and repair expenses from mold damage he causes. This is important because it can cost you a lot of money later, and some landlords have been sued for allowing mold in their properties.

Additional Addendum Information

Take a look at the list of essential forms available online at the LPA at www.thelpa.com/lpa/forms.html. One thing that is great about this site is the uniqueness of many of the forms—some that address situations we'd never know how to handle without, like how to notify a tenant of a strange odor or how to inform her of her inability to have a motorcycle. Other forms include:

- Furnished lease with an inventory checklist for every item
- Lease with purchase options
- Rental application
- Urgent late notices
- Urgent eviction notices
- A template for a payment booklet (how convenient!)
- All the qualifier forms you need to qualify a tenant over the phone and in person
- Notice of charges due
- Grounds violation notices
- Smoke detector addendum
- Intent to enter premises (very important if you're going to enter the tenant's home; although it's your home, remember the tenants' rights!)
- Motorcycle addendum—yes they can be an issue!
- Odor notices
- Satellite dish/cable TV addendums
- Quick-glance tenant charts

MOLD ADDENDUM

This addendum is made this _____ day of _____, 20____, and is added to and amends that certain agreement by and between _____ as Tenant(s) and _____ as Landlord(s), which agreement is dated _____ day of _____, 20____. Failure to comply with the terms of this addendum is a violation of said agreement constituting grounds for eviction and tenant's liability for any damages as a result of tenant's failure to comply.

1) **Acknowledgement** Tenant acknowledges that the rental is free of mold and agrees to take responsibility for preventing mold growth that can become a health hazard to occupants of the rental.

2) **Liability** Tenant agrees to be responsible for any defects or damages concerning mold during or as a result of the tenant's occupancy, and agrees to check for mold on a regular basis. Tenant accepts full liability for the entire amount of cleaning expenses and damage reparations caused by mold or mildew during or as a result of tenant's occupancy.

3) **Maintenance Care** Tenant agrees to take full responsibility for keeping the residence clean and dry and free from moisture accumulations where mold could be allowed to grow. (The kitchen and bathroom(s) are the most common places mold is known to form.)

4) **Climate Control** Tenant agrees to keep the temperature and humidity within reasonable levels as to prevent the growth of mold.

5) **Violation of Agreement** Violation of any of the provisions in this Mold Addendum shall constitute a material default of the terms of the Lease Agreement and subject to the remedies and/or penalties concerning lease violations stated in the Lease Agreement.

6) **Contract** The parties acknowledge and agree that this addendum once signed shall be a part of the above mentioned lease, and that no other agreements concerning mold shall be valid unless such agreement(s) are written and signed by the parties.

Tenants have read and acknowledge this addendum and agree to carry out the responsibilities described above.

Owner/Agent_____   Tenant_____ Date_____

Lease Clauses

A clause in general creates some sort of dependency—if this, then that. A clause can state that the individual may have guests over, but if the guests cause damage, the renter is liable. Rental and lease agreements are full of clauses. As you read through the samples provided in this book and those the LPA provides, you will see numerous clauses. What you need to determine is which clauses are sufficient to cover your property. Does the tenant have the right to use all furnishings, but anything not returned in the condition borrowed is paid for by the tenant? If so, how is cost determined? Anything that needs to be stipulated can be a clause.

> Normal wear and tear might be one clause you mention in your agreement. One thing that is important to note to your tenants is what is considered normal wear and tear and what is not.

Here are some things the www.buyincomeproperties.com/html/RentalNormWearnTear1.html website notes that are critical:

- Dishwashers cannot be run through the dial because the tenant can strip the mechanism.
- Water heaters wrapped in blankets can cause problems and void the warranty.
- Electric ranges don't last nearly as long as a gas range and if elements aren't properly put back in, they can short out the range.
- A filter not changed in a furnace can burn out a motor.
- Concrete can crack from having a heavy object in the same spot for long periods of time (such as heavy cars).

If you weren't aware of even one of these things, check out the site for more information!

Legal Considerations

Remember that your lease agreement and its addendums are your legally binding documents between you and the tenant. This creates the tenancy, which is very powerful in the United States. Tenants have significant rights, and the only way to protect your rights as the homeowner is to document them clearly and succinctly in the lease agreement. Get each cosigner or coapplicant to sign the agreement also, and consider running your final lease agreement by a real estate attorney, particularly if this is your first one. Also, make sure that your lease agreement abides by all local, state, and federal laws so that you—and your tenant—are protected.

6

Getting Your Property Rented

Now that you have your ducks in a row and have your applications ready and your advertising campaign beginning, you need to get your property rented. Most of us want to rent our property quickly, but there are some downsides to rushing for renters—primarily that the one you rent to will turn out to be a bad tenant. It's better to forgo a month's rent (although it might not feel like it right now) than be stuck with a tenant who destroys your home.

Sometimes it is faster and easier to get the property rented through a property manager, but sometimes not. Either way, you will need to communicate with your property manager on a regular basis, so it's imperative you find someone who returns calls or emails, stays on top of problems, communicates with you promptly, and makes you feel comfortable when asking questions without feeling dumb. Property managers usually have a lot of experience to share, and it's okay to ask them how they'd handle problems. It's also okay to ask them when you can expect them to interface with you, when you can expect statements, if they provide online services, and so on. It might help for you to make a list of the top qualities you feel would be important when dealing with a property manager and then make notes as you interview him. I've found that if he doesn't return calls to get a listing from you, he probably won't return tenants' calls or your calls after you become a client. Beware of

TALK FROM THE TRENCHES

"If you are sentimentally attached to your home, please consider letting a property manager lease out your home and stipulate what you want the property manager to do for you." Perhaps another good reason to use a property manager.

these types of property managers! Remember that you are paying him a monthly fee to take care of you and your property!

If you travel a lot, this might also be another good option, but look for a company with direct deposit. If you aren't around to deposit checks, you might find yourself stressing to pay the mortgage, and that negates the reason you're probably renting the property to begin with.

If you do find yourself wanting to rent your home and wanting to hire a property manager, don't feel bad or as though you're wasting money by bringing in a professional. For some, time or family constraints or even living out of town might really create a need for someone else to do the day-to-day work. That is perfectly reasonable, and you might find the manager's paycheck is worth fewer hassles. Do be sure you check whether this has any tax ramifications, though. If you were claiming to be a real estate professional on your tax return and you outsource this, you might no longer qualify. Find out from an accountant specializing in real estate.

Working with a property manager can provide you with many benefits. I find the biggest benefit is in the event that someone doesn't pay and needs to be evicted. It's a legal annoyance, but it can also be maddeningly frustrating, particularly if you aren't living in the state that your property is in. Providing a 24/7 contact number for tenants is beneficial, and not having to take calls at all hours of the night when something small happens or not having to take calls from tenants who can sometimes be squeaky wheels can be a big benefit. You might even want to test the property manager's 24/7 responsiveness sometime or ask your tenants what it is like when they call for maintenance.

Periodically perform checks on your property management company and its managers. I wasn't aware of a bad property manager until a tenant told me that she couldn't get in contact with the manager; that is obviously a big problem. Upon further investigation, I found that the property manager, who had four of my homes, really wasn't doing her job with any of the properties, and I subsequently had to find another property manager (which, by the way, is harder than hiring one to begin with, so choose carefully!).

Another benefit is that property managers often have teams of individuals working on behalf of property owners. They know the law and will generally protect your rights, and they also know the tenants' rights. They will run the credit checks, run background checks, verify income, and so on. They have the resources to do this quickly and cheaply, and they know the maximum amount they can charge for various services.

A property manager is by definition a middle man between you and your rental money. There are drawbacks: if the money is collected on the first of the month, you might not see it until the fifteenth (all things to find out ahead of time!). You might have to wait for a check in the mail (if you can, use companies that offer direct deposit), and you might have to make many phone calls if the check doesn't show up. You generally would not contact your tenant directly after the tenant enters an agreement with the property manager (and you enter into an agreement to let them act on your behalf), so you shouldn't be phoning the tenant unless the property manager has completely disappeared. If you want to check on the status of something, you might need to wait until the weekday instead of the weekend, which can be frustrating.

You Want to Rent But Don't Want to Manage It Yourself

If you decided to rent with a property manager, she will most likely have a landscaper and a housecleaner to take care of some maintenance issues, but be prepared to pay the property manager money for the "maintenance bucket" to get it going. My last property I rented through a property manager required a $700 check to hire pest controllers, clean the house, clean the yard, and so forth. Even though this was a brand-new property, dust gets in, and I even had a vagrant living in the home for apparently a few weeks. These are the chances you take with new homes. Thankfully, nothing was seriously ruined. The property manager will ask for keys, do an inspection, and determine how much you will need. Ask for a breakdown of the items that need repair or sprucing up. You want to know what you're paying for.

TALK FROM THE TRENCHES

Forty percent of people who used a property manager said that deciding on the property manager they wanted to work with was either hard or very hard. This is most likely because property manager talk is confusing. One may give you a higher percentage of the first month's rent, but may not handle direct deposit. It's also tough to tell who will do a good job, but you can get around that by asking for references and calling them! Check references, monthly percentage rate, and finder's fee. If they are all in line and you enjoy working with the property manager, go for it. Personality is important too—remember your tenants are going to interface with this person that represents YOU!

What to Look for in a Manager

What do you want to look for should you decide to hire a property manager? Reputation, integrity, and a significant period of time doing business as well as a license for his state. Integrity and reputation can be hard to gauge, so it's vital you ask for references.

Ask plainly what the benefits are to using his service. For example:

- Does he offer tenants a 24/7 number?
- Does he have his own maintenance team?
- Does he get bids from multiple contractors to save you money?
- Does he regularly check the property and if so, how often?
- How often does he drive by versus doing an in-house inspection?
- How does he feel about renting a home when you have it for sale also?
- Does he run credit and background checks?
- What are his criteria for tenants?
- Does he offer direct deposit and online statements?

I have had two drastically different experiences with property managers. I have one in Texas who has done such an incredible job that he even offered to split costs with me when repairs exceed his estimate. He routinely stays in contact via cell phone and email and provides documents online within a day. He directly deposits rent and sends online electronic statements. In short, he makes my life easy. He's worth the 8 percent management fee and full month's rent he charges for finding a tenant—and then some. (For the record, if you would like a property manager in Texas, contact Austin Real Pros' Bill Evans and tell him Dani Babb sent you!)

I've had other experiences, though, including a manager who didn't drive by houses for years quite literally. I didn't know this until a real estate agent phoned me and told me I should / could not sell my house as there was "two feet of trash piled up outside"—apparently because the tenant didn't want to pay for trash service. I've had neighbors who sued because a tree wasn't cut down—a tree that the neighbor warned the property manager about for months and that eventually fell and smashed the neighbor's car—all the while the property manager had never informed me of any problems. Other problems I've experienced include property managers who don't cooperate with my agent when I choose to sell in an area I don't live in, late rent checks, and no communication when a renter leaves. I've also experienced property managers who had a maintenance company under another name and then billed out services at a higher rate to the property manager, while the owner double-collected for services. You name it, I've had it. Check out your property managers before you invest your time, money, and emotional security. Drawbacks to property managers are minimal unless they are not reputable.

You should test responsiveness immediately by contacting the property manager in your preferred method to inquire about the issues I'll talk about next: fees, areas they cover, services provided, experience, and so on. If it takes the property manager three days to secure a new property, how responsive do you think he will be after you've already handed the keys over? Personally, I expect same-day communication whether by email or phone. Whichever your most preferred communication method, make sure the property manager regularly supports it. For instance, if I email someone, I want a response by email not by phone—a property manager who returns my email by phone isn't in tune with my needs and requirements. For me, that won't work. If you prefer phone and the person responds to you by email, that might not work for you.

Look for experience; it counts here in a big way. The property manager needs to know the area, the types of tenants, and how to handle problems. He needs to know by ZIP code and street what the house can rent for. Don't be afraid to flat out ask how many years he has been in the business, how he advertises, how he finds tenants, what the average time to rent is for that area for that particular company, and what criteria he uses to qualify renters. Find out how he deposits your funds, when you can expect checks, and what kind of deposits he requires from tenants, and ask for a copy of the rental agreement that he gives to tenants.

Read it thoroughly and see what agreements he makes. Does he keep all late fees for himself, or does he share them with you? Does he go for eviction, covering court costs and trying to recoup costs from the tenant on your behalf, or does he let the tenant go with little recourse? What are his income criteria and credit criteria?

TALK FROM THE TRENCHES

One respondent to the survey had this to say: "Keep the relationship business. Don't let too much time go by before you file an eviction. Don't hesitate to go after your money in small claims court." This goes for property managers, too; they need to be comfortable should the need arise to evict a tenant.

Find out whether the property manager is a licensed real estate professional and if he's going to lock you into selling the property through him! Yes, I have seen this. I immediately demanded this be taken out of the contract (and subsequently changed property managers to the aforementioned Austin property management company!). You might want to sell by owner, and you don't want to have to sell through a company just because it collected rent, took a cut, and passed money onto you for a few months or years.

Perhaps most importantly, find out what the property manager does to check on your property! I've run into big issues with property managers not checking on properties and having serious issues I didn't find out about until I went to sell the property—issues such as trash piled up outside that would have been spotted if the property manager had ever driven by the house.

Management Fees

A big question of course is what the management company charges. Remember in many cases that you're going to get what you pay for. You might ask for a multi-property discount if it applies to you. I always ask potential property managers for this; some will give it to you, and others won't. Expect to pay between 6 and 10 percent of each month's rent collected, and expect to pay between 50 percent of one month's rent to a full month's rent to find tenants. This usually covers advertising costs, but be sure to ask if you're footing the bill for those costs on top of the fees. If you are, you might want to consider going elsewhere. Find out how much the property manager charges for finding a tenant, and what the monthly management fee is. Find out if they require you to list your property with them if you decide to sell (if they do, I recommend eliminating them from your list).

Property managers will often say that they charge the first month's rent as the finder's fee. This is normal, but you may ask, "they don't know how much I'll rent it for, so how can they do that?" They will tend to start higher and come down if the place isn't rented. Whatever price it rents at will be your final fee for finding a tenant. Taking $\frac{1}{12}$th (if the tenant stays a year) is tough; so ask if this is negotiable.

Find out what the management fee includes. How can tenants deposit funds to the property manager? Do they require a mail-in payment? How quickly do they follow up with late tenants? Will they pay you via direct deposit, or do you have to wait for a mailed check? My property manager in Austin not only directly deposits rental payments, but also emails statements in PDF format! Talk about convenient! If you travel a lot, look for this option.

Your cash flow statement will look a little different, primarily because your property manager will take two "cuts" of your income. The first is in the form of a finder's fee, which can vary from $0 to only advertising costs to a full month's rent. This is generally negotiable if you have more than one property you are renting, but not so much if you are renting only one with the property manager. The second is in the form of a monthly payment, which is usually a percent of rent collected. The property manager will also hang onto the tenant's deposit as a credit in your account and is responsible for taking repairs out of the deposit. The property manager will also, based on state rules, give the tenant her deposit back within the allotted period of time.

Maintenance Options

There are benefits and drawbacks to working with a property manager that has their own maintenance company. They could be pulling a scam by running the maintenance company as a separate business and up-charging you for repairs! I ran into this in Austin, Texas, until I found Austin Real Pros.

They might have maintenance as a part of their company, though, and might just pass costs on to you, which can often be cheaper than outsourcing jobs to other contractors. You often won't have to wait as long for repairs either if the maintenance person works for the company. Find out what the property manager does for maintenance and if they provide a 24/7 paging service for emergencies for tenants of your properties.

TALK FROM THE TRENCHES

Twenty-seven percent of those surveyed said handling maintenance issues on their own was either hard or very hard—something to consider when deciding on whether to use a property manager and the importance of the maintenance piece.

Find out how they handle maintenance issues. Most have a value they won't exceed without checking with you first but will take care of items less than, say, $200 without checking. Find out what that limit is and whether it's negotiable to your comfort level.

I always recommend asking the tenant at some point how he feels about the service he receives, usually via a mailed survey. Even though the property managers might frown on this, I do this until I am comfortable that all issues are being handled properly. Another thing you can do is to check your monthly statements; you should expect minor repairs once in awhile unless the home is relatively new. You might also want to check in with the property manager on occasion to see when he last did a drive-by, how the property is looking, and to forecast any big-ticket items for the coming year. After all, you need this for planning purposes anyway.

If you want to do your own survey, try this. Go to www.surveymonkey.com. Type in your survey, and email your tenants the link. (Yes, you will need to get their email address! Your property manager should have this, and it should be on a copy of the agreement that they send to you.) What questions do you ask? How about these for starters:

- Have you requested any maintenance from the property manager that hasn't been done yet? If so, what?
- Have your phone calls been returned promptly (e.g. within forty-eight hours)?
- Have you requested emergency service? If yes, was your issue handled promptly?
- Are you greeted and treated with courtesy by the property manager?
- Do you find making rental payments easy? If not, what can the property manager do to improve?
- Is the property manager in any way hindering your desire to continue your lease? If so, how? What can be done to remedy the situation?
- Are there any specific concerns or compliments you wish to share?

Understanding How the Money Works

Throughout the time you rent your property, money will be trading hands with your tenant. Here is an example of what you might expect on a one-year lease and how it can affect your balance sheet:

Month 1: Rental deposit made to landlord. First and last month's rent paid.

Month 2: Rent paid. Utilities paid by tenant and landlord (vary by state and contract) and will remain throughout the year.

Month 3: Renter paid for a maintenance problem, asks to be reimbursed. Rent paid will not include maintenance repair, but the tenant will send a receipt with rent.

Month 4: Rent is late. You assessed a $50 charge. The rent and the $50 are paid within five days.

Month 5: Rent is paid on time.

Month 6: The renter adds a pet. You are made aware, and you add a $100 pet deposit. You add $100 to the deposit amount on record, and add this to the balance sheet.

Month 7: Rent is paid on time.

Month 8: Your association fines you $100 for leaving cooking oil on the fence for longer than thirty days. You assess the renter the fine in added rent, and the renter pays an extra $100 with regular rent. You use this to pay the fine.

Month 9: Rent is paid on time. You have $800 worth of repairs to do, and you don't have a way to know if they are tenant-caused. You have to pay for the repair bill.

Month 10: You send out two-month notifications that their lease is about to expire, and offer a one-time discount for renewing early. You remind them that you report them to credit agencies and to the Landlord Protection Agency if they are late or leave the property in bad condition. You receive normal rent.

Month 11: Renter contacts you asking about a $500 discount to renew. You offer a $200 credit for month 1 of the new fiscal rental year, and the renter accepts. You send the renter a new contract, and the renter signs. You do a periodic inspection after sending out the forty-eight hour (or greater, depending on the state) notice of entry. You do not raise the tenants' rent to try to keep them there longer.

Month 12: Renter pays on time.

Month 1 of the new year: The renter pays rent, minus $200 credit ... and the process begins again!

7

Getting Your Home Ready to Rent

So, now you know whether you're going to rent your home yourself or hire a property management company, but what do you need to do to the home to get it ready for showing? This chapter covers all the ins and outs of your preparatory work.

First, make sure the home is clean and presentable. Then be sure you are ready for your applicants. You know you're going to need to run credit checks and background checks, and you know what you're going to be checking for—you might even want to create a checklist for yourself.

Get the home in sale-ready form: fresh paint, fresh carpet or newly cleaned carpet or floors if needed, if you're providing any appliances get them in and ready (you don't need high-end goods, but the more you offer, like a refrigerator or a washer and dryer, the more appealing your property will look over your competitors, particularly to someone who doesn't have these things for themselves), and get the yard landscaped and maintained. Get a housecleaner to do a good thorough deep cleaning, get all the bushes and trees trimmed back, and get the home looking sharp. If you are offering the place furnished, remove any furnishings you don't want included. When a potential tenant does a walk-through, what he sees is what he should get. Put in the drapes or curtains and window coverings discussed earlier, too.

Home Inspection and Walk-Through

When the tenant moves into the home, she will have certain expectations that it's your job to meet. You can do this yourself, or you can hire out and have others do it for you.

After you have selected a tenant, notified her of her acceptance, and she is moving in, you will need to do a home inspection and walk-through with that tenant. The rental car analogy works well here. You walk around the car, noting all the dings and problems that existed before the rental, so you have something to compare to when the car is returned. The same thing occurs with your home. The garage door window has a small crack in it? Note that. The carpet shows significant signs of wear along the staircase? Note that.

Here is a list of things to look at, but be sure to check out the LPA's complete list:

- Overall condition of the property.
- Condition of the floors or carpet, including stains.
- Condition of the cabinetry.
- Condition of the doors and hinges.
- Condition of all the bathroom and kitchen fixtures.
- Condition of the appliances.
- Any burned-out lightbulbs.
- Smoke detectors—working and in good order.
- Stovetop, oven, and other appliances—all in working order.
- Whether the refrigerator is clean and the freezer and refrigerator are working.
- Grounds and lawn are trimmed.
- Property is free of trash.
- Countertop and tile condition.
- Hood/fan/lights in the kitchen are working.

- Mirrors are not broken.
- Fireplaces work.
- Windows are all screened and open and shut properly.
- Garbage disposal works.
- Walls and ceilings in all the rooms are free from damage, dents, nicks, painted wells, and so on.
- Toilets are all working well, including freely draining.
- Grout is clean.
- Towel bars are installed, including other accessories.
- Windows and doors open and lock correctly.
- Washer and dryer work.
- Balcony/deck/patio is in good shape, no wood rot, and so on.
- Fences and gates are all working, including the locks.
- All security systems and locks are working properly.
- Garage and storage areas are free from debris.
- Parking area is clear and available for parking.
- Keys provided are X (indicate number 1, 2, 3, etc.) Note: if you are including mailbox keys, provide the location of the mailbox and what number it is if applicable.
- Heating and air-conditioning work.
- Heating and air-conditioning filters are all new (and should be when the property is returned to you).
- Home is free from cigarette smoke.
- Gutters are cleaned and free from debris.
- Tubs and showers are not leaking, have no cracks, and all plumbing works.
- Electrical outlets in the home are in working condition.
- Utilities that are required to be turned on by the owner are turned on and are working.
- Window coverings are in good condition and are working, not bent, and so on.

TALK FROM THE TRENCHES

One accidental landlord had this to say in the survey, "Think about a variety of worst-case scenarios and develop back-up plans in case any of them happen." Good advice!

The condition of the home must be documented and signed off by both you and the tenant during the walk-through phase. The requirement is that the tenant returns the home in the same condition it was rented to her, less normal wear and tear. This is similar to renting a car. You aren't expected to pay for the depletion of tire tread, but if you get into an accident, you are expected to pay for the damages. Take care of everything you need to (and should) up-front so you have a happy tenant moving in and can clearly delineate between any damage or wear caused by the tenant and anything that was preexisting.

Minimal Repair and Maintenance

Many landlords are reluctant to do anything expensive to homes. Admittedly, I still cringe when my property manager tells me a home needs new carpet or paint because I know it can get expensive. Remember, though, that this is an investment to buy you time to make a decision and to keep a property in good condition. You owe it to your investment and decision as well as your tenant to keep up the maintenance. Install light-colored, inexpensive carpet that can be dyed if you intend on renting the house for years, and apply a fresh coat of paint whenever it's needed between tenants. I just try to go with the cheapest bid here and someone I know will do a good job. If you have a property manager, he should provide you with a bid up-front. Here are some of the basics you should always do:

- Replace all fixtures that aren't working.
- Make sure all plumbing works.
- Make sure all appliances work.
- Make sure all toilets work properly.
- Make sure the garage and all parking areas and storage areas are completely clean and free of debris.
- Make sure all locks work.
- Make sure all doors are secure.
- Make sure all windows and window screens are secure.
- Make sure all lights and lightbulbs work.
- Make sure all electrical outlets work.
- Replace any worn or tattered carpet.

- Apply a fresh coat of paint.
- Install any towel bars or other necessary accessories.
- Make sure proper window coverings are installed.
- Make sure the oven vent works properly.
- Make sure landscaping is complete, neat, and clean.
- Make sure all utilities you are required to have on are turned on and that trash pick-up is also available.
- Make sure neighbors know who to call if there are any issues.
- Remove any personal items you don't want a tenant to believe are included in the rental, such as furniture, pots and pans, shower curtains, and so on.
- Make sure all fireplaces are cleaned out and are working properly.
- Make sure any cable, satellite television, or Internet connections you are providing with the home are working and that the cabling is in good condition.
- Make sure the moldings and trim are free from nicks, scratches, or anything else that might turn off a potential tenant.
- Make sure any vinyl flooring is repaired, any granite is sealed, and any porous materials such as travertine are appropriately treated, and do a thorough cleaning and appropriate maintenance on hard wood or other flooring or counters throughout the home.
- Make sure the water heater is in good condition and is providing hot water.
- Make sure that all your association fees are paid and that you have forwarded any bills you will continue paying, such as water, trash/sewer, and definitely tax and association bills to another address (a post office box or a service like the UPS Store are helpful for this sort of thing, particularly in keeping the tenant from having your home address).
- Make sure you have copies of keys made to all gates, deadbolts, storage sheds, and so on.

Whether to Furnish

Furnished homes can be more attractive to tenants, but they will also potentially exclude families that already have their own furniture. Ask yourself some simple questions: What will storage of my furniture cost me? Do I need the furniture in my new home? What kind of tenant in this area will I attract with furnishings? Without? How expensive are my belongings? How much will this increase my insurance? Does that offset the cost of storing the items? Do I have a tenant who wants to move in now with (or without) furniture? In general, I don't furnish homes, but I have rented my home with all its furniture for a short time while moving 30 miles or so. Remember that you might pay more for insurance if you have your own belongings there (usually if your personal items exceed $5,000 in value), but you may be able to get considerably more in rent. You might attract a renter, though, who doesn't have much for herself, which might not be a good financial sign. Weigh the financial pros and cons, and determine what your things are worth. You can always add a deposit for furnished homes, but there are state limits on how much more you can charge.

Safety and Security

It is your job to provide a safe and secure home. If you are aware of broken locks, broken windows, or anything else that would create an insecure environment, get them fixed before the tenant moves in!

You must also require your tenants to get their own rental policy—for your safety and security as well as theirs. Ask to see a copy of the individual's rental policy (he needs to get one to protect himself, and you!) within fifteen days of renting the property or sooner if it makes you more comfortable. Rental policies are generally inexpensive and cover the tenant's personal belongings. You still have an obligation to provide a safe and secure rental. To do this, you need to be sure that all locks work, that the windows aren't broken, that any security system in place can be activated (and paid for) by the tenant (but you must have the code, too), and that any reasonable threats are documented.

8

Advertising and Marketing Your Home

This chapter is vital to getting your home rented quickly, to the right renter, and in a way that is in-line with your own financial needs and goals. We will walk through identifying the market that your home is in, understanding how to advertise (and how to stay out of trouble), how and where to list your home, online tools, how to create marketing buzz, and what renters—your clients— will be looking for. All of this information ties together neatly as you begin to market your house as a package to potential buyers!

Identifying Your Market

You will need to identify the market for your specific home, which is harder than it sounds. Let me give you a firsthand example. I have a single-family home that is continuously rented by four college students. Sounds scary, right? Not so much. The house is in excellent condition, they pool their money, and their parents have backed the lease. They weren't my target tenants, but when they were interviewed and checked out, there was no reason for me not to rent to them.

By identifying your target tenant, I am not implying anything that is discriminatory. What I mean is: what types of people are going to want to rent your place? If it's furnished, that might not appeal to families. If it's in a neighborhood next to clubs and bars, that might not appeal to families, either. If it's next to a top-notch public school and has a big backyard, it might appeal to families. The target tenant will dictate how you spend your advertising dollars, and that is why it matters. You can never target a tenant based on anything deemed discriminatory under the law.

Legal Terms in Advertising—Keeping Yourself Out of Trouble

When you start advertising your home for rent, it is very important that you are aware how *not* to advertise your home. The Department of Housing and Urban Development (HUD) has a list of words that are considered discriminatory. Local newspapers will also have their own list of words even more strict than HUD, so these are unlikely to run ads that will get you into trouble.

Remember that some classes are not protected by federal law but are protected by state or local laws. Check locally for laws regarding marital status, sexual orientation, and source of income (for example, small business owners, commissioned workers, and so on).

Words that will get you into trouble are *restricted* (might imply to a certain group), *adult*, *single*, *<religion> only*, *individual*, *no children*, *woman/man*, *retired*, *no more than* X *children*, *older children only* (or *younger*, or *no teens*, and so on), *<race> only*, *employed* (discriminates based on income when the person could have millions in the bank and be capable of paying the rent), and *heterosexuals* or *homosexuals only*. Anything that on the outside could be deemed discriminatory should be avoided. Even phrases that seem innocuous like *mom will love that big closet!* might imply that no gays, single people, or single parents are allowed. Be careful, and try to stick to what is relevant and LEGAL. You might want to include some things that are borderline, like "quiet tenants only" or "mature" tenants (be careful here, too, though!) or listing which churches a home is close to (informative, though saying it's close to a Catholic church could imply that only Catholics are welcome). In general, I just recommend staying away from all such phrases and words and keeping things simple.

How to List Your Home

Be sure you clearly spell out what you are and are not willing to accept from rental applicants when you advertise your home for rent. You will want to include:

- Whether pets are acceptable
- The amount of the deposit
- The lease and Term, or if it's month-to-month

You will also need to have your own rules and requirements for your tenant. For starters, you want a tenant with good income (this is up to you; I recommend that you use the same formula as banks and not allow the rent to exceed 40 percent or so of the tenant's income, depending on her other obligations)—some landlords decide that a 2.5:1, 3:1, or 3.5:1 ratio is acceptable depending on the house or multifamily unit in question. This would mean that the tenant's income has to be 2.5 times, 3 times, or 3.5 times the rent. If utilities are included in the rent, you can make the percent lower because they're covered.

You also want a tenant with verifiable income (the tenant needs to prove to you she has a job or a reliable income stream). This means that you can verify the person works where they say they work, and make what they say they make.

When you submit your advertisement, you will want to make it thorough enough that questions are answered and so the ad screens tenants to some degree, but loose enough that you don't weed out every potential renter!

The advertisement should be thorough enough to completely describe the property and the terms. Some of the things you might include in your listing are:

- Rental amount—what you want to rent the house for
- Potential discounts you're willing to offer
- Preferred leasing or renting terms
- Property features—number of bedrooms and bathrooms
- Washer and dryer, or only hook-ups
- Appliances included
- Upgrades that might be of interest (marble bathrooms, granite counters, and hardwood floors)

- Square footage of the home
- Views it might have (ocean, mountain, golf)
- Utilities included—if so, which ones
- Cable or Internet prewired or included
- Landscaping and/or housekeeping included
- Deposit requirements
- Central air-conditioning or window A/C

Some great words to include are:

- Upscale
- Luxury
- Bottom line
- Opportunity
- Value
- Lively market
- Energetic neighborhood
- Quiet
- Tranquil
- Free
- Profitable
- Underpriced

Also be sure you include pictures of the inside and outside of the home and any special views it may have. Remember that people want the outside to look nice, not just the inside. Talk up the great points—is it on a cul-de-sac with a large lot? Does it have a pool, and is it close to parks? If the site you're using requires that you pay more for the added information, pay it. The more information, the more attention your ad will get.

There are some great sample leads (the heading that everyone sees immediately) with headlines and details available to you at www.alllarentals.com/sampleads. html. Here are a few examples from the site:

Westwood $795/mo. Private Guest Apt. Attached to house, with private entrance. Spanish style home. Downstairs, quiet & private. Major cross street: near Beverly Glen, on quiet residential street. Hardwood floors. Deck, Yard & Garden. Lots of trees. Front yard. Lots of greenery. Garden view. Breakfast room. Sunny, Light and airy. Security entry. Security system. View of Century City's Twin Towers, through tree-filled garden. Other info: Fabulous Location, 5 minutes to UCLA and Beverly Hills, near 4 bus lines, quiet furnished room with private entrance in Spanish style house. Safe upscale neighborhood of single-family homes with easy permit parking. Like being out in the country, trees all around.

Granada Hills $625/mo. *Guest Unit! Nice & private. Private 3/4 bath. Mini-kitchen with Refrigerator and microwave. *Located in 1-story home with a private entrance. Residential area with street parking available. Carpet and blinds. Air-conditioning. Includes all utilities (paid).

Landlord.com offers the following sample listing:

3br/1½ ba town home, $1500/mo, enclosed garage. Park district. Quiet, comfortable, roomy. Landscape maintenance, major appliances included. Small pets ok. Call Zebulon, XXX-XXXX.

You can access their information on writing informative, effective ads at www.landlord.com/classified_ad.htm.

Using Online Tools

The wonderful world of the Internet has lots of fantastic tools to make your life easier! Take advantage of them! Blogs, online community forums, craigslist, and even MySpace can have great opportunities. It's all about networking and getting your property out there. Consider videotaping your property and putting the video on YouTube. Consider posting video links hosted on a video site (there are lots of them that are free!) and then letting potential renters take their own video tour! Why not walk around with a video camera, take video of your home, and include it along with more information about the house to drum up interest?

My favorite site of all is the Landlord Protection Agency at www.thelpa.com. This site is comprehensive and has everything from free forms to more advanced paid forms, to the ability to check credit, report bad tenants, and even look up rental comps. This is truly a one-stop shop! You can access the site from www.drdaniellebabb.com. One thing that I find incredible is the ability to report bad tenants; this is something accidental landlords never had the option to do before the Internet.

Here are some other great tools:

- U.S. Record Search at www.usrecordsearch.com
- Family Sex Offender List at www.familywatchdog.us
- U.S. Search at www.ussearch.com
- Public Background Checks at www.publicbackgroundchecks.com
- RealCheck at www.realcheck.com
- eRenter at www.erenter.com

Many of these tools even search utility records when they are public, so you can learn a lot about your potential tenant online and for a low cost. RealCheck is particularly useful and beneficial in that it will handle most aspects of your tenant verification. It also provides rejection notifications that are required by law.

Remember it is illegal to discriminate against an applicant due to race, national origin, religion, marital status, gender, or physical disabilities. Beyond this, it is your property.

Craigslist is a good site to post your house on (I post my homes even if they're advertised through a property manager because it doesn't hurt to get more publicity), and you should even consider sites like roommates.com, which allow you to list rentals for a nominal fee.

Creating Some Buzz!

Even when I've hired a property manager, I've still created my own advertising buzz! I've contacted human resources individuals at local companies to let them know about my rental in case anyone moving there for a job needs a place to live,

I've advertised on craigslist even when I do have a property manager (referring the potential tenants to the property manager and telling them to say, "Dani sent me!" so the property manager knows I got the listing), and I've even advertised on services like roommate.com or any of the following sites (some of which do charge a nominal fee):

- U.S. Rental Listings at www. USRentalListings.com

- Rent Marketer at www.rentmarketer.com

- Craigslist at www.craigslist.org (list here anyway!)

- Rent My Home at www.rentmyhome.com

> **TALK FROM THE TRENCHES**
>
> According to the survey, 68 percent of landlords said finding a good, qualified renter was either hard or very hard!

Don't ignore the local newspapers, and be sure you put up signs if your association allows. I've held rental open houses, too, just as if I were selling my home! Consider using military sites, too. This was particularly popular in the survey. Consider those who are stationed for a shorter period of time for your home and those serving our country. Check out the site www.militarybyowner.com for some interesting options for renting your home to military personnel. This is useful if your home is near a military facility. (I had three homes in Tucson and had a military family in one of them. Although their tenure was shorter due to a relocation required by the government, they were excellent tenants, kept the house immaculately clean, and always paid their rent on time. This won't always happen, but my experience was good and many people concurred it in the survey).

You might also consider colleges and universities and allowing multiple people to lease with you. I know this sounds a little odd at first, but I've done this near a university in Texas, and it has been outstanding so far. As one of the senior members moves on, the juniors find a suitable replacement. Consistent property reviews have turned up no problems; they pay their rent on time and often cover for one another if one tenant cannot pay. If you think about it, three to four people will be losing their home if they don't pay, so they're more likely to find a way to pay their rent. Also, often they are backed financially by their parents, who are glad they're living in a safe place and not a party-laden dormitory. The key here is to interview them and make sure they appear responsible. You might even ask to see their grades as an indicator of whether they're going to use your house as

TALK FROM THE TRENCHES

One landlord wrote, "Tenant qualification is probably the best investment a landlord can do to get the right tenant and it's pretty smooth sailing from there."

a party house or a study house, with partying on a limited basis. I recommend making sure the neighbors know how to get in touch with you in case there is a noise problem, which could tip you off to potential partying. This works best, of course, with three- to four-bedroom homes that allow for each renter to have a room to herself.

Be as detailed as you possibly can in your listing, including pictures. Also, include any perks. Are you willing to offer the first month's rent at half off? First month's rent free? Free housekeeping? Free landscaping? Free phone or utilities? These might be very important to potential tenants and set your house apart. Is cable TV included? List it! You might choose to start off slowly and add incentives if you aren't renting the house as quickly as you had hoped for.

Finding qualified renters can take some time, so be patient. In general, in hot markets you will need two to four weeks to find a good tenant; in average markets, you'll need one to three months; and you'll need even longer in slow markets or in markets where houses can be purchased cheaply and there is less need to rent. If jobs are moving away from your home's town, you might also need to factor this into the length of time it will take to find a renter. The first thing you will need to do is advertise. Find any way you can to advertise—from signs to notes at the local grocery store, to ads in the college newspaper, to using online sites (which is imperative today).

TALK FROM THE TRENCHES

One landlord commented in the survey, "Consider posting your property/house as 'military/owner' for sale or rent if you live within a reasonable distance to military communities. Many military want to rent or buy from another military member."

The key here is *qualified*; the tenant needs to have the money and income to pay for the property, show a history of paying bills on time, and be willing to lease or rent on your terms.

Marketing Hooks—Creative Ways to Get Tenants In!

I've used and have seen others use lots of creative ways to get tenants in! This has ranged from use of a boat already in a boat garage with the rental (and a greater deposit), to something as simple as letting the tenant choose the paint color for the walls and you painting it for him. You can get creative, or you can get down to money and offer a month's free rent, half the deposit (which is really half off one month with a real deposit), one half of a month free—you name it—be creative and the sky's the limit. One thing I do with new homes is I let the tenant choose from three or four landscaping options. After all, he is living there, and I want him to stay and to be happy.

You also might want to offer a broker co-op fee of 2 percent of the rents collected for a year or a month's rent so brokers will bring tenants your way, too.

Another thing I have done that has proven wildly successful is to contact the human resources departments at the organizations that are local to the home I am trying to rent. Often new-hires are looking for a place to move into quickly. Although they won't accept kickbacks in most cases, local companies are often very glad to have a quick list on hand for new-hires to be able to move into a home quickly so their move isn't delayed. This is often the reason people don't start new jobs right away (lack of housing or difficulty finding a new home).

You might need to find creative ways to get tenants into your home. I've seen landlords offer the use of cars or boats, a free month's rent—thirteen months for the price of twelve— anything to keep the property filled. Don't look too desperate, though!

What Renters Look for

Renters look for different things depending on their life situations, marital statuses, job statuses, and so on. Renters will look for either quiet or vibrant. They will look for newer or older (or not care). They might look for a high-tech house or a yard—or not. Think of all the things your house has, and then try to determine what type of individual would be happiest there. Is it the single person who needs to be within walking distance of restaurants that would be best suited for your home? Or the family that needs playmates for their kids?

Renters are going to look for a good deal, but they're also going to look for someone who appears responsible, which to a renter means someone who's going to take care of problems right away. A landlord who protects herself is understandable; a landlord who is overly protective is annoying. Tenants want (and have a right to) their privacy, and they won't want to deal with an intrusive, frustrating landlord. Try to remember this as you make the house that once was your home into a rental. Many tenants are overly sensitive to this, so it's important to just be yourself so you can make sure you and the tenant are a good fit.

Money Matters

9

Your money matters. If it didn't, you wouldn't be renting out your home! You want stable income, tenants who won't trash your house, tenants who will care about the home, tenants who will report problems, and tenants who will pay the bills. You also want some sort of gain out of this—whether it's to live in your home again in the future, be able to sell it when the market rebounds, or move back in after awhile. It isn't too difficult to get all these things if you have done your homework on the tenant and if your monthly losses aren't too steep (even if they are, it might still be worth it to rent it as we've discussed).

In this chapter we'll go through all the matters related to money. We'll discuss how to collect it, what to pay, how to pay renters their deposits, and more.

Determine How You Will Collect Rent

Collecting rent is one of the reasons many potential landlords choose to use property managers; they believe that collecting rent is frustrating and difficult. It can actually be quite easy if you've done your homework on the tenant. The key to collecting rent is to not bug your tenant—unless he is late with payment! Offer many ways for the tenant to make deposits to you so it's more convenient for him.

TALK FROM THE TRENCHES

"For 20 years I have had great success with an early payment discount. Payments received on or before 7 a.m. the first day of the month receive a discount amounting to $25 (average). Every Halloween one renter brought her kid by for candy and left me a check ...."

Pick Up the Rent Yourself

If you live in the area where you are renting, you may just go and pick up the rent check yourself. I would not recommend giving out your home address (you never know what an angry renter can do), but picking it up is an option. This also allows you to check out the home while you are there, which can be a really big benefit. Many don't want this hassle though and prefer direct deposits (remember you can offer discounts for this!) or mailed checks.

Direct Deposit

You might want to work with your bank to set up business direct deposit. This is where the renter can use either online banking transfers or actual direct deposit from her paycheck into your account. You also might want to offer 1 to 2 percent off rent or a flat amount off of the rent ($20, $50 etc.) if the person changes a portion of her paycheck to directly deposit into your account, unless she has a history of losing jobs!

Mailed Checks

The tenant can mail checks the old-fashioned way. Make it easy for him, though—whatever the lease period is, give the tenant that many envelopes (plus a few extra) that are already self-addressed and stamped. You might even choose to include a payment coupon book you create in a word processor with the due date and rental payment amount. Staple the coupons together, along with your self-addressed stamped envelopes. The key here is to make it as easy as you can for the tenant so he has no excuses to not pay rent!

```
           RENTAL PAYMENT COUPON

ADDRESS: <PROPERTY ADDRESS OF RENTAL>

PAYMENT AMOUNT: <RENTAL AMOUNT>

DUE DATE: <INCREMENT THESE FOR EACH MONTH OF THE
LEASE>

REMIT TO: <YOUR ADDRESS>

CHECK HERE TO RENEW LEASE FOR _____ MONTHS. (A new
rental or lease agreement will be mailed for your
signature)
```

TALK FROM THE TRENCHES

Learn from Natalie Sterling who writes from Charles Town, West Virginia in the survey: "Be very careful and never…(give keys) before the check clears….Checks have bounced on me, and they already had the keys and a signed lease, but I had no money at all; they started off on the wrong foot and getting money paid was difficult and set the tone for bad checks, late rents, (and) runarounds. Eventually I had a painfully costly eviction on my hands. Had I insisted on certified funds or even went to the bank itself to cash I could have seen that they were not people I should have ever rented to in the first place."

On the last two coupons of the leasing period, you might want to offer a checkbox similar to the one shown previously: "please renew my lease for X months to ensure my lease price does not change." If the renter checks this box, send him a new lease to sign with another self-addressed stamped envelope. If any conditions have changed, include an addendum. You can choose to increase the lease amount, and if you do, be sure to let your renter know well in advance.

Regardless of which method you choose, mail the tenant a receipt each month. It can be a simple receipt that looks like this:

LPA
The Landlord Protection
AGENCY ™

Rent Receipt

Date: _____

To: Address:

Received from _____ the sum of $_____, as rent for the period of
_____ for the premises described above.

Landlord/Agent: _____

Balance Due: $_____

Paid By: Cash Check Money Order
(Circle one)

LPA
The Landlord Protection
AGENCY ™

Rent Receipt

Date: _____

To: Address:

Received from _____ the sum of $_____, as rent for the period of
_____ for the premises described above.

Landlord/Agent: _____

Balance Due: $_____

Paid By: Cash Check Money Order
(Circle one)

LPA
The Landlord Protection
AGENCY ™

Rent Receipt

Date: _____

To: Address:

Received from _____ the sum of $_____, as rent for the period of
_____ for the premises described above.

Landlord/Agent: _____

Balance Due: $_____

Paid By: Cash Check Money Order
(Circle one)

Have the Renter Deposit for You

Many of my friends have their renters make deposits for them. Along with the previously shown rental payment coupon or something similar, they include a stack of deposit slips. This works very well if you bank with a nationwide bank that has banks in many locations. You might want to offer a slight discount—1 percent off the rental fee for instance—for making the deposits for you. This generally means that the renter has the money to pay, and it certainly relieves you from the burden of checks potentially lost in the mail. Using online banking, you can generally see when the deposit is made, and monitoring it online is much less intrusive than calling the tenant to ask where the rent is.

If you use a national bank that has branches in the area you're renting the home in, it's easy to do. Give the renters a year's (or more) worth of deposit slips and tell them when the rent is due (stipulated in your rental or lease agreement). If you use online banking, you will know immediately when the check is deposited and when it clears. You also can choose to offer discounts to tenants who do this because it will save you a lot of time and hassles, and it will encourage the tenants to pay on time.

Cash or Cashiers Checks

If the tenant has a not-so-great history of paying late or not paying and you decided to let him lease or rent from you, you might ask for a cashier's check or cash. Some landlords do this anyway for the first month or two to ensure the tenant is paying. If the person is paying consistently in cash, you won't want him to send it via the mail. Have him make a deposit for you at the bank or drop off the funds at a mailbox (I like to use UPS Stores or similar mailboxes and let them handle things like this). Cashier's checks are a bit easier. If the tenant is paying in cash, you might want to verify his identification again because you might have a noncitizen working for you or someone who earns a lot of his wages under the table. Keep in mind that these payment methods often are turn-offs to potential tenants because they cost money to obtain, so potential tenants might not want to do this.

Raising Rent

This lovely thing called inflation means that rental amounts won't stay the same forever! Yet many landlords won't raise rents due to a fear of confronting their tenants, rocking the boat and having tenants leave, being unable to afford to make the tenant angry and cause a vacancy, because the tenant feels more like a friend, or because the rent is "high enough." Still, there might come a time when you have to raise rent. You should raise rents regularly even if only by small amounts. If tenants are used to the same amount of rent over a long period of time, they might actually get offended when you do increase the rent. Small increases annually are usually easier for tenants to handle. I recommend putting the raising of rent issue into the lease agreement and planning for scheduled rent increases. Even if the increase is only $25, it will likely cover increasing costs. Remember that your tax bill, association bill, and even some utilities you cover can increase. You also might need to raise rent if the cost of living or inflation increases, you have significant negative cash flow, you have a high-maintenance tenant or property, you want to make the tenant leave the rental, or the tenant isn't taking care of your property. Use a rent increase letter (check out the forms in Appendix B) to notify the tenants about the increase in rent, when it will take effect, and the new payment amount. If you took my earlier advice and provided payment coupons, include more with the new rental amount. Be polite, but give adequate notice, which is thirty to sixty days before the first day of the next rental period. If your lease doesn't allow the increase until the leasing period ends, send it along with your notice of lease renewal. The Landlord Protection Agency recommends sending these two along with a tenant's intention to vacate letter should the tenant not agree to the rent adjustment and would rather move out. Sending the letter lets the tenant know you're okay with the concept of having her leave.

So, how much more should you charge? Check the rental market, the quality of your tenant, how badly you want her to stay, and the availability of new qualified tenants. If I like a tenant, I keep the increase to a minimum. You can include a form letter showing an increase of X percent, cross it out, and then handwrite a new increase amount over it. This will give the tenant an idea of what the increase would have been if you didn't value her tenancy. (Thanks for the great idea, LPA!)

Check out the rental increase reminder example here.

The Landlord Protection
LPA
AGENCY ™

```
.............................
:          Your            :
:       Letterhead         :
:          Here            :
:                          :
.............................
```

ANNUAL RENT INCREASE REMINDER

Date: _____

Dear _____,

Address:_____

_____

Your rent is due to increase as agreed in your lease. As of _____ your new rent amount will be $_____ per month. Early payment discounts as agreed will remain in effect.

Paying Your Taxes

In earlier chapters I explained that you must pay your own taxes on rental properties, and this is absolutely essential! One thing you need to be sure you do is to change the mailing address with the county for the tax bill when you move to your new address. I personally prefer to use a confidential mailbox (such as a UPS Store) so the tenant doesn't have my home address and I can call to see whether I've received any checks (and packages too—a convenient bonus). You still need to get your property tax bill, so have the mailing address changed. Some counties support a simple online form; others require a phone call. Either way, you must do this.

It isn't a bad idea to check out the tax assessor online either just to make sure they do in fact have the correct address on file. This is another reason you should use a mailbox or PO Box—if you can get your home address at the assessor's office, so could an angry tenant.

Insurance Changes as You Rent Your Home

When you rent your home, you will want your tenant to get rental insurance. But you also need to change your insurance to a landlord policy. Sometimes it's less expensive; other times it's a bit more. It depends on the state, the value of the home, what the contents were insured for, and a variety of other factors. Usually your current insurer can help you make the transition. You should be sure to cover for any accidents the tenants might have and may sue you for. Remember our discussion in Chapter 2 about umbrella policies, too.

I talked about umbrella policies, but this is a good time to reinforce doing a full check on your assets and then talking with a good insurance salesperson to think through your needs and ensure all your assets are covered. The umbrella policy companies need to know which homes are rentals and try to find a policy that covers renter accidents or lawsuits. This is where it also can help to incorporate your "business"—that is, your rental business. Talk with a tax authority about this option and how it might or might not separate your personal assets (your new home) from your business (the home you are renting). You don't want a renter suing you and going after your personal home, too. Although these instances are rare, you need to consider them and protect yourself to your comfort level and within what is reasonable.

Keeping Track of Costs and Income

Remember to keep track of your costs and all income received that is associated with the property. After you convert a property to a rental, when you sell it and you're not a real estate professional, the costs might come out of potential capital gains.

If you do qualify as a real estate professional, you might be able to expense monthly losses and create a business out of your rental(s). Talk to a tax accountant about the tax and legal ramifications of doing so. Either way, keep track of all costs, repairs, and fees associated with the property; all taxes; insurance; association fees; utilities—anything associated with the rental unit.

One way to do this easily is to use the QuickBooks version that provides for property management and rentals. You can also export it into an easy-to-use file format for any accountant and save yourself some money come tax preparation time!

Deposits

Keep track of all deposits made, including deposits made for having pets in the home or any deposits associated with addendums. You will need to show these as liabilities as well as income; a tax preparer can help you do this. The aforementioned QuickBooks property management software also makes this easy. Remember you need to appropriately track all deposits and all rent checks made by the tenant so you can ensure that any monies owed to him are in available funds and so you know what is in the deposit-kitty come time to terminate the lease or rental, for whatever reason.

TALK FROM THE TRENCHES

Remember that according to the survey, 45 percent of the respondents said that collecting rent was hard or very hard—nearly half! It shows you how delicate of a situation this is, and why it's important to learn as much as you can about all of the options to collect rent, including direct deposit, deposits made to the bank by the tenant, and mailed checks.

Collecting Rent

Anytime you collect rent you need to include it on the credit side of your balance sheet (remember debit-credit from accounting?). Be sure you keep accurate records. You might want to hang onto a copy of your own rental receipt form. I scan them all into my computer and print them at the end of the year to store in my tax folder, as well as keep a soft copy on my computer. Also, if you want to take out a home equity line of credit or a second mortgage on the home, having these files in computer format is easier. Remember that the underwriters at banks will want copies of your rental agreements and proof that the tenant is in fact in the home, and this is far easier done with scanned copies (especially in PDF format).

Association Fees

Generally speaking, unless you pass off the costs in the form of higher rents, association fees will also be paid by you, the homeowner. I ran into a situation in Austin, Texas, where the homeowners association was sending bills to the home rather than to my mailing address in California. After two years, they hired a lawyer to find the owners who weren't paying; I received a letter asking for the two years' worth of association fees. After contacting the association, they admitted it was a recordkeeping error on their part, I paid what was owed, and they updated their address records. Tenants will typically toss bill such as these! Most tenants won't even notify you, and they don't have to. So, be sure you update your mailing address to continue receiving any bills you will be paying yourself. Be sure you let the association know about your new billing address, too.

Subcontractor Costs

Anytime you hire a subcontractor, including a gardener or a housekeeper or just someone to get the home ready for rerental, you need to keep track of receipts and costs. Again, these offset gains, which is critical come tax time. In some states, if you do the work yourself you cannot deduct the labor, which is costly in time. Check the LPA's state-by-state rules to know precisely what your state allows—or perhaps more importantly, doesn't allow.

"Potential" Tax Deductions

Insurance, property tax, maintenance, and other items are deductible against your income. They help offset gains and you must record these and keep accurate records and talk to your tax preparer about how these are deducted. The method of deduction depends on your status as a real estate professional and the status of the home as a second home or if you officially converted it to a rental property. There are rules about appreciation and depreciation here too so talk to a tax authority!

Pros and Cons of Incorporating Your New "Business"

I noted earlier in this chapter the possibilities of incorporating due to risk. If you incorporate your properties into an LLC, then your LLC—its own entity—has its own properties at stake if you were sued. For example, I have deeded all of my properties to my LLC. Even though the mortgage is in my name and social security number, my LLC is the primary deed holder, after of course the bank. This means that if a tenant sues me, they're suing my LLC and only assets in the LLC are at risk. Your LLC must also be a named insured on not only your umbrella policy, but also on your landlord insurance to be fully covered.

Some people also choose to deed their properties to a business that protects them from being personally sued. This is often the case with an LLC, but check with an attorney on the pros and cons of doing this. Most of the time your LLC won't have sufficient credit to buy the home, and most lenders won't loan to a corporation anyway, so chances are you're buying the properties with your personal credit at stake. It doesn't mean you cannot do a quit claim deed, deed the property to your LLC, and then update insurance records to add another "named insured."

Evaluating Tenants

10

Evaluating tenants is absolutely vital. It will save you from destructive tenants, tenants who engage in illegal activity in your home, nonpaying renters—you name it, screening is the key to a successful tenancy. The first part of the evaluation process is the application; the next is the subsequent checks that follow after you have this information. This section of the book might be the most important, cost-saving, stress-busting section you read.

What to Do to Evaluate a Tenant

Evaluating tenants is not easy. There are a few steps you should follow to ensure that you save yourself some hassles and grief throughout all steps of the process, including moving back in or selling the home when the tenancy is over.

> Before I even tell you about the application, if you're still considering not putting in the effort to screen applicants, check out the following graphic reasons why you should change your mind: Warning, not for the faint of heart! This is a reminder because it is incredibly important! Check out the photos on this website: www.thelpa.com/lpa/eviction_pictures.html.

The Application

You should have your tenant fill out an application so you can screen him, and you should supply him with rental policies forms. These will spell out clearly why you might or might not turn down an applicant and will keep you out of legal trouble.

I learned a lot from the *Profitable Tenant Selection Guide* by Robert L. Cain, via the Internet (electronic guide). This is an online self-published manual that they email to you, and I've incorporated some of his suggestions into my own work. You can get your own copy at http://rentalprop.com/Merchant2/merchant. mvc?Screen=CTGY&Store_Code=RPRS&Category_Code=LM.

In his sample rental property application and policy document, he notes some of the rules that he obeys and the integrity he upholds. While you can find the full verbiage on the Internet, the general policies are about providing equal housing, not discriminating, maintaining the quality of the neighborhood, screening tenants, and so on. His application procedures indicate that anyone who wishes to fill one out is welcome to—hence nondiscrimination.

The forms are reviewed in the order received and the property is rented to the first qualified tenant. He also notes the time frame in which they are processed; up to ten business days. You may change this based on your own requirements, travel schedule, and so on. Using the LPA's credit and rental check history database you'll be able to quickly and properly screen your tenants. He also indicates that applications must be fully filled out or they will not be considered and will be returned. Similar to a job application, all information is needed for a reason.

He also indicates he will screen and personally meet every adult who will move in. He also states that all information must be verifiable, which might include things such as telephone numbers, places of residence, employers, and so on. He indicates the amount you must earn per month to qualify, and uses it as a "percentage" of the rental; in this case 2.5 times the rental amount. By doing this, he can use the same information for every tenant without having to change specifics.

He also clearly states what scrutiny you will be under; a credit check, a background check, and so on. He notes clearly his application fee; but note that this could change depending on the state you are renting your house out of. In general, the entire screening process at large is documented.

The author also clearly states why applications will be denied, such as unpaid collection notices, bankruptcies, judgments, evictions, landlord reports, felonies, and so on. This is important also to show you are not being discriminatory and to clearly state up front to your potential tenants why they must be denied. When you send denial letters you will indicate which of the items you used to deny the application.

> Note that each state has its own laws about how much you can charge for screening. Verify your state's laws at www.thelpa.com/lpa/forms/state-lease.

You should also have potential tenants fill out a rental application, which you will hand them along with the rules you determine work for you. There are other forms in Appendix B you may want to provide, and you can access them from the Landlord Protection Agency, too. You might also check out www.buyincomeproperties.com/, which has a lot of free forms available on its site.

In general, you're trying to collect references, five years or more of job history, five years or more of residence information, stated income, and stated debts.

> One test of honesty is comparing this information to what you see when you run your own checks.

You will want to ask the individual whether he has been convicted of a felony within the last seven years and, if so, have him describe it. You might want to ask additional questions, but check with an attorney as to their legality before asking or requiring disclosure. Never ask about race or religion or anything that could be construed as a basis for discrimination. You might want to ask about marital status if the individual is using spousal income to qualify for the rental.

In the next sections, I will tell you about some checks you need to run on your potential tenant. Remember that you should charge an application fee to cover these credit and background checks. Usually $100–$150 will cover it, but again it depends on what your state authorizes you to charge. It is generally nonrefundable, but you may want to apply it toward the deposit if the individual checks out.

Making it nonrefundable deters people who are committing some sort of fraud from even applying.

As John at the LPA puts it, "I learned that the easiest and cheapest eviction is the one when the tenants never get possession of your property. Screen them out, so you don't have to kick them out."

Credit Checks and Public Records

Credit is fundamental for all loans; credit card companies, automobile manufacturers, and banks use them for just about everything. A credit check needs to be run on anyone who applies to rent your home. You must tell the potential tenant the name of the screening services and/or reporting agencies you will be using, so you might want to list this in your initial document that you hand to the tenant along with the application as I do. Be sure your ad includes this as a "subject to" so the renter knows up front that you will be verifying her credit. Another good tool to use is an online credit verification system for landlords. One I recommend is RealCheck. You can also get online rental forms, use their collection services, run criminal checks, and run rental history reports! There are rules you must follow if you deny someone on the basis of her credit, so be sure you review Appendix B to ensure you are in proper compliance with the law. This is very important.

How to Run a Credit Report

Running credit is relatively easy. You can simply ask the individual to supply a credit report and have it emailed to you through any variety of online credit reporting agencies. You do need permission to do this! Keep in mind that these can be modified if they are emailed or in text format (even Adobe PDFs can be modified), so you might want to have the individual do this in your office or at your home so you can print it and then view it immediately.

If you decide you want the applicant to get the credit report for you, have him contact one of these companies:

- **Equifax**—PO Box 740241, Atlanta, GA 30374, 1-800-997-2493. This generally costs $8 per report. Maryland and Vermont citizens can get one report per year, and Maine residents must pay $3. The consumer can make the request and charge it over the phone with a credit card.

- **Experian**—PO Box 2104, Allen, TX 75013-2104, 1-888-EXPERIAN, www.experian.com. The report is $8; $2 for Maine residents, $5 for Maryland residents, and $7.50 for Vermont residents.
- **Trans Union**—PO Box 390, Springfield, PA 19064-0390, www.transunion.com. The report costs $8.

If you go this route, the reports will probably be mailed, which will take longer to receive. Have the applicant mail the report directly to you.

> Remember everyone is entitled to one free copy of their credit report per year, but most don't know how to get it. You can safely order this from two sites: www.ftc.gov and www.annualcreditreport.com. To order by phone call 1-877-322-8228 or by mail print out the form available on annualcreditreport.com and mail to Annual Credit Report Request Service, PO Box 105281, Atlanta, GA 30348-5281. You can choose to accept these from tenants, but understand that PDFs can be modified—so be sure you are getting an authentic report. I would personally always run credit myself anyway.

You can also use tenant services like the aforementioned Landlord Protection Agency. You can go to www.thelpa.com/lpa/credit.html to run a credit report.

How to Interpret a Credit Report

Many of you might have questions about how to interpret what you read. A lot of codes are used on credit reports, including the following:

O = This indicates an open account, such as with a physician.

R = This indicates a revolving account, such as department store cards or credit cards.

I = This indicates an installment, such as money borrowed from a bank, credit union, and so on.

These codes apply to the status of the account:

0 = Too new to rate or approved but never used. If the person has a credit card and never charged on it, it might show a 0.

1 = Pays within the thirty-day period. Not one day past due.

2 = More than thirty days from the payment due date but not exceeding sixty days late.

3 = More than sixty days late but less than or equal to ninety days late (or three payments past due).

4 = More than ninety days late but less than or equal to one hundred twenty days late (four payments past due).

5 = More than one hundred twenty days past due (more than four payments late).

7 = Makes regular payments under a debt plan.

8 = Repossession (there should be some kind of note about whether it was voluntary).

9 = Bad debt (uncollected, the company wrote it off).

Credit Score (you want someone with at least a 640 credit score, and if her score isn't that high, she needs to be able to explain why).

If excessive inquiries are creating the lower score, you might want to overlook that; however, you might also want to find out what the person has been applying for (multiple applications with other landlords, perhaps?). There will be a summary of contributing factors at the top or bottom of the report depending on which company you use, and I've listed them in this section. Review them carefully.

If you see anything like bankruptcy, foreclosure, substantial late payments, late payments beyond sixty or ninety days, unverifiable addresses, or credit limits exceeded, these are all red flags that the individual might be overextended. You need to determine what to do on a case-by-case basis, but in general I don't rent to anyone with a score lower than 640 unless it's due to inquiries to rent from me. If I'm desperate for a renter, I sometimes drop this to 620 if other factors check out okay, such as income and references.

Remember that a credit score above 800, according to Empirica, generally means that the person has a 1.1 percent chance of "performing negatively," or being late with payments or not paying at all. Numbers continue to stay in the 1 percent range until you hit the 760—779 range, where it drops to 2.1 percent. A score of 740–759 is 3.2 percent, and we see a big jump at 720–739, which is 5.1 percent. A score of 700–719 is approximately an 8.1 percent negative performance risk, 680–699 is an 11.8 percent risk (680 is the magic number banks often use), and it continues to decline from there. Someone with a 600 credit score falls into the 35 percent chance of negative performance category. Why would you want to take such a high risk? Someone with a score lower than 500 has a whopping 83.5 percent chance of having negative performance!

You should also look at the Equal Credit Opportunity Act (ECOA) Chart. These codes apply to who is responsible for the account:

I = An individual account that no one else is responsible for paying

J = A joint account shared with someone else

A = An authorized use account (one person has responsibility, but another person can use it and does not have responsibility)

U = Undesignated (There isn't enough information to assign the account a code.)

B = On behalf of another person, or someone else has financial responsibility for the account (for instance, when a child goes off to school and a parent opens an account in the child's name)

T = The subject's relationship to the account has terminated (such as after a divorce, where one person maintains the account but another isn't related to it anymore)

M = Maker, meaning that it's an installment loan but a comaker or cosigner had to ensure the loan would be paid (find out why!)

C = Comaker, meaning that the person has been the cosigner for another loan

S = Shared, where the person or company giving credit knows the person and at least one other person shares the account, but not enough information is available to make it a joint account or an authorized use account

So, which of these ECOA accounts are red flags? In my opinion, anyone who has co-signed accounts or is a cosigner is a red flag. This means someone had to help him establish credit because he couldn't get it on his own. Find out why and get more information. He might still make for a good tenant, but you will want to dig deeper. If you have a very young person or a college student that is relying on their parents, that is a far less scary reason than someone who has three foreclosures and two bankruptcies!

You will also see a lot of industry codes, which are two-letter codes inside the account number after the name of the creditor on the report. Here are some examples:

B = Banks

    BB = Banks

U = Utilities

    UF = Fuel Oil Dealers

    UZ = Miscellaneous

    UW = Water

R = Real Estate, Hotels, Etc.

    RA = Apartments

    RH = Hotels

    RZ = Miscellaneous

K = Contractors

    KG = General

    KS = Subcontractors

    KZ = (as with any Z, Miscellaneous)

F = Finance

    FA = Auto Financing

    FS = Savings and Loan

    FP = Personal Loan

    FC = Credit Unions

V = Government

VC = City and County

VF = Federal

VS = State

Y = Collections (Be careful here! It means that some accounts are in collections, and the person hasn't paid their bills! Why would they pay yours?)

Look at each of the creditors, and see what the loan-to-balance ratio is. Is the person using his credit to the max? If so, he might have high payments and might not be able to prioritize rent. If he has high debt to available credit maximums, has he been late with payments? Maybe he just likes to use his credit cards for cash back or miles or convenience. Try to speculate based on all the information you gather because it will give you a better idea of the whole picture.

Calculate the prospective tenant's monthly payments and check his overall debt ratio. You don't want his debt ratio (excluding your rent) to exceed about 30 percent of his income. If he makes $4,000 per month and his debt is $2,000 per month, chances are he won't be able to pay your $1,500 rent! On the other hand, if his balances are low and he has a lot of credit available to him, it's an indication that he has been responsible.

Look for late payments, which are often reported as 0s and then 30, 60, 90, and so on in the credit report. The number 0 or a dash indicates the person was on time that month; a number represents the number of days he was late with his payment. Excessive lateness is not a good sign, and you might want to wait for another tenant. Look for any notes from creditors, such as "account in dispute" (which could indicate the prospective tenant is disputing a charge on the account), "account closed at consumer's request" (which means the person chose to close a credit account), "paid off obligation or debt paid" (which means it was paid in full), or "account closed" with no other explanation (which you might want to follow up on to find out more information). Read the notes carefully and don't be afraid to inquire what it all means. After all, this is your house and your livelihood. I can personally attest to the tremendous financial burden not having rental income can create in your life, particularly if you're renting more than one home or the mortgage is a substantial portion of your income.

Check previous addresses and even employment history that might be noted on the credit report, too. See if it matches with the application the person filled out. The application now becomes relevant beyond just data collection because one of your goals is to determine how honest the individual was with you. If he says he has had four homes in five years, is that what his credit report says? How can he explain any discrepancies?

Check for abbreviations that can indicate some problems in the report. Here are some examples:

BKRPT = Bankruptcy

DV FD = Divorce Filed

FORCL = Foreclosure

GARN = Garnishment (The person might be making $2,000/month, but $1,000 a month might be garnished! Be careful here!)

WEP = Wage Earner Plan (Be careful here. This is a plan that individuals who have filed Chapter 13 bankruptcy go on as an alternative to full bankruptcy. This is a negotiated settlement between an individual and people they owe money to. Their income must have been higher than reasonable living expenses, so check job status carefully!)

ST JD = Satisfied Judgment (This is a judgment that was placed against the individual, but that was at some point satisfied or paid. It shows a history of nonpayment, but ultimately paying based on terms and conditions agreed upon.)

SECLN = Secured Loan (Find out what is securing it and why.)

DV FL = Divorce Final

LIEN = Tax Lien (Be careful here, too, because tax liens can eventually come directly out of someone's pay or assets can be seized.)

COLL = Collection (This means the account went to collections; in other words, the person didn't pay his bills.)

Where to Locate Public Records and What to Look For

You might be unaware that it is possible for you to run a nationwide criminal background check or even check for traffic tickets in some counties! Lots of data is available online. The one I prefer is Intelius because it can run nationwide searches and, although it cost me quite a bit of money, I was able to learn a lot about individuals. You can access it at www.intelius.com. You can choose a variety of options, and the more information you have about the person (including previous states where she has lived from the credit check), the more thorough you can be. Remember that you should select a multistate felony check, too, and should rely on the credit report—not just the application—for the list of states the individual has lived in. The LPA also has the ability on its site to do a record check.

Be sure to at least look for felonies. To do this well, you need a Social Security number (include this in your application, and it will also be on the credit report), full name, and date of birth. This will weed out false positives. At the very least, look for crimes and outstanding serious debt, such as owed taxes—which can also be a search criterion using online tools.

When you get the civil and criminal records, you will find a lot of information that can be useful to you, particularly along with a credit report. Sometimes felony charges are pleaded down to misdemeanors, so watch for that. Look for anything having to do with domestic violence because these tenants might cause you no end of grief, including taking out walls and doors, not to mention giving a home to someone who beats someone else.

Here are some standard criminal abbreviations and what they mean. There are hundreds, but these will probably be most relevant to you as they speak to character (at least at the time of committing the crime).

Drug-Related

PCS = Possession of a controlled substance—you don't want these people in your home! This often leads to MCS (manufacturing a controlled substance) or selling the drugs out of your home.

Theft

BUR = Burglary

ROB = Robbery

TH = Theft

UUV = Unauthorized use of a vehicle

FRG = Forgery

Physical Threats, Rape, Abuse

RPE = Rape

SA = Sexual Abuse

ALT = Assault

SOD = Sodomy

KID = Kidnapping

ESC = Escape (This might mean from an officer's control, running from the police, or escaping from jail— don't rent to these people.)

Miscellaneous

FTA = Failure to Appear (Will the person meet your obligations if he doesn't show up to court?)

DWSF = Driving While Suspended Felony

HBOF = Habitual Offender

If something is on your mind or bothering you, you might choose to decline the applicant or to get more information. If you decide the latter, make sure all the answers are completely answered to your satisfaction and ask in person (unless there are physical assaults and such, you might want to just send a decline letter).

Note that there is no national criminal record database available in the United States other than the FBI's. This is why addresses are so important from the credit report and the application because you will need to search those counties or states. Credit reports don't contain any criminal information, only money-related information. Searches with common names might provide false positives, so Social Security numbers and birthdates can help validate information. Check at least two to three previous counties the individual has lived in. Remember that you don't need the tenant's approval to check criminal history, although you should disclose that you will do a check on the rental application. Also, run checks on all applicants so you're not discriminating against anyone.

Validating Information

Part of validating information is making sure you have a match on birth date, Social Security number, previous addresses lived at, outstanding debt, felonies on record, and so on. You might want to tell the potential tenant that she didn't qualify for the rental. State and county laws dictate whether you need to do this in writing or if a verbal confirmation is enough, and whether you need to give a reason to the tenant.

Always be sure you call the applicant's employer. Most employers are not legally allowed to provide more information than just that the individual is employed and what her title is. Stick to the basics, but this is important. You may even want to drop by, unannounced, at her current residence and see what it looks like. Is the yard clean? Does the house look like a mess? Are there enough cars in the driveway for ten residents?

Be sure you follow up with your references. Call previous landlords. Ask the landlord what kind of tenant the individual was, leaving the question open-ended. Find out if the landlord knew the tenant was moving and why she's moving, and see if it matches information you collect during the personal interview. Ask what the previous rent was, what the dates of tenancy were, whether the person's rent was ever late, how many people lived with her, if neighbors ever complained, if the tenant had pets (yes, tenants will lie about having pets!), and if the landlord would rent to the tenant again.

Call the employer and see if they will tell you information about the individual—what type of person the applicant is, how much they make (they might not say, but you can ask), if they are a full- or part-time worker, and if they would rent to the person.

Check personal references, too, but these will be less likely to give accurate information. Also, be careful because some professional cons will list friends as their previous landlords. Look up the phone number on a free web site that does reverse look-ups, like 411.com and whitepages.com. If something doesn't match up, I recommend rejecting that applicant. One thing you might want to do is call the customer service department of the landlord's company (assuming it's an apartment or another property manager) and see if the landlord the applicant listed actually works there! If the applicant sold her home recently, ask for the name of the agent. If she says it was a for sale by owner, ask for the name of the buyer. Ask about the condition of the property when it was sold, the sale price, and anything else you think could be important.

Identification

You should make copies of the following at the very least:

- A valid driver's license or state identification card
- A visa if the individual is here on a student or work visa
- A second form of photo identification, such as a passport
- Social Security card

Keep and retain copies of this information for your files, and validate it against what you find in your search. If you suspect the individual who wants to rent from you is not a legal citizen, continue reading "Renting to Noncitizens" later in this chapter to see what to do if you encounter this situation.

You will, of course, want to do as you say in the rental policies form and interview each potential individual who will live there. Ask a lot of open-ended questions to get them to talk to you because this is a good way of discovering some potential problems. Some questions I generally ask are: Why did you last move? How long have you been looking for a place? When did you decide to move? What kind of place did you last live in? What did you enjoy about your last apartment or residence? What did you not enjoy? What hobbies do you have? What did you like about your last landlord? What do you expect out of a landlord? What have your experiences been with your neighbors? How big is your current place?

Sometimes the tenants will ask questions as well, and some of the questions might not be legal. For instance, if an individual asks you how many Hispanics live in the neighborhood, you should always say, "I don't know; I've never counted." Try to turn these questions around. For instance, you might say, "Why do you ask?" instead of answering the question. Try to get a feel for what the person is like and what potential issues you might run into; this is one of the reasons you are conducting the interview!

By the way, many people ask me if they can turn down someone because the person is a smoker. The answer is YES! The smoker will cause unnecessary harm, not just wear and tear, to the home. This is a legitimate reason to turn down a renter. When you meet him in person, be on the lookout for paraphernalia that would lead you to believe he is a smoker—walk him to his car and try to smell the car. This is all perfectly legal. You can also choose not to rent to someone because he is too new to the area. Frequent moves are not a good indicator of stability, and this is a valid reason not to rent. You might also turn down a renter if he has too many vehicles (this can irritate neighbors and cause unnecessary wear and tear on the home), is a drug user, has pets, shows any evidence of illegal activity (landlords and police departments will know!), has insufficient income, has been convicted of a crime in which a threat to property existed in the past five years (including burglary, drunk driving, and robbery), has been convicted of manufacturing or distributing controlled substances within the past five years (you might want to check with an attorney here), or has too many debts or a history of late payments.

Here's another important point: if the individual has on his application that he was born in California but the first three digits of his Social Security number begin with 001–003, you know his Social Security card was issued in New Hampshire! You can look this information up yourself at http://genealogy.about.com/library/blsocialsecuritycodes.htm.

Note that not everyone lives in the state where their social security card was originally issued, so if they moved then you might find a different number. This isn't a red flag, but you should investigate prior residences.

The asterisk (*) means that certain numbers were transferred from state to state, so look over the individual's application a bit more carefully. The applicant might not be lying to you after all, but do check. There is also a site where you can type in the Social Security number and get information: www.csgnetwork.com/ssnmbrcalc.html.

Spotting Potential Problems

You need to spot potential problems right up-front. Recently, I had a tenant who applied to rent a home I have in Austin. The tenant checked out well, but then at the last minute didn't move in because the house had "bad karma" (yes, bad karma!). So, it isn't always possible to spot the crazy people with documents, but they sure help. Shortly after this, another tenant applied. She has good credit but still owes a previous apartment complex $3,000 in repairs. She contends that the repairs are bogus, and after some time looking at her other documents, I decided to let her rent. So far as of writing this book, she has been a good tenant. I personally never, ever compromise on application dishonesty, inability to verify identification, and inability to verify income.

If you do run across someone that seems like they are probably going to be good but something tells you otherwise, you may offset this risk with a higher deposit. If they don't accept, then move on. If they do, maybe they are serious and legit after all.

So, what are some things that might be red flags? For starters, a change in marital status in the past year or two. Although you cannot discriminate based on marital status, you might discriminate based on damage guests could possibly do to the home. Try to assess what type of risk the other spouse is to the property. Be sure to get a lease from a recently split couple or individual because if the renter reconnects with her spouse, you might be left with a very short-term tenant! Each vacancy costs, at the very least, one month's rent plus advertising costs. Beware of people who are in a big rush to rent. People know that credit cards may take up to thirty days to report a late payment, and they might be trying to sneak in before their credit reflects their late payment. Beware of people moving from out of town who have no references and of people who are self-employed, unless you can verify with taxes their income. Beware of people who have changed jobs in the past year because if they're unstable in jobs, they might be unstable in their rent payments too—plus, they may have to move quickly to go where the jobs are. They also might be less prone to have savings if they've been unemployed for awhile. Verify the length of time the individual says she lived somewhere versus what the landlord says—look for "missing" locations! This is not a good sign, and based on the untruthful application clause, I would not rent to one of these tenants.

Also be wary of individuals who haven't lived in the same home before. This has worked for me in Texas by offering a four-bedroom home to several college kids (they cycle in and out, but two are responsible for making sure the rent gets paid). Often these are 20-somethings who are just moving out of their parents' homes and don't know what it will be like to live with someone else. They also don't know the ramifications of moving out without meeting rental obligations, so they're less inclined to actually give proper notice. I'm also wary of tenants who have "always been the victim of bad luck." Once or twice is believable, but every year, every job, every home, every dime of savings? Their stories can make you want to rent to them to help someone down on his luck, but send them packing. These people will tell you that they had the worst bosses, they had the worst jobs, the most unreasonable rental rates—their dog died, their aunt got sick, they had a lot of bills—you name it and it's happened to them in the last year.

As John Nuzzolese, President of the Landlord Protection Agency (LPA) says, "It is far better to have NO tenant than to have a BAD tenant."

> **TALK FROM THE TRENCHES**
>
> One respondent said this in the survey, "A MUST—check/verify, make calls, do whatever it takes on prospective tenants' previous addresses, employment. I also get emails, cell phone numbers, etc."

> Anything you find in your document search that seems odd deserves a follow-up. Sometimes making one or two phone calls can save you six months of headaches.

Renting to Noncitizens

Many of you might be faced with whether to rent to noncitizens of the United States. More than 6 percent of California's population are illegal residents, as are 4 percent of Nevada's and Texas's. Most illegals are unable to get mortgages, so you must be aware of this because you stand a reasonable chance that someone not here legally will ask to rent a home from you.

Legality

The first question I'm always asked is, "Is it legal?" The short answer is yes, unless your state has a particular law against it, which you should check either online or with a real estate attorney. If an individual has identification and her credit checks out, you might have no way of knowing whether she is legal. If it's legal in your state, then whether you choose to lease to these individuals is up to you. Also please know that some cities don't allow it and have passed acts forbidding leasing. The best thing to do is to Google your city or call your county or city to determine if this is legal. Some places, such as Cherokee County, Georgia, have even considered fining landlords who rent to illegals. Cities in Texas, California, and Pennsylvania are notorious for having antirental laws. San Bernardino, California, voted (despite its large illegal immigrant population) to disallow landlords to rent to illegals and to face fines if they violate this law (*The Wall Street Journal*). Bottom line—check with your local officials.

Potential Problems

Illegal residents often have multiple people living in one home. This is more than a stereotype; it is a well-documented fact. As laws change, you might become out of legal compliance if you are renting to someone you know might not be legal. An illegal immigrant also may have less job stability than documented workers and might need to move more often to accommodate job changes.

An illegal immigrant might also leave quickly if he needs to due to family obligations or authorities finding out about his status, which might mean your home is vacated and you only find out when the rent check doesn't arrive.

Benefits

Undocumented workers tend to pool their money to pay their bills. If they lose a home or a place they are renting, an entire family no longer has a place to live. That can make them great tenants because they are motivated to keep the house. They also know that if they leave, they might not easily rent another place—yet another motivation to stay in the home. Landlords say that illegals often don't make many complaints that aren't well-founded (real repairs or maintenance issues), though I'm not quite sure why that is; nonetheless it is a widely reported phenomenon. Your applicant pool is larger than your supply and demand equation, so you should be able to rent the property more quickly. In fact, *The Wall Street Journal* reported in October 2007 that illegal immigrants are 18 times less likely to default on mortgages than subprime borrowers who are legal citizens and are only half as likely to default as prime borrowers. That might make for some very trustworthy renters in terms of cash flow.

Instincts and Information

Sometimes the information we collect about someone and our gut don't necessarily mesh. When I rented my own home in Southern California (described in the introduction), the renter's qualifying information wasn't exactly stellar. She didn't have great credit, and she didn't have a stable job. I felt I knew her, though—that she'd take care of the place, she'd be very clean, and my home would be in good care. I was right, and she always paid her rent on time. Sometimes I advise that you meet every adult who will be living in the home. You might have a good feeling about one person but not about the other, for instance.

TALK FROM THE TRENCHES

"Do NOT go with your heart—go with the facts. I 'felt' that someone needed a break after a bad divorce, and now they are constantly late payers. But the signs were there—they had bad credit and they asked me not to call their prior landlord. On the good side, I have inspected the property and they are clean. The property is in good shape. If a tenant is late, get on them RIGHT AWAY. Do not let weeks go by, as you will use up your security deposit and if you have to kick them out, you have no financial recourse." What a lot of stress you don't need as a landlord.

What If Your Gut and Information Don't Align?

The truth is, sometimes the information you collect and your gut won't tell you the same thing. The example I documented is one time when my gut and information didn't align. Sometimes you collect information that would indicate someone would be a great tenant, but you just don't get a good feeling from the person. That happens, and you ultimately decide who gets to rent your home. If your reasons aren't illegal (race, religion, and so on), feel free to say no.

How to Tell a Renter "No"

Different states have different rules about whether you have to document in writing your response to a tenant's request. In the next chapter, I list some good websites you can go to for specific rules from each state, and these are essential to follow and understand. Unfortunately, though, they also make the landlording business more complicated.

There are federal requirements for rejection notifications. Telling the individual why you rejected her will help protect you against Fair Housing complaints. You must also let her know why in almost all cases. A "yes" response is obviously far easier than a "no" response, particularly if the person had a really strong reason to want to live in that home (good schools, close to work, and so on). However, remember that ultimately this is your home. I find that telling people by mail is the best option, but that is based on my personality and comfort level with the process. Don't feel obligated to say yes just because you feel bad for someone. You really need logic to rule here! If you're incapable of doing that because you like the person, but her documentation just doesn't make sense, ask someone you trust to look it over and offer his opinion. Sometimes another set of eyes makes saying no a little easier and usually reinforces what your gut is already telling you. Use a form letter that explains or just checks a box as to why the applicant was rejected—unsatisfactory references, inability to verify income, and so forth. If you reject someone due to credit, you must indicate (Fair Credit Reporting Act) which agency the information was from so the individual has an opportunity to contest information contained in the report. You do not have to wait to rent the property, though. Some reasons you might want to list that are legal are:

- Unable to verify information provided
- Inaccurate information provided
- Lack of references
- Incomplete information on application

- Lack of insurance required (rental insurance, history of insurance)
- Consumer credit agency report
- Undisclosed pets
- Unstable rental history
- Unsatisfactory references
- Insufficient income
- Unstable income
- Unverifiable income
- Another applicant who applied first was accepted (Be sure to return the application fee!)

When you do find the tenant you want, call him and see if he's still interested. Call him immediately because if he's looking at other places, you want to be the first one to make the offer. Be sure not to tell the others "no" until you've found out if your first choice is available. If your first choice found another place to live while you were running your checks, you don't want to lose out on other good candidates.

TALK FROM THE TRENCHES

One wise landlord said this: "It's all about whom you choose to rent your property. Be sure to spell out all the rules on paper and verbally while meeting with them. Friends and family rarely work." Yet another had similar sentiments: "Don't rent to family or friends! Most (not all) people rent for money reasons and your tenant's money problems can easily become yours."

Legal Considerations in Evaluating Tenants

This is always tricky. You cannot and should not for legal and ethical reasons discriminate on the basis of age, gender, race, religion, or any other protected class. However, you might decide you don't want pets or a bunch of fraternity brothers sharing the home together. If you have a valid reason to exclude groups, generally it is legal to exclude them, but you should check with a real estate attorney or online. As a general rule, if an employer could rule that particular person out, so can you. Keep in mind, though, that you can have set rules on income, verifiable sources of revenue streams, employment, references, credit checks, and so forth,

TALK FROM THE TRENCHES

> **TALK FROM THE TRENCHES**
>
> Another landlord in the survey said this: "NEVER rent to any one who you would feel guilty for evicting! NEVER rent to family or friends. Check in often with www.thelpa.com for great advice." Having done this myself, I can certainly verify that renting to friends or family is tough.

and you can deny renting to an individual based on the criteria that are legal and that you set forth.

In general, these are the legal standards you can use: 1) the application was completely (and honestly, which I'll talk about in a bit) completed; 2) the tenant(s) income is verifiable; 3) the tenant has identification; 4) the tenant has sufficient income to cover your requirements as stated in the preceding paragraphs; and 5) the tenant has the ability to cover whatever you require up-front—the deposit, first and last month's rent, for instance.

Just be sure you're verifying to the degree you are comfortable with. Asking for two months' bank statements, W2s, pay stubs for two to three months, letters from employers, personal references, and more is not outside the scope of what you are entitled to ask for. You are also allowed to verify that the individual has no felony convictions, has no prior evictions, has no notices of any kind with regard to rental agreements, doesn't exceed the maximum number of occupants that will be living in the home (be sure you review Fair Housing Laws for complete sets of information on this topic), actually resides at the address noted, gave sufficient notice to the previous landlord, and has no negative marks on his credit. If your reason for turning down a tenant is legal, you should feel completely free to do that.

Taking these steps and noting them in your advertisement ("subject to <insert any of the above, or more!>") usually keeps those who won't qualify away because they know you're going to be diligent and check, but some will try anyway. Stating your requirements doesn't guarantee that all applicants will meet them, so it's your job to do your due diligence and pull information as needed. This is another good reason for the application fee. You weed out the people who aren't serious renters, not to mention those that cannot afford to pay the application fee.

Discrimination

Tenants have won $100,000+ in lawsuits against rental owners for violating Fair Housing rules. This is one reason I strongly suggest throughout this book that you consult a real estate attorney and use a lease that has been reviewed by many experts, such as those on the LPAs site. Often property owners aren't even aware of practices that are discriminatory. The laws affect all aspects of renting, from advertising to tenant screening and selection.

TALK FROM THE TRENCHES

Fred Becker of Big Bear Rentals responded to my survey and had this to say about screening tenants: "You must screen, screen, screen! And even when you do all that and you think you have a good tenant, all it takes is one bad month and you have a major problem on your hands. I charge $5 a day late charges after rent is not paid in full. Because I started enforcing my late fee policy I have evicted more tenants than ever before. Once they get behind, they seem not to be able to get back. I feel being a landlord is a major responsibility if you want to make money at it. You can't give your tenants any reason to think they can get something over on you." Lots to learn from Mr. Becker.

You cannot ever discriminate on the basis of race, color, religion, national origin, sex, age, familial status, or disability. Some states and locales have additional laws that might include sexual preference, gender identity, occupation, source of income (particularly government-assisted, Section 8 housing), educational status, medical status, and even the size of a person's body.

Some owners aren't even aware that they did anything wrong until they are charged with discrimination. One form of such discrimination is *steering*—this is guiding an applicant toward where you think he should live on the basis of one of the protected areas (sex, age, and so on) noted previously. Not showing or renting to certain groups is also steering. Assigning a person to a specific floor or a specific building is also steering. What does this mean? If you have two properties up for rent and the tenant wants to see both, you can't not show one property based on one of these factors. In short, everyone gets to see everything that they want.

Sometimes owners have good intentions. You know that a family might want a single-story house so they don't have to haul laundry upstairs, but if you do anything that might restrict housing options, you can be charged with discrimination.

No matter what the status of families and people with or without children, you must be fair to all applicants. This is why we rarely see adult-only housing, except for HUD-certified senior housing. You might think that your house doesn't have any good areas for kids or is too noisy for older adults—but this is not your decision and must be left up to the tenant. You also cannot charge applicants with kids higher rents or security deposits, nor can you offer different rental terms. If there is a very specific safety issue involved (like a pool, for instance), you might require that someone over the age of 16, for example, accompany any children, but you cannot exclude them from being allowed to rent from you.

Another area of discrimination we are seeing is tenants with disabilities. All owners must make reasonable accommodations at their own expense for tenants with disabilities so that they have an equal shot at the home. The key here is *reasonable*. If the individual needs you to rebuild the downstairs kitchen, that might not be reasonable. However, this is still a gray area in the law. You must also make reasonable adjustments to your requirements, procedures, or services when practical. This generally applies more to multifamily units where, for instance, wider or closer parking spaces might be needed, but it does legally apply to anyone providing any housing. Disabled tenants must also be able to change their living conditions or their living spaces at their own expense as long as the change is only what is required for safety and comfort (which is rather vague) and the modifications don't make the home unacceptable to another tenant (and if they do, the tenant must return the home to its original condition at her own expense before she leaves). In addition, the tenant must obtain your approval as the owner first, the work must be done in a professional way (including getting any and all permits), and the tenant must pay for the work into an interest-providing escrow account to ensure that all work is completed and that there are no liens left on the property at the end. (Remember: any work done to the home may result in a mechanics lien if you don't pay the contractor, and this holds true even if the person requesting the work is the tenant. Have the tenant put the entire payment for all the work into an escrow account up front.)

> Mechanics liens exist in every state. They protect contractors and subcontractors in case they aren't paid for their work. By filing a mechanics lien, they ensure that when the property is sold the lien is paid (subordinate to other liens, like mortgages). Mechanics liens are often filed before major work is done, and then removed once the work is complete and paid for.

There are some exceptions:

- If a home was built in 1991, there are limited requirements.
- If the home was built after 1991, there is a different set of rules.

The following website lists the rules based on the Department of Justice's (DOJ's) set of criteria: www.usdoj.gov/crt/ada/adahom1.htm. Note that the DOJ works closely with HUD and that they do investigate ADA complaints.

Red-lining

Red-lining is another discriminatory practice that denies or increases the cost of something based on race. One of the most devastating times in history is when red-lining occurred in the mortgage business. The term was coined in the 1960s by community activists in Chicago because of the practice of marking a physical red line on a map to show where banks would not invest. Most of the time this practice was used, it was used in black, inner-city neighborhoods. In the past, the most affluent areas—those which were considered desirable for lending purposes—were outlined in blue and known as *Type A*. *Type B* neighborhoods were yellow and not as wealthy. *Type D* neighborhoods were in red, and most black neighborhoods were Type D. Many private companies used this to determine who they would or would not give money to for mortgages and home purchases.

How do you avoid being accused of red-lining? Be fair. Don't do anything discriminatory. Keep your practices ethical.

Words to Use in Advertising

Be sure that none of the words you use in your advertisement would be discriminatory; you have to think outside the box here. While it's doubtful people will be looking for a discriminatory problem where it doesn't exist, people who are turned down for a place that they want to move into suffer hits to their egos and might plead discrimination even when there wasn't any. Be very careful and pay attention to the words HUD lists as discriminatory—and then some.

Here is a list generated online: www.hud.gov/offices/fheo/library/part109.pdf.

Here is also a great site from Lee County on identifying discrimination that will help you understand what is and is not legal: www.lee-county.com/equalopp/How%20to%20Recognize%20Housing%20Discrimination.htm.

The previous site lists some of the following as red flags:

- Adult Living
- Adult Community
- Adult Building
- No Children
- Singles Only
- For Mature Adults
- For Active Adults
- Mature Citizen Discount 45+
- Adult Living 50+
- Hispanic Area
- Christian Female to Share Apartment
- Prefer Bright, Healthy Person
- Male or Female Only
- Restrictive
- Catholic Church Nearby
- Near Synagogue
- Chinese Business Area
- Any religious symbols in the ad
- Any national flag symbol
- Any male or female symbol

What is acceptable:

- Exceptions to no pets policy
- Gated Community
- Parks Nearby
- Near Houses of Worship

- Quiet Residential Area
- Housing for Older Persons
- Handicap Accessible
- Senior Complex
- Private Club
- 55+ Community

Note that in the last section of acceptable words, even though you're excluding certain age groups, you are referring to the community and not to your specific building.

Here is another site to check out with great information from the City of Dallas: www.dallascityhall.com/fair_housing/advertising.html.

Move-In Day

On move-in day, you will need to be available by phone for your tenants should they have any questions or any urgent needs. Usually I've noticed that tenants have found any problems that will exist, like running sinks, small leaks, or plumbing problems, within forty-eight hours. The key here is to be available for them, to do the walk-through, and to document the property condition for both your sake and the tenant's.

You should never give a tenant the keys without having a cleared deposit, first month's rent, and all paperwork in order! You should collect as much as you can before move-in day; although some tenants will wait until move-in day to pay. You may disallow them to hold the property until they pay the deposit.

Walk-Through

Some owners feel awkward doing a walk-through with the tenant. Before you hand the tenant the keys, you should do the walk-through and make sure that all areas of the property meet your expectations. This will set the right tone for the entire duration of the rental period. Also, you can point out things you are already aware of (think car rental here!) and then give them one to two days to add things to the list that you didn't know about. This gives some level of comfort on both sides and sets the "trust tone" with the tenant right away. It also makes it clear to them that you know what you are doing, and you aren't going to let them get away with property damage.

Property Condition Report

There is an example of the property condition report in the forms section at the end of the book, but the property condition report is a move-in and move-out checklist that is signed by the tenant on move in and notifies her that the condition has been fully documented. Notify the tenant that this protects her and you—it's mutually beneficial. When you do the move-out checklist, do it alone so you aren't distracted by the tenant or more likely to go easy on her when she should rightfully pay for a repair. To charge a tenant for the items in the charge sheet, you'll also need to be sure you documented it was working to begin with, so this form is really important. The form will also help you make calculations for charges. Take a look at www.thelpa.com/lpa/forms/ef-property.html?mv_pc=1566.

TALK FROM THE TRENCHES

"Keep very good records and pictures of condition of property at move-in and move-out, including all receipts. Pay someone else to repair damages, clean, etc." Note that in some states anything you do after move-out isn't tax deductible.

Setting Expectations

Set expectations—both what you expect and what the tenant should expect of you—right away. Will you handle all non-emergency repairs within forty-eight hours? Then say so. Will you provide immediate access to you via cell phone? Then give the tenant the number. (Be careful you don't give it to a nagging tenant, though!) Do you have expectations on communication from the tenant? State so clearly. Be up front right from the get-go with your tenant and ask that he be up front with you, too. You both should know what you're getting into, so to speak.

TALK FROM THE TRENCHES

"Don't be bashful in making a list of rules with your lease, i.e., no parking of extra vehicles or trailer, etc., expectations on the appearance, especially street appearance, carpeting and wall expectation (i.e., steaming, patching, and professional touch-ups when they leave), require co-signers of young couples, make clear that your expectations of the home being returned as it was rented to them are high, and that they will be charged a fee if it isn't."

11

Managing Your Property Yourself

If you've chosen to use a property manager, managing your property will not be difficult at all. Just be sure you manage (not micromanage) your property manager by asking for reports you are entitled to, and keep in good communication with your manager if you receive city notices, association letters, or anything else that affects your property.

Managing your property yourself is the biggest cause of anxiety for a lot of landlords, so there is much you need to know. Whether you are using a property manager or managing it yourself, you will need to do a few things to keep the property in good condition during its tenancy, regardless of what you are going to do with the property after the tenant moves out.

Regular Maintenance

When a tenant makes a repair request, you need to act on it quickly. You can provide the tenant with forms he can mail or fax to you, or you can just provide an email address, which for expediency is my preferred method. I want to be informed of problems because I'd rather deal with issues when they are small before they become large. For instance, an air conditioner leaking Freon is a small issue—until the system dies on you because it doesn't have any pressure! Now a $200 fix is going to cost thousands. Remember, too, to track which maintenance issues are really tenant repairs because the tenant caused the problem. If the tenant didn't regularly replace the filter on the heater and the unit went out, that might not be covered under maintenance but might come from the tenant. It all depends on who or what caused the problem, which is where your tenant checklist upon entry comes in. Sometimes though situations like this are difficult to prove. You may wish to create your own routine monthly or quarterly maintenance schedules and do it yourself or hire a contractor to take care of it.

> I recommend giving the tenants maintenance request forms on move-in day with their packet, along with utility forms and so on. This makes it easy and clear for them to request maintenance; you may also provide a website or email address.

Sometimes you'll have tenants who feel the need to excessively complain. Sometimes these tenants are lonely; others feel they want you to work hard for their hard-earned money! If the complaints are frivolous, talk with the tenant and warn him that each minor complaint is logged and counts as an incident. When the lease is up for renewal, this can actually increase the rental amount. Sometimes this alone is enough to get the renter to stop complaining. You can require the repair in writing, which takes time and discourages tenants from making frivolous requests. You can also state in your lease that any repair costing less than x dollars is a minor repair and the tenant's responsibility! This might discourage some from renting from you, but if the rental market where your property is located in is healthy, you might get away with this and avoid dealing with small problems altogether. The risk of course is that the tenant won't fix issues that could become big problems down the road. Some tenants have even been known to break things so the repair exceeds whatever your minimum amount is for "minor repairs," hence creating a bigger problem altogether. You might find that a repair wasn't really a repair after all, and then warn the tenant that bogus complaints in the future will cost them.

Remember that maintenance and repairs can also be a great excuse to go into the home. One thing I have noticed is that tenants who don't ask for anything—ever—to be fixed are often hiding something, as was the case with my tenant in the horror stories section. You might want to calendar a six-month air-conditioning filter replacement for instance, send the tenant a note that you'll be in the home, and then use it as a good chance to check out the status of the property.

When You're the Repairman

In your agreement, you will have a time period that you will handle repairs. It is the tenant's responsibility to make you aware of repairs that need to be done, but it is your job to do them in a timely fashion. Anything affecting health or well-being must be done immediately upon notification, within the fastest possible time frame that you were capable of doing so. Failure to remedy a serious situation can cause you to be held liable for health bills and so forth. Many of us tend to repair issues immediately because happy tenants are tenants that more often pay on time. But, sometimes you have to wait for parts or time to get there. The key here is to communicate with your tenant and set expectations. This is the method that will lead to the least problematic solution. If you want to wait until you can do it, you still must meet the specification in the lease. If you don't, you aren't holding up your end of the agreement. If this is the case and you don't have time to handle a repair, you should very seriously consider hiring a repair person.

> Some renters will get fed up with delays if you are handling a repair yourself, and demand a repair person—or call their own and expect you to pay for it. You might be surprised with a bill accompanied by a lower-than-expected rent payment.

Repairs vs. Upgrades

Remember that legitimate repairs do need to be handled by you, the landlord—and handled promptly. You must provide a safe environment for the tenant. You also have a moral and legal obligation to provide good living conditions for your tenant no matter how inexpensive the rent is.

Sometimes tenants ask for upgrades, and that is another matter. I had one tenant request a fence be built for her dog, and then she moved out three months after I built her a $3,000 fence. I chalked it up to a very expensive lesson learned. In general, now I do an upgrade only if it's required by the association or makes for a standard living condition, such as window treatments. Get several competitive bids; unless you are living there or it's a high-end home, you don't need to install something like automated blinds!

Working with Subcontractors

If you are working with a property manager, this becomes a bit easier, but you should compile a list of good subcontractors you trust and work with them consistently. They can also report back to you any potential tenant problems they notice. It's good to establish rapport with these contractors as they can provide invaluable information and insight into what's happening at your home, and because they are working for you, I have found they are more likely to be honest. I would not recommend working with any subcontractor the tenant recommends. Why? There are reported cases of subcontractors kicking back to the tenant money for the repair, or if they are friends, not reporting information you need to know.

Also, remember that you should always ask the contractor what caused the problem. If the tenant did, you need to ask the contractor or repair person to document that for you so you can require the tenant to pay for the repair. The tenant might fight you on it at first, but if you have the opinion of an expert and you have your walk-through checklist, the law is on your side on this one.

> The Better Business Bureau, online at http://welcome.bbb.org/, can give you some insight into the records, status, and filed complaints against contractors. Don't hesitate to make one yourself if you find that a contractor was misleading or didn't perform a service, and then wouldn't remedy the situation.

Purchasing Home Warranties

Home warranties can save you time, provide peace of mind, and save you money. If your home is relatively new, a builders' warranty may still apply. If it doesn't, consider a home warranty.

Home warranties generally cover mechanical systems, electrical, plumbing, appliances, the roof, and more. Whether your home is new or old (older homes may cost more), big or small (bigger may cost more), you can find flexible plans that could save you money if you run into a big home problem. Home warranties are available for single family homes, multiunit complexes, duplexes, town homes, and condos, and are available even if you are renting out your home. One that I particularly like is Blue Ribbon Home Warranty because of the flexibility in service offerings. Also, if you decide to sell the home, there is evidence that these homes sell faster than nonwarranted homes.

You can find many home warranty companies online and get competing bids. Whatever company you choose, be sure to Google them and check the BBB to make sure there aren't any serious nonremedied complaints against them.

Safety and Security

You have a legal obligation to take care of any security or safety issues immediately. I recommend creating a checklist and doing a routine inspection of things such as smoke alarms, making certain the tenant has working fire extinguishers and an escape ladder for a two-story home; I've even gone so far as to provide small emergency kits for tenants (this isn't required by the way). What is required is a safe, secure environment within reason. This is another reason the premove-in checklists are so critical; you will have documented that all these items work before the tenant moves in.

Checking Up Without Invading Tenant Rights

You have the right to check up on the property you've rented. After all, it is your house! But tenants have rights, too, and you have to abide by those rights and rules when you check up on the house. Use the tenant notification entry forms, many of which are available online and noted in previous chapters, to ensure you follow the law.

> Tenant notifications change by state. Be sure to check out the rules according to the LPA on how much notice you must give to enter a home.

Drive-bys and Walk-ins

Drive-by inspections are easy and quick. You are checking whether the property appears to be maintained on the outside. If it is, it's a good indicator that the inside is also being maintained. A more thorough inspection is of course the walk-in. Tenants generally feel invaded when this occurs, so unless you have reason to suspect the tenant is causing trouble, I usually don't recommend doing this often, if ever. Before renewing a lease could be a good time for a walk-through. If you notice anything unusual, disorderly, or unacceptable, you will need to provide written notice of that. Use the forms in Appendix B to notify the tenant of her noncompliance and what must be done to remedy the situation.

There are many stories online about tenants who have trashed houses, have done walk-throughs with landlords and then gone back in after with copies of keys and destroyed homes, have drastically hidden problems, have lied to landlords—you name it and it's out there. Know this is a small minority of tenants and not the majority, but the cost of being in that minority of affected landlords is so significant that you will want to do everything you can to protect yourself.

I can personally share a couple of horror stories to start with, and then I'll go into those shared in my survey. Most importantly, I'll share what to do to avoid the problems from ever occurring to begin with!

I had a tenant in Bullhead City who was "quiet"—this is a good thing when you are a landlord. Although the property was rented through a property manager, the property was not being followed up on often enough. Apparently, the tenant had her dog living in the garage and had not cleaned out the dog's feces for awhile (months) and when neighbors complained, the property was followed up on. Even though the property manager gave the tenant a three-day clean-up or evict warning, he didn't follow up, so the feces continued to pile up until the renter just one day left—and left her dog's feces behind. Two months later I was still dealing with the tenant and the fact that she left, unwilling to move without a fight and unwilling to clean up her act. The city got involved, and it was costly and stressful.

Do you want another one? I had a tenant (unfortunately in the same house) pile trash up four feet on the front lawn and have human feces throughout the home. It wasn't until I hired a real estate agent who went to check out the property that I found out. The real estate agent called me and said, "Dani, I cannot sell this property. Have you been in there?" Again another letter went to this (new) tenant, and the problem lingered, quite literally, for awhile. This can make rerenting or selling these homes nearly impossible without significant repairs.

So, what can you do to avoid this? First, have a pet policy! Next, at least drive by the property often enough so you know what is happening with it. The smell would have been strong enough had anyone driven by that it would have been dealt with earlier. Also, give neighbors your phone number (if they don't appear too obnoxious). Often they can report trouble first. Also, anytime you hire a repair person, ask for a report on how the property is doing, looking, and smelling! One last reminder, get a good deposit and be sure you call previous landlords. Chances are, if your prospective renter destroyed a previous home, she will destroy yours, too.

Right of Entry

Remember you have a right to enter the property but only with proper notice. Check out the requirements by state: www.hud.gov/renting/tenantrights.cfm.

Due to the significantly different rules by state, another good place to look for a second opinion is the Department of Consumer Affairs for your particular state. For instance, check out all the information provided for California: www.dca.ca.gov/publications/landlordbook/index.shtml.

There are many other rules you can look up here, too. As you can see, the DCA defines who the landlord is, who is a tenant, how to look for a rental unit, unlawful discrimination, reading the fine print, refunding security deposits, dealing with problems, living in rental units, retaliatory actions and evictions, terminations (of leases or rental agreements), having repairs made, moving out, and how to resolve problems. This is useful information for you as the landlord, even though much of it is aimed at the tenant because these are the types of rights your tenant is being advised that he has. I had a tenant in California who was not happy I was selling a house and kept throwing rules that her attorney-friend told her about in my face. He was misinforming her, but I did have to write letters in response to each one of her queries, which made for a very stressful rental termination (and this was only month-to-month!).

Tenant Privacy

You might want to check up on the property by either driving by it or going inside. If you decide to do periodic walk-in checks, you need to let the tenant know—although driving by is fairly innocuous and doesn't require advance notice.

In general, the tenant has exclusive possession of the unit she's renting. This means that only the tenant and members of the tenant's household or those invited by the tenant have a right to be there. The landlord cannot enter the house whenever he wants. In a lease, there is a covenant called the "covenant of quiet enjoyment," which promises that the tenant has control over who comes into her rental.

Landlords can enter if invited by the tenant, or if workers or landlords must go into the home to inspect the property or perform repairs. The landlord can inspect the property within "reasonable periods." One would expect daily is unreasonable, but every quarter is not unreasonable. I prefer to spell this out in the lease or rental agreement. Also, the landlord must inspect the property only at reasonable times; 2 A.M. for instance is not reasonable. The tenant must also receive reasonable notice, which is usually determined by the courts to mean in writing and at least one day (although some states require up to five days' notice). Emergencies can be handled by anyone doing work on an as-needed basis. In other words, if there is a major leak in the home, you don't have to write and wait five days to fix it! You might not need to give any notice, but you should try to give some kind of notification—a call, for example. If you want to show the home to other potential tenants or buyers, you must also give notice to the tenant of at least twenty-four hours and you must enter during reasonable hours. Again, be sure to check the Housing and Urban Development's website for state-by-state rules. Here is the address again: www.hud.gov/renting/tenantrights.cfm.

Legal Considerations

When you lease or rent your home, you're granting exclusive use rights to that tenant. This means the tenant has a right to privacy. You own the home and you have an obligation and duty to protect your property, but the exchange of rental or lease monies does forfeit some of your rights. You cannot enter the property without proper notification, for instance. This site has all the housing laws you must abide by, in addition to state laws: www.hud.gov/offices/fheo/FHLaws/index.cfm.

Be sure you don't step on the tenant's toes with regard to her rights, and be sure you give proper notification for everything you do, including maintenance that the tenant asks for. Even if the tenant asks for the repairs, you are obligated to inform her of when or how the repairs will take place. One of my rentals had to have a fence, as required by the neighborhood association. I informed the property manager of the upcoming fence construction, but the manager did not inform the tenant. The tenant was quite upset when contractors began showing up at "her house" to build a fence. Remember that tenants look at the home as their own; they are paying you rent in exchange for their right to privacy and their right to use. You must respect these privacy rights because they're guaranteed not only by the law, but also by ethical standards that govern proper landlording. If you follow these rules, you will have happy tenants and tenants who know you mean business when it comes to following the law.

12

Tenant Troubleshooter

Most likely your tenant is a good one; surveys indicate you are far more likely to get a tenant who pays on time and doesn't cause damage than you are to find a bad one. But sometimes tenants ask questions or do things that cause problems for landlords. This section is a tenant troubleshooting guide, discussing the most common problems and what to do about them.

What If My Tenant Won't Pay Rent?

This is one of the biggest problems we face as landlords. Not paying rent is a hassle and a financial burden. Sometimes tenants pay partial rent payments, and leases should cover what the consequences are if there are past due charges and late fees. Unpaid added rent is the same as unpaid rent, and it is also grounds for eviction just as not paying rent is.

According to the Landlord Protection Agency, when a tenant doesn't pay rent you must follow a legal process. First, don't wait too long! Don't buy into a tenant's "I'll pay tomorrow," particularly if he has a history of not paying. It doesn't matter how good of a family or couple you think they are, you have to remember that this is a business. Send your five-day notice out immediately!

Don't wait one day longer than you have to. Send it certified mail or use a carrier like FedEx that provides signature confirmation. Your tenant must know you are serious.

TALK FROM THE TRENCHES

"There are good tenants and bad tenants, and sometimes circumstances (such as job loss, divorce, etc.) can turn previously good tenants into bad tenants. Overall, my experiences have been positive, but I have learned to be diligent in keeping regular contact with my tenants so that I am not caught by surprise."

Be sure to issue a late rent notice immediately after rent isn't paid within the grace period. Use a late notice form that informs the tenant of all late fees. If two to four days pass after delivering or mailing the late notice, call and find out what's wrong. Give the tenant a heads-up that late fees are building daily. Inform the tenant that as of a certain date, the account will go to the attorney's office for eviction proceedings and that any attorney fees will be added to the balance owed (be sure your lease covers this!). If you work with a real estate attorney, ask her to then send an attorney's warning letter instructing the tenant to pay all rent and late fees before eviction is imminent. You might also send this along with a notice to pay rent or quit and a demand for payment. Be sure the tenant knows you will report the missed payment to a credit agency.

TALK FROM THE TRENCHES

Thirty-four percent of survey respondents said that they had to file a complaint officially about a tenant. This is one reason it's so important to deal with problems early on before they become habitual.

Eviction is costly and troublesome. It's best to avoid this by screening tenants—the importance of this cannot be overstated. Sometimes, though, even the best screening process still results in a nonpaying tenant, and you should follow through with proceedings as quickly as the law allows. This tells your tenant you mean business; it also gets the tenant out and a paying one back in as quickly as possible.

You can begin the eviction process yourself though. It is easier with an attorney, but it is also most costly. Remember you can evict if they are paying partial rent! Partial rent is not fulfilling their contract unless you agree to it. (If you do, get the payment plan in writing.) On the fifth day (if the state you are in allows five days for example), generally speaking, you must go to the court or magistrate's office and file what is usually referred to as an unlawful detainer. For example, in Virginia, after X number of days have passed (X referring to the number in your state—five in this case), the sheriff would go to the home and serve a summons. If you accept any money from the tenant (and they are likely to call you at this point), decline unless you want to work with them or believe they're going to change. Accepting money starts the process over in most states. You would then appear before a judge with the summons and copies of all of your evidence. After you win your case, the sheriff's office posts an eviction notice on the door of the residence, and arranges a date with you to meet them at the house. In many states, anything left behind in the home becomes your property.

In many states the court or magistrate's office can help you with the legal proceedings; you might want to begin the process and let an attorney handle it.

If, based on your state's laws, the eviction notice expires and you still have not received rent, start the court eviction. I always recommend using an attorney who is familiar with tenant evictions. If the tenant still owes you money, use the Landlord Protection Agency to report bad debt. This goes onto the tenant's record and stays there for seven years. You're doing other landlords a favor.

Remember you can and should begin the eviction process yourself with your notice to the tenant. In most states, five days after rent is due you can send the notice; check the LPA for your state's guidelines.

TALK FROM THE TRENCHES

"If they are late on the rent, don't give them another month to catch up. They will always be behind. Don't rent to friends, or relatives. Do stick to the contract or rental agreement. Charge late fees and call as soon as they are late."

Courts

Going through the courts can be a very time-consuming and expensive process. Whenever possible, try to get the tenant out of the home by putting pressure on her through an attorney or directly. Anytime you feel threatened, though, let the attorney handle it.

What If My Tenant Wants to Use the Security Deposit as Rent?

This happens more often than you might think! The rent isn't paid, and the tenant asks, "So, can you just take my rent from my deposit?" Or one of my favorites I've heard several times, "I'm moving anyway; you have to use our security as our payment." NO WAY!

The security deposit clause in your lease should explain how security money is used and how it may not be used—as rent! The security deposit clause is important. Make it clear to the tenant that the security deposit is kept in a special account for the entire term of the tenancy and cannot be used for any reason other than physical or financial damages as a result of the tenant not complying with the contract. Also specify that failure to pay rent is cause for eviction and will destroy the tenant's credit—remind her that you do report to credit bureaus. Also remind the tenant that the lease agreement explicitly states (and be sure it does!) that deposits can not be used as rent, so asking for that means the tenant is breaking a contract. Let the tenant know that any default on rent, late fees, collection fees, and attorney fees will be billed to her. When it comes time for a rental increase, you might choose to increase rent to get the tenant out so you can find a more suitable replacement.

What If My Tenant Gives Me a Partial Payment?

You might be thinking that some money is better than no money. Well, only if you have the renter sign a form stating that you accept his partial payment but are still allowed to continue with the eviction process until you receive payment in full.

Remember some tenants are "lifetime tenants" and know the rules on their side extremely well—sometimes better than most landlords. Don't get caught up in their tricks.

You can have the tenant sign a repayment schedule if you wish, but it might delay your ability to get the tenant out. In most states, once you accept partial payment, your entire time to evict starts over again! Be very careful, if you accept partial payment, have the tenant sign documentation that they understand this does not stop the eviction proceedings. Better yet, refuse partial payments.

What If My Tenant Is Engaging in Illegal Activity?

If your tenant is engaging in illegal activity, you could be sued for any damages caused by the activity or called into court to testify about the activity. If you didn't provide a safe environment for the neighbors, you might also be called into court for that. If you knowingly rent to someone who, say, possesses cannabis on your property, you can be contacted by the Drug Enforcement Agency (DEA). This is an example of what can go wrong if you don't do your due diligence. The DEA has sent property owners notices in California notifying them that they may face criminal prosecution or asset forfeiture (that is, their homes) for knowingly renting their properties to medical cannabis facilities, for instance. You are partially responsible if you knew of anything illegal happening in the home. Federal laws do provide for an "innocent owner" clause if the owner truly wasn't aware of any problems, but you don't want to get into this predicament. Get any tenant out immediately who is causing this kind of disruption, and use clauses you've documented in your rental agreement to do so. Usually law enforcement agencies want landlords to evict the tenants, and that is their purpose for contacting you.

Who's Responsible for Property Damage Caused by My Tenant?

If the tenant causes damage that requires a repair, it's the tenant's responsibility to pay for it. Sometimes it's tough to figure out whether the damage is tenant-caused or just the result of normal wear and tear—and some tenants will do their best to hide the problem. If you can show that the item could not have been damaged except through neglect or misuse, you can demand the tenant pay for the repair. This is where information from a subcontractor or the repairperson can help, particularly if you need to charge the tenant for the repair.

What's Required for Eviction?

First, always be sure you read the laws for your particular state regarding eviction. You don't want to get into trouble financially or legally for inappropriately evicting a tenant or not following the rules.

Generally, tenants are evicted for one of two reasons: either nonpayment, in which the tenant must pay or vacate, or conditional/unconditional quit or vacate notices, which are demands for some corrective action to be taken, other than paying rent, or vacating the premises. Eviction can be quite expensive, involving courts and law enforcement. At this point, if you need to evict a tenant who refuses to leave, I recommend securing a real estate attorney who is knowledgeable about evictions and charges a flat rate. You can find many such attorneys online; a good resource is online forums where other landlords meet and share valuable information. The LPA has many forums you can post to. Here is another source for finding attorneys who deal with evictions: www.thelpa.com/lpa/attorney.html?mv_pc=904.

Remember that the only way you can evict is to go through the entire legal eviction process. You can do this for not paying rent on time and giving written notice of this by, in writing, demanding the tenant pay full rent or move out (note the specific law for your state on the number of days you must give the renter to rectify the situation), essentially forcing the tenant to pay or move. This is where partial payments come into play—remember not to accept them! On the fifth day after the warning was issued in most states, generally you can evict the tenant in county court. Tenants can contest your eviction by filing an answer on or before the time set by the court. If the tenant does not appear on the date indicated on the eviction papers, she usually has forty-eight hours to vacate or be removed by the local law enforcement. If the tenant breaks any terms of the lease (including oral, though those are hard to prove in court), you can evict them—be sure that you keep complete documentation of what has occurred.

What If My Tenant Asks for Unreasonable Repairs or Upgrades?

Upgrades are entirely at your discretion unless they are required for Americans with Disabilities (ADA) accommodation, as you read about in Chapter 8. Unreasonable repairs—that is, repairs that do not materially affect the living conditions for the tenant or cause a safety or security issue—are at your discretion.

However, if you don't make the repair, you run the risk of alienating your tenant. If you do make the repair, though, you run the risk of setting a precedent where the tenant starts asking for numerous repairs or upgrades.

This is really a decision that needs to be made based on the tenant's history, how troublesome he is, and how reasonable (and costly) the request is. Ultimately, it's your decision if the request isn't a safety or security issue. If it will help you sell the house later or seems reasonable and/or the tenant doesn't ask for much, you might want to take care of it just to make the tenant happy. I have a great example. I had a tenant in Bullhead City who wanted to landscape the yard, even though it wasn't association-required. I gave her a monthly credit of $100 for six months and let her spend it on landscaping; in return she had to submit receipts to me (which I could use for taxes and to verify that she actually spent the money she said she would). I requested pictures every two months. As a result, she signed a longer lease, she knew I cared about her staying, and she got a yard landscaped the way she wanted. It also increased my resale value for very little money out of pocket. You can find creative ways to work with your tenants on this issue.

> Be very familiar with ADA laws and regulations. While many repairs or modifications are at your discretion, some are not. Be careful not to break these rules.

What If My Tenant Is Disrupting the Neighbors?

This can be a tough situation because often the tenant says he isn't doing anything disruptive. If the neighbors complain, you will want to serve the tenant with a written notice to cease the activity that is causing disruption. If the behavior continues, ultimately if it's within your lease or rental agreement to evict on the basis of disruption, you have the right to do so. I usually find it's better to try to work these things out with the neighbors.

Sometimes neighbors are just resentful that you are renting your home and "bringing down neighborhood values." In this case, the tenant might actually be right. You might choose to find times to try to observe whether the tenant is really engaging in disruptive behavior, and perhaps even meet the tenant and neighbor at the same time to settle the disagreement. I have found this often diffuses situations because most likely both sides have exaggerated their behavior (or lack of it) a bit, and ultimately they are able to come to an acceptable resolution. However, if the tenant is being disruptive, a cease notice should be sent and you can evict the tenant for disruptive behavior if it's within your state and local laws to do so. I've had neighbors call the police on noisy tenants, and police reports are very serious and reflect negatively on you. You will want to handle these types of issues right away.

You can also get copies of all documentation on your particular home by calling the police department. They will generally give you a form to fill out and charge a small fee ($5 to $10) to give you a history on your home of every time law enforcement had to show up to the home, and what it was for.

Keep the local law enforcement involved; let them know you need information on your property. Being able to prove disruptions and violations helps to give you leverage if you need to evict. After a crazy situation erupted in one of my homes in Bullhead City, Arizona, I asked the local police for a copy of all reports filed for my address. For $5 I got a three-year listing of all the times (too many to count) law enforcement was at the home and what they were out there for. They broke about every noise and "using the home for illegal activity" clause in the lease.

What If My Tenant Wants to Stay and I Want to Live in My House or Sell It?

The tenant's rights, after the termination of the lease or rental agreement, do not supersede your rights. If the lease is up and you want to move in, send the tenant a notice to move out with specifics (all in the forms section and on the LPA); the tenant will have to leave. This is not the tenant's call. However, if the lease is still active, you cannot ask the tenant to leave unless you are evicting her for nonpayment or other issues. This can be one advantage of doing a month-to-month rental rather than a lease; if you anticipate needing to move back in. If you do want the tenant to leave before the lease is up, one option is to sit down and talk with the tenant and consider incentivizing her to end the lease early on a mutual agreement—often foregoing rent for a month or two or paying her deposit on another place will convince her to move out. This is between you and the tenant, but the tenant does have the right to stay in the place whether you want to move back in or not if her lease is current.

What If My Tenant Is Subleasing Without My Permission?

You have clearly indicated in your lease agreement whether you allow subleasing or subletting. If the tenant is doing this without your permission, it is against his lease and you can terminate the contract. Send him a notice regarding the problem marked urgent in a certified letter; then you can remove the tenant if he is not holding up his end of the lease agreement by subleasing. Another option, if you choose, is to put the additional person on the lease officially.

> Remember the lease or rental agreement is a legally binding contract! Your tenant doesn't have the right to just break the rules without consequences. Know the law and know your rights as a landlord.

What If My Tenant Is Running an Unauthorized Business Out of My Home?

Some businesses are not necessarily an issue; the online teacher, for instance, might not be disrupting the neighbors. Other professions, such as auto mechanics or daycare, can not only create insurance nightmares (and might not be legal), but can also seriously disrupt the neighbors and surrounding neighborhood. Make it very clear to your tenant in the lease or rental agreement that any undisclosed and unapproved businesses shall result in five-day cease-and-desist or lease termination warnings. This is a serious issue because if anyone is hurt or sued due to this business or if the business is illegal, you can be in legal and financial jeopardy, too.

What If My Tenant Upgrades or Changes the House Without My Permission?

Tenants are not permitted to make structural changes or changes to the home without your permission unless they completely return it back to the way it was when you leased it to them. If they don't return it in the same condition, you can charge them to do so. Additionally, if they make any changes that result in permits being required, taxes being assessed, and so on, you need to consult a real estate attorney immediately because the tenants will most likely need to pay for these damages and you will most likely have to sue them. Make it clear up front that the tenants are not to do these things without first contacting you and should submit a work order request (available in Appendix B) to you for any and all work to be done to the house. I've had tenants who wanted to make minor upgrades that were mutually beneficial, and who even helped with the costs.

What If My Tenant Refuses to Let Anyone Onto the Property—Including You, the Landlord, and Any Contractors?

If you have provided the appropriate warnings ahead of time by written letter (a follow-up phone call is also often beneficial), the tenant must allow you or the contractor onto the premises. The key here is to look up your specific state rules because some require that the tenant acknowledge your letter, some tenants might claim right to privacy and disallow your entry according to state rules, and others yet will just make it difficult for you to inspect the property because they don't want you to see their mess. Anytime this happens, it's good reason to check out the property—there might be something going on there that the tenants don't want you to see, which is something I would list in the red-flag category. Note that the tenants are not permitted to change locks; they can submit a work order request and call you for immediate service if there is any danger to them or their property, but they need to make arrangements with you for this. If the tenants are obviously in immediate danger and change the locks and provide you with a key, you might not want to make an issue out of this, even though it is technically a breach of the contract (if you use the recommended forms).

What If the Tenant Leaves Things in the Home After Vacating?

Every state has its own laws (use the LPA) to address this issue. This is called Abandonment of Goods. This applies only once the tenant has left but left their things behind, too. You may dispose of anything perishable immediately. The Residential Tenancies Act defines any abandoned goods as those which are left at the premises either after the tenancy has expired or been terminated or if the tenant abandons the property. You must keep very detailed records of what you find and how you handle it. This site has excellent resources on ending a tenancy and abandoned goods: www.nexsenpruet.com/assets/attachments/271.pdf.

Generally in the United States, if a tenant abandons property and leaves goods behind the landlord can take possession of the property ten days after the tenant receives personal service of notice or fifteen days after a notice is mailed. This does change by state so when in doubt, ask an attorney or check the LPA. The landlord may sell the property at a public sale, and the tenant is even responsible for storage fees. You must use the last known address as "sufficient notice" in these matters.

After you give notice, be sure to store all personal property in a safe place and exercise reasonable care. Any costs you incur to do this are charged to the tenant and you should collect them in cash when or if the tenant picks up the items. If the tenant responds back that he/she wishes to pick up the property and then doesn't, you may take the property fifteen days after the date of intended pickup. In most states you must notify the tenant of sale to their last known address at least ten days before you intend to sell, easily stretching the holding time to a month. Most states do protect landlords from being sued if they remove or dispose of property within the states guidelines.

Any proceeds from the sale though generally must go to, in this order, 1) reasonable expenses of holding and selling the property and giving proper notice, 2) any rent due from the tenant, and 3) then any balance given to the court for holding for six months. If not claimed for the tenant, the money often goes to the county. Check your local state and county laws before disposing of property.

Sound complicated? Just be glad you don't live in Canada! To give you an example on how convoluted things can get, the rule of thumb is that if items left behind have a market value of $2000 or less, you can just dispose of them. If a landlord believes they're worth more than $2000 but it costs more than they are worth to remove, sell, or store the items, you can dispose of them in a reasonable way. If it's unsafe to store the items, you can remove them. If they are worth more than $2000 though and won't be damaged by storage or are worth selling, you have to hang onto the goods after the tenant has left, in general, for thirty days. After that you can sell the goods, but you need permission by a court. Proceeds must be sent to the Department of Building and Housing along with photocopies of the order, and the department pays out money owed to the landlord per the order. Any money left over is held in trust for the tenant to collect.

What If My Tenant Goes Bankrupt While in My Home?

This is a very real and scary problem for many landlords. Some states have very strict laws protecting tenants if they file bankruptcy. For instance, in some states like Arizona, serving a five day notice while a tenant is going through bankruptcy can result in very steep fines. Landlords must know the rules to protect themselves and know what rights tenants can exercise, and what available options you have.

> Any rent owed before the bankruptcy was filed is a pre-petition rent or unsecured claim. This is the very last type of claim that is paid out of bankruptcy and will almost always be discounted.

If the tenant stays in the premises any time after a bankruptcy is filed, the claim for rent for this period is considered administrative. An administrative claim is paid before other claims, regardless of the type of bankruptcy. Therefore, rent incurred after the bankruptcy commenced is often paid. Sometimes though there isn't enough money to pay everyone so monies are paid proportionately.

When your tenant files for bankruptcy, all collections against the tenant must stop, including efforts to collect money. You must have court permission to pursue and collect any rent. Thankfully, most leases (be sure yours does!) have a clause that says if the tenant files for bankruptcy, the lease is breached and the tenant is evicted. But, many state laws mandate that a landlord cannot evict a tenant for bankruptcy. This is when an attorney might be helpful. You also cannot require that the tenant pay more rent or a higher deposit.

Note though that any time a landlord terminates a lease before they file bankruptcy, they have no right to continue the lease after they file. Under a lease agreement, when tenants file Chapter 7 or Chapter 11 bankruptcy, the tenant must assume or reject a current lease within sixty days of filing. Before the sixty-day mark, the tenant can file an extension request for another sixty days and then you are told what day the new sixty day period is good through. Keep close watch on your costs and motions and deadlines set by the court. If your tenant assumes the lease while in bankruptcy, they are agreeing to pay. If they were already in default, they must make up any existing debts owed to you within a "reasonable time period." If within sixty days the debt isn't paid, the tenant must go back to court to request additional arrangements.

In many cases, the tenant won't accept the lease. If he or she rejects the lease, it automatically cancels it. You can negotiate a new lease though if you like, that then needs bankruptcy court approval.

This particular site on tenant law has some great information that will help you: www.bernsteinlaw.com/publications/tenant_res.htm. This is really a good time to call an attorney. Be sure you follow the rules or you could be in a lot of trouble.

This is a great case study to show you what can happen: www.mcmlaw.com/pubs/719079_1.pdf.

13

Time to Sell or Time to Dwell

So you want your house back. You are moving back in, you're selling it, your tenant has left, or you want a new one—regardless, you will need to get the house back in order. It is not okay for the tenant to leave a mess, including his discarded items! This is his trash, and when you remove it you will be billing the tenant for this or adding it to any balance owed to you.

When the tenant leaves, you should provide a security settlement statement to the tenant. It's recommended that, regardless of the reason or the initiator of the move-out, you send a pre–move-out letter of instruction to the tenant at least three weeks before he vacates. The unit should be returned clean; unabused; and free of debris, trash, or worse.

When Can You Legally Move Back In?

You can legally move back in when the tenant has vacated the property. If the tenant left items behind, be sure to read the section in Chapter 12 on goods that tenants leave in your home. You must still store the items in a safe location under certain circumstances.

You may legally move back into the home after the lease or rental agreement is up, the tenant has been properly notified, final inspections have been done, and all the appropriate documentation has been sent to the tenant. We will go through each step of the appropriate documentation in this chapter, and the reference material and forms are available on the LPA's website and in Appendix B of this book.

Notifying the Tenant

You must follow certain procedures based on who is initiating the tenant removal. If the tenant is choosing to leave, the tenant will either be violating the lease or leaving in accordance with the lease.

If the tenant wants to vacate the tenancy properly, she must give you a notice to vacate in the time frame outlined in the rental agreement. This should provide you ample time to find a new tenant. If the tenant has abided by the lease, normally the following occurs:

1. Notify you in writing within the terms of the lease. This is generally at least thirty days before the last day of a full month's occupancy. You can require more and feel free to request it in your lease. If you didn't specify, most states require a thirty-day minimum. The tenant should use the tenant's notice to vacate form, which you should provide her upon signing the lease or shortly before the lease ends.

2. After notice is given, make arrangements with the tenant to show the property to new prospects. This is required per the laws regarding tenant's rights.

3. Two to four weeks before the tenant's proposed move-out date, send a move-out reminder letter to tell her what she's expected to return to you, how to return the keys, and what to do to be entitled to a security refund.

4. You might choose to send the move-out, cleanup, and debris letter, which reminds the tenant that she must leave the rental the way she found it.

5. Inspect the rental for damages. Tenants usually prefer to do the walk-through with you. Both the LPA and I do not recommend this. Do this without the tenant present because, as the LPA says, most damages are

found after the tenant leaves. In fairness to the landlord, you cannot make a full, careful list of security deductions with the tenant watching. It takes time to do a good inspection.

6. Avoid confrontations if you can. Let them move out smoothly, and then be in charge of the refund. Remember most of the damage you will find will be after the tenant has left. Remember the case of the tenant painting around the couches?

If you are kicking the tenant out, things change a bit. If a tenant is consistently breaking the rules in the lease and you're sending proper notification as outlined in this book, you have the right to evict the tenant. Almost every state has its own guidelines, so be sure to check the laws in your state. One law most states have is that the tenant has an opportunity to be heard, particularly before a law enforcement officer removes her from a property. This is part of due process. Almost all evictions start with your written notices and giving the tenant the opportunity to fix the problems within a specified period of time, catch up on rent, and so on. These notices are crucial in that they establish that you have communicated requirements to the tenant. There are many laws to protect tenants from vicious landlords, so know what is legal and what isn't for your state. But you have very serious, well-documented rights if part of your lease agreement is broken.

> Be sure to study Appendix B! These fast forms will help you move tenants out and properly refund money without getting yourself into trouble.

Many people ask whether they can remove a tenant for no reason whatsoever at the end of a lease period. Yes, you absolutely can, but you must give the tenant notice to leave and serve that notice within a specified period of time before the end of the rental period, as outlined in your lease agreement. If the length of time isn't specified, notice to vacate requirements generally are as follows:

One year or longer lease—three months' notice

Six months to one year—one-month notice

One month to six months—ten days' notice

One week to one month—three days' notice

Less than one week—one-day notice

Any written notices you provide the tenant for any reason should always include the date, the address of the unit, any dollar amounts involved, any violations, any remedies, any options for the tenant, and a landlord signature.

> You should always send all documents with receipt confirmation for your own protection. You can use Return Receipt Requests through the post office or a company that requires signature confirmation. This is especially important for any documents that have time limits, like pay/quit notices, eviction notices, or notices for goods left behind. Many landlords have needed these confirmations in court.

After the Tenant Has Moved

After the tenant has vacated the property, you must be sure you handle the situation legally to prevent hassles, stress, and financial damages. If the lease agreement was met, most likely the property will be in acceptable condition so you can rent it to a new tenant. This also means the tenant has paid for his lease through the term of the agreement and doesn't owe you any more money.

If there are charges against the security deposit, even if the tenant has done a great job complying with the lease agreement, you will minimize damages and clean up by using the letters I've described thus far from the LPA. You need to be sure you send the tenant four documents:

1. A property condition report checklist, which documents the condition before and after the tenant lived there
2. A security settlement statement, listing the charges made against the deposit and notifying the tenant of any additional charges owed to you above the deposit
3. A settlement charges guide, which shows how much you should have charged the tenant for some of the usual damages
4. The "security settlement challenge crusher," as LPA calls it, which is a form that helps to eliminate unfounded claims to get security money back from you

There is a reasonable chance, particularly if the tenant didn't leave under the best circumstances, that he will try to argue about deductions from the deposit. Sometimes these tenants threaten a lawsuit, but don't let them intimidate you. The arguments and phone calls from former tenants can lead to harassment and can waste your business's time and money—leading to a countersuit. You should let any tenant who is getting to this point be aware that you know of your rights.

Be sure your documentation tells the tenant, in no uncertain terms, that careful thought has been put into the handling of the security settlement. You can ask him to bring in a copy of the lease, settlement statement, and all other supporting documents to his own attorney for review and explanation. (This alone gets a lot of tenants to drop it!) By asking him to go to his lawyer, you're showing the tenant that you aren't intimidated. I've provided a sample of the LPA form recommended that you send to tenants under the "Settlement Charges Guide" section in Appendix B!

Abiding by State Regulations

Every state has its own rules. You can use Google to look them up, or use the trusted LPA to check them out by state. Here is a good link to use to get the information: www.thelpa.com/lpa/lllaw.html?mv_pc=6.

You must abide by the law where the home is located; therefore, even if you don't live in the state you're renting the home in, you must be familiar with the laws there to be a landlord.

> Always check state rules and laws! Every state is different, and you must abide by the rules of the state the home is rented in.

This is an example of one particular state's requirements, California, which happens to be my home state:

California, as of 4/23/07, requires thirty to sixty days' written notice based on the situation to terminate tenancy.

The period to cure a default on a lease in California, or reinstate a lease, is three days.

The late charge option is whatever is "reasonable" as agreed to in the lease rental agreement. A flat late fee that is so high that it amounts to a penalty is not legally valid in California.

Landlords can charge a bounced check fee under California's "bad check" statute, and the landlord can charge a service charge instead of the dishonored check fee. The charge can be up to $25 for the first check returned for insufficient funds and up to $35 for each additional check.

California limits security deposits on unfurnished dwellings to two months' rent, and three months for furnished dwellings. Uniquely, if the unit has a waterbed, the landlord can require three and a half months' security deposit!

The security deposit in California can be called the "last month's rent," "security deposit," "pet deposit," "key fee," or "cleaning fee." The security deposit can be a combination of the last month's rent plus a specific amount for security. Regardless of what you call them, the law considers all of them to be part of the security deposit.

In California, as a landlord you can not charge more than $37.57 per applicant to screen. (Yes, I'm not kidding!)

California State requires that rental property owners include the following notice in their rental agreements according to California Civil Code:

Language concerning "Megan's Law" required on and after April 1, 2006:

[Notice: Pursuant to Section 290.46 of the Penal Code, information about specified registered sex offenders is made available to the public via an Internet website maintained by the Department of Justice at www.meganslaw. ca.gov. Depending on an offender's criminal history, this information will include either the address at which the offender resides or the community of residence and ZIP Code in which he or she resides.]

In this case, the landlord would be required to copy and paste everything in the brackets into the agreement or use a lease addendum form.

Can you see why looking up your state's requirement for landlords is so vital? How would you ever be aware of most of these laws or the maximums? It is impossible to know them all, but you can use the LPA to help you. You can also use Google to search for various laws, but you run the risk of getting outdated information.

Under almost all circumstances, you are not legally permitted to lock out a tenant without a court order because you are interfering with the right to peaceful possession until a legal court eviction. You can be sued for damages, so don't try this.

Selling Your Property to an Investor with a Tenant

Investors often buy homes to rent them and hold them, and finding tenants is one of the many hassles they go through in their acquisition to build their portfolios. Often having an existing lease with a decent amount of time left on it is very attractive to investors! You may wish to sell the home to an investor with your tenant! If this is the case, the tenant still has the right to maintain the lease. Once the new owner takes over though, he or she may give the tenant notice to move. You need to make your tenant aware of your intention to sell and be prepared for the tenant to break the lease. Sometimes the best time to do this is at the end of a lease.

You can incentivize your tenant to stay though, too. I have sold many properties to investors with tenants and have reassured the tenants that they would have a home based on my contract with the new owner. I have also purchased property that had a tenant with an existing lease. If you take one of these over, be sure to do a walk-through right away. Also, if you do sell the house, be sure the tenant knows where to send rent. Give copies of the lease or rental agreement to the buyer.

Getting Ready to Sell or Move Back Into the Home

After the tenant has left, it's time to fix any damages and do repairs that you have taken out of her deposit. If you are going to sell the home, consider selling the home yourself to save 5 to 6 percent in agency fees, particularly if the market is reasonably stable. Make sure you run a new comparative analysis and know what the home is worth. You might decide to rerent, to move back in, or to sell the home.

When the tenant moved in, you went through the house methodically. Whether you are going to live there or are going to sell the home, do the same after the tenant leaves. Have the yard landscaped (or some of the landscaping replaced if it's needed), and get the home professionally cleaned if you don't have the time to do it yourself (or don't like cleaning up other people's messes). Remember that the security deposit can cover regular cleaning, too.

Selling Your Property While It's Rented

If you are wondering whether you can list your property for sale while you are renting it, the answer is yes. But ... your tenant likely won't appreciate it. There is a reasonable chance you will lose your tenant as the tenant either breaks the lease or leaves as soon as he legally can. Remember also that you must provide the tenant with the use of the home, and that means you cannot be invasive and must respect his privacy rights.

You must provide the tenant with adequate notice when you are selling the home. Do this in accordance with state and federal law. Also be aware that if the home is for sale or lease, most tenants won't consider renting the home from you unless you take it off of the market once they move in. People don't like strangers showing up and walking in or driving by their home all the time. Respect the tenant's rights; it's not only the right thing to do, but also is the law. If you want to show the property, you must do so within reasonable times of the day and with adequate notice, based on your lease agreement and what the law requires for your state.

14

Refinancing Your Rental Property

At some point during the period you own your rental, you might decide a refinance is in order. Refinancing can occur before or after you rent the home, but you will get a better rate if you refinance it before it becomes a rental property. Why? Rental or investment properties carry a risk for the bank, so banks charge more for the loan in interest. They also might require a higher loan-to-value ratio, which means you might actually have to come in with cash to close your refinance loan. Not exactly the ideal situation for most homeowners.

Consider the possible need to refinance prior to renting while it is still your primary residence. Talk with your lender (direct to lender is a better deal than a mortgage broker) and find out what the rules are with regard to how long you must live there before converting it to a rental to maintain legal compliance. This means if you do intend to refinance, you will need to plan this in advance.

What Is a Refinance?

Refinance, referred to as a *refi* in the lending world, is the process of converting one loan into another. It can mean that you change banks, giving your loan to another bank entirely, or that you refinance into a different type of loan program or a different interest rate with the same bank.

You might also be taking a cash-out refinance, which means you want to take money out along with the refinance (perhaps a good thing to do if you need to take cash out for your move into another area or another home or if you want the security of having that money in a liquid asset such as stocks or bonds).

When Should You Refi?

People refi for a variety of reasons. You might want a cash-out refi that keeps some of your money in a liquid asset. You might need to drop your monthly payments so that you can at least break even on your rental, take less of a loss, or perhaps if you're fortunate to even cash flow positively on rent each month.

You might have had a teaser rate loan or a negative amortization loan (often referred to as a *pay option adjustable-rate mortgage* or *option ARM*) and need to solidify your payments and stop adding to the principle each month as you move into your new home, retire, or just wait out a market recovery.

Should You Refi with the Same Bank?

Refinances are generally a bit faster and easier if you use the same bank that has your original loan. However, the same bank might not have the best rate, and that is essential if you need to cut your payments down. Remember though our discussion about combined loan to value. The bank, when you refinance, will look at all loans outstanding against the value to determine the CLTV, which determines your rate and qualification abilities.

> Your first mortgage, second mortgage, home equity line of credit (HELOC), or even your third mortgage don't have to be with the same banks! You can have a first mortgage with one, and shop around for another good rate on a HELOC or second for the same home. Go with who has the best rate and cheapest price.

Comparing Banks, Loan Options, and Rates

It's vital that you make a good decision when you refinance. You need to take into consideration the following:

- How long will you rent the property for?
- Do you intend to move back in after you are done renting it?
- What is your cash flow situation?
- What is your current loan type?
- Does your loan keep you up at night? Maybe it's a great payment or rate, but the worry about adding to the balance each month creates anxiety.
- What are the costs to refinance?
- What is the break-even point on the refinance?

There are some great websites like bankrate.com that compare loan values at many lending institutions all on one site. You can compare loan types as well. After you narrow it down to three to four banks, go directly to the bank websites and check out their current rates, usually posted on their home pages. Some of the top lenders to check out are:

- Washington Mutual (www.wamu.com)
- Bank of America (www.bofa.com)
- National City Mortgage (www.nationalcitymortgage.com)
- Indymac (www.indymac.com)
- Countrywide (www.countrywide.com)
- Wells Fargo (www.wellsfargo.com)

Some smaller lending institutions such as Ditech (www.ditech.com) and eTrade (www.etrade.com) might offer great rates, too, so they're worth looking into before you make any final decisions.

After you have two to three institutions that appear to have the best rates, get in touch with a local branch office representative. You can apply through the website, but I've had terrible luck with my loans going to call centers in India. Having someone personally handle your loan creates a relationship that might last over the long term, and you will have someone to ask questions of (like the aforementioned "how long do I need to live in the house after the refi?").

The Refi Process

The refi process can take from two weeks to four weeks depending on the loan circumstances and the lender, as well as how quickly their underwriting department works (and how backed up they are from other refinances in the current market). Expect the worst, but there are things you can do to speed up the process.

Application Process

The lender or mortgage banker will usually take your application over the phone. You can go into the branch to do this, but often it's faster to just give the information over the phone and let the bank pull your credit. Your FICO score, discussed in this book in detail, will also impact your interest rate. If your FICO is on the border of being prime (these days considered 680 or above, even though just one year ago 620 got you a prime rate at many banks), find out what you can do to improve your score. If you can wait a month and pay off small debts to get your score up, you can save $1/4$ of a percent to 2 percent, depending on the loan type and the bank. This can mean hundreds of dollars in interest each month.

Expect the banker to ask for income information, employer information, and what you intend to do with the refi (Pay off a loan with no cash back? Cash out? If you're going to cash out, what will you do with it?). Home improvements or paying off high-interest debt are looked at more favorably by the bank than going on a lavish vacation because they decrease the likelihood you will let the home go back to the bank or sell it quickly, which means the lender makes very little money off of you and might not even break even on its costs of completing the loan.

The home also cannot be on the market. Banks check the Multiple Listing Service (MLS) and, if the home comes up as being on the market in the last thirty to sixty days, you will have some explaining to do. I recommend keeping it off the market for two months if you intend to refinance.

Good Faith Estimate

The goal at this stage is to get a good faith estimate (GFE). This lets the lender run an appraisal and verify your income and loan-to-value ratios, which will help her accurately predict the loan options and payments available to you.

It is not a bad idea to compare two or three GFEs to ensure you are getting the best deal. The GFE will have the cost-to-close and will break down the costs you are paying. Some things to look for are who is paying the appraisal? Try to negotiate this if you are paying so the bank does. What are the loan fees? Are there any points? Find out if you can "buy down" the interest rate. Are there prepayment penalties that will penalize you if you refinance or sell the home (these are referred to as *soft* and *hard prepays*, respectively). If the GFE doesn't have all this information, be sure to ask your lender. Even though she might not change the short-term payment, she can cost you dearly in the long term.

Have Your Paperwork Ready

Every time I have applied for a new loan, a refinance, a home equity line of credit, or a second mortgage, I have sped up the process by several days by having certain paperwork ready and emailing it to the lender. Here are some things you will need:

- W2s from the past two years and any 1099s you have
- Current mortgage statement, including current balance and interest rate
- Documents showing your current interest rate (this also is usually on the mortgage statement you receive monthly or on your loan documents or the company's website)
- Two months' pay history via pay stubs
- Asset statements for two months or one quarter (401(k)s, brokerage accounts, money markets, bonds, stocks, and so on)
- Two months' bank statements
- Last two years of tax returns

If you have this information in a readily usable format such as PDF, you can just email it to the lenders. How do you do this? Take the current information and scan it into a PDF format using almost any scanner. If you have an electronic copy from your company or can pull it off the Web, get a program like CutePDF Writer or ScanSoft PDF Writer that lets you print to a PDF format.

> One quick tip I use often is to scan all my pay stubs and relevant statements monthly so if I need information while traveling or immediately, it's always available.

Send all of your documents to the lender's fax or email, and she should be able to prepare your documents to get to the underwriter fairly quickly.

Doc or No Doc?

Remember you can probably do a "no-doc" loan, which means low or no documentation (pay stubs are usually sufficient), but it often means you pay a price in interest rates because you are a higher-risk borrower—the same holds true for being an investor. You're more likely to let your investment property be foreclosed on before your primary residence so banks charge a risk premium in the form of interest rates and/or prepayment penalties. Having your documentation means you might qualify for a full-documentation loan. It's more of a hassle but can drop your rate, monthly interest payments, and payments substantially. If you have the paperwork, it's worth it to go through the process. Penalties can be as much as 2 percent in interest with some banks! On a $200,000 home, this is $400 per month in needless interest!

Refi Equations

After you get the good faith estimate, you can determine what your break-even point is in months for the loan. You will need a few pieces of data, most of which your lender can supply. Remember that lenders can get creative; if you have equity, you might be able to pay off a high-interest second mortgage with one first mortgage and consolidate loans. You might be able to split up your first mortgage into a first and second mortgage to lower your overall monthly costs and avoid paying private mortgage insurance (PMI), a monthly insurance premium you pay to the lender if your first mortgage loan-to-value ratio exceeds 80 percent. Here is an equation you can use that is very simple to calculate:

X = The amount saved per month with the new loan

Y = The amount the loan will cost you (in fees) to refinance

In this case, let's assume a refinance will save you $200 per month and cost you $3,000 in fees and points.

Divide Y by X

In our example, $3,000 divided by 200 is 15.

This means that it will take about fifteen months to break even on the new loan. If you intend to sell the home before the fifteen months are up, it is not worth refi'ing because you will pay more over the long term than if you just kept your existing loan. This is a simple way to determine if it's worth, financially, the cost of refinancing.

Pay Option ARMS

The equation gets a bit more complicated if you are adding to the principle each month. If you are, you need to add the amount you are adding to the principle to X. Your new equation becomes:

X = The amount saved per month with the new loan + the amount you are adding to the balance on your existing loan

Y = The amount the loan will cost you (in fees) to refinance

In this case, let's assume we save $200 per month, and currently we are adding $300 per month to principle due to having a negative amortization loan or paying the negative amortization amount on pay option ARM. Now the monthly savings is $500.

Divide Y by X

In our example, $3,000 divided by 500 is 6.

In six months, you will break even by refinancing. The difference is that the money will come out monthly, so you will be paying now rather than waiting until you sell the house to pay off the extra debt.

What About Another Negative Amortization Loan?

If you need your payments to be low or you have varying income from commissions, tips, or the like, it might be important to have the option of paying less than the full interest amount some months. In this case, if rates are lower than you are paying now it might still be beneficial to refinance and to do so into another negative amortization loan. Just be aware that the interest you are paying on this option ARM will be higher than a fixed-rate or adjustable mortgage.

The Emotional Equation

There is another equation, though, and that is the emotional one. Sometimes knowing you are adding to the principle while watching your home value decline is so stressful that even if you have a great interest rate, you need to refinance to sleep at night. This has no value; it is priceless. If the stress of the loan you have causes you distress, my suggestion is to refinance. Consider opening a home equity line of credit (HELOC) that lets you tap cash and equity in the home if you need it just for emergencies. (Remember, however, that this reports on your credit like a revolving charge account so it affects your credit more than a second mortgage and usually has a higher interest rate.)

Solidifying the Loans

In the last five years, a variety of loan options has made homes more affordable but has also confused a lot of people and helped create the situation many are in now—a home worth less than what a homeowner owes, a higher rate of fore-closure, and the biggest new-home start decline by homebuilders in twenty-five years. The loan you're in might in fact have led you to need to make a decision to ride out the market by renting your home, so you might understand this problem firsthand.

Beating Up the Lenders

By this point, the lender should have sent a preapproval and/or a qualification letter to you, and you can now compare them side-by-side. Don't be shy in sharing GFEs with the other competing banks. Let them compete for your business. They might not be able to budge much on interest rates, but they certainly can on fees. If they want your business, they will negotiate.

Types of Mortgages

Knowing the types of mortgages, their plusses and minuses, and what is available to you is essential to making a good decision. We will go through some of them now. Check out the MortgageProfessor.com for some great information, too.

Mortgage Classifications

All mortgages can be put into two categories: conventional and government financing. Then, subcategories include fixed-rate loans, adjustable-rate loans, and a combination of both of these two. So, your loan will fall into one of the first two categories, and then one of the two second categories. For instance, it might be a conventional fixed or a government-backed adjustable.

Unless your mortgage is backed by the Veterans Administration (VA) as a VA loan, is government backed by the Federal Housing Authority (FHA), or is a Rural Housing Service (RHS) loan, it is conventional. There are rules that must be complied with for government loans, but they can save you a lot of money.

State, County, or City Assistance

Some states and counties also have additional help for borrowers. Some states, counties, cities, or townships have low to moderate housing finance programs, down payment assistance programs, or programs that are designed to help first-time buyers. (Mortgage Professor, 2008) Usually they help with regard to leniency for qualification, lower fees, loan assistance programs that offer rates lower than the market, or programs that allow for tax credits for part of your interest payments. Check with your state, county, or city for more information on possible programs, particularly if you have low income or are a teacher.

Government Loans

I'll explain government loans first because you can save a lot of money if you qualify for some of these programs.

FHA Loans

The FHA is part of the United States Department of Housing and Urban Development (HUD). FHA loans will allow you to close with a lower down payment and are generally easier to qualify for than conventional types. One big problem with FHA loans is that they must fall under certain government requirements for maximum home values, which in some states is nearly impossible. These will be changing throughout 2008, so check out www.hud.gov for more information on FHA financing. Most lenders will work with FHA loans so you should ask if you qualify.

VA Loans

VA Loans are guaranteed by the United States Department of Veterans Affairs. This is a benefit for service personnel to obtain a loan with really good terms, often without *any* down payment. VA loans are usually easier to qualify for, and most banks will work with VA borrowers. There is a limitation, though, of $203,000 on the home. The VA must determine if you are eligible and issue a certificate of eligibility, which you must use and take to the lender. The VA has a lot of information on its website so you should check it out at www.va.gov.

RHS Loan

RHS loans are rarer than VA and FHA loans. These are loans that are guaranteed by the United States Department of Agriculture and allow people living in rural areas to close with minimal closing costs and usually no down payment. Talk with your lender to see if you qualify for such a loan.

Conventional Loans

Conventional loans can be grouped into conforming and nonconforming loans. It's important to understand the difference because it can affect your rate, fees, and down payment.

Conforming Loans

Conforming loans have terms that follow guidelines set by Fannie Mae and Freddie Mac. These are stockholder-owned corporations that buy mortgage loans as long as lenders follow specific guidelines. Lenders package these into mortgage-backed securities and can sell them on the secondary market or to Fannie Mae or Freddie Mac. If the loans are bundled and sold to Fannie or Freddie, they also can sell them on the secondary market to investors. Companies like these help keep money flowing for borrowers.

There are a lot of frustrating guidelines to qualify for a conventional loan. As of the day I wrote this chapter, a single-family residence first mortgage cannot exceed $417,000. If the home costs $500,000, you need to put down the rest in a down payment. This means many people on the coasts and in the South are excluded from borrowing under this type of loan. The government is looking at increasing this, particularly in some states where this is insufficient.

You can get a conventional loan, interestingly enough, on a duplex, threeplex, or fourplex. The limits for these are $533,850; $645,300; and $801,950 as of January 2008, respectively.

In Alaska, Guam, Hawaii, and the United States Virgin Islands, the maximum loan amount is 50 percent higher than these stated amounts. If the property you are refinancing exceeds four units, it's considered a commercial building and has a different set of rules. These numbers have increased from 2007—a good thing. 2007 and 2008 saw considerable jumps in the maximum, which has helped a lot of families.

Jumbo Loans

Jumbo loans go above the maximums established in the last section—those that Fannie and Freddie use as lending guidelines. They are called *jumbo loans* because they are bought and sold on a smaller scale and have slightly higher interest rates than those that fall within conforming limits. These interest rate penalties seem unfair to those who live in states where it's nearly impossible to get a home for just slightly more than $400,000.

B- and C-Rated Loans

In the world of credit, *paper*, or mortgages, are rated as A, B, and C. They are also put into subcategories such as A- or Sub A paper, but A, B, and C is sufficient for your comparisons.

A rated loan highly depends on the lender. Just as the conforming limits are set by Freddie and Fannie, so is the rating of the paper. B, C, and D do not meet lending requirements by Freddie and Fannie; A paper does. B or C loans might be offered to those who have had a bankruptcy or foreclosure or late payments on their credit reports. The purpose of these loans is to let applicants buy time at a higher rate to prove they're capable of holding A-rated paper. The interest rates and programs available to B-, C-, and even D-rated paper varies by bank, the individuals' financial history and credit report.

Fixed Rate vs. Variable Rate

Fixed-rate and variable-rate mortgages are precisely as they sound—either the rate is locked for the entire length of the loan or it's locked for a shorter period of time. Usually adjustable rates are tied to the London Inter Bank Offering Rates (LIBOR). Fixed-rate loans are tied to our bond market and our federal reserve rates, which are usually higher than adjustable-rate mortgages.

Fixed-rate Loans

A fixed-rate loan or mortgage fixes the interest rate and payment for the entire period of the loan. This can be anywhere from ten years to forty years, in increments of ten, fifteen, twenty, twenty-five, thirty, forty, or even fifty years. The interest is better on the shorter loans than the longer ones, so over the life of the loan you pay less interest. But, the longer loans obviously change the payment and lower it substantially. If you take the entire time to pay off the home, you will pay double, triple, or more overall for your home over the life of it. However, if you expect to have a huge sum of money, say, from an inheritance in thirty years, you might want a fifty-year loan to keep the payment low and pay it off in thirty years, saving yourself twenty years of interest. This is where your own personal strategy based on your financial situation comes into play. For instance, a fifteen-year loan usually means you will save more than half the total interest cost than on a thirty-year loan.

The Mortgage Professor has an outstanding graphic that helps to depict this and an excellent tool available online at www.mortgage-x.com/calculators/amortization.htm. For instance, one of the vital pieces of information it graphically depicts is a scenario like this: 15-year loan, $200,000 loan amount, 5.75 percent rate (keep in mind 15-year rates are almost always lower than 30-year rates), with a payment of $1660.82. Over the entire life of the loan, you pay $98,947.23 in interest. But, if you choose a 30-year loan with a 6.25 percent rate and take all 30 years to pay it, you will pay a whopping $234,316.39 more for your home!

These fixed-rate loans are referred to as *fully amortized loans*. This means that each month you pay down principle as well as interest. As time goes on, more money goes to principle and less goes to interest. The intent is that at the end of the loan your loan is paid in full, and you officially own your home!

Another graph from the mortgageprofessor.com shows how the payments apply principle and interest differently as time goes on and shows you how you pay down your loan more quickly as time goes on. Some people who want to pay off their loans rapidly choose to make extra principle payments.

If you make an extra principle payment, be sure you send it separately and note on the check: APPLY TO PRINCIPLE NOT AS A PAYMENT. Lenders will automatically apply this payment to your next month's payment and not to your principle! How kind of them to do. You might need to verify each time you make an extra payment that the bank has applied it correctly by phoning them.

Some people also realize the benefit of paying their mortgage every other week, called the *biweekly mortgage payment*. If you pay half your monthly payment every two weeks, you will repay your loan much more quickly. A typical thirty-year loan will be paid off in eighteen to nineteen years because you are paying interest on a lower principle amount every two weeks. This simple trick can lower your payments dramatically!

Mortgage-X also has a biweekly mortgage planner that shows you how much you will save over the life of a loan if you pay your mortgage biweekly rather than monthly. For instance, a thirty-year loan can be paid off in eighteen or nineteen years! This saves you an incredible amount of interest. Check out their accelerated payment calculator at www.mortgage-x.com/calculators/extra_payment_calculator.asp

Balloon Loans

Balloon loans are also short-term fixed-rate loans that have monthly payments which are fixed and short terms such as three, five, or seven years. They generally have lower interest rates than thirty- or fifteen-year straight fixed mortgages. There is one major downside, though: at the end of the short term, you have to have the entire amount or balance to pay off your lender, either by refinancing again or through your own financial means. This is tough for most people to do. Some balloon mortgages have an automatic refinance option at the end of the short term to allow the owners to automatically convert the mortgage at the end of the balloon period to a fixed rate based on whatever the current balance is. The problem is that there are usually considerable conditions, including the need to requalify (what if you lose your job in the meantime or miss a credit card payment?) and the reappraisal requirement. These conditions make these loans very risky for the relatively small savings in interest. You also have to pay new fees, and whatever the new rate is at the time is what you will be paying. If rates go up, you might be stuck with a much higher rate.

Adjustable-Rate Loans

Adjustable-rate loans or adjustable-rate mortgages (ARMs) vary or adjust according to the index on which your loan is created. LIBOR is a common one, but there are others. Periodic adjustments are made to the adjustable-rate mortgage, which could be monthly, yearly, or at a different interval entirely.

Caps on Adjustables

A cap most adjustables have is a lifetime cap. Say your interest rate is 4 percent and the index is 8 percent with a 3 percent margin. This means your new interest rate would be 11 percent. If the lifetime cap is 4 percent, the new interest rate is 4 percent for the initial plus 4 percent for the lifetime cap—or 8 percent total, not 11 percent. This can save you a lot of money and can be a point of negotiation with lenders. Mortgages might also have a periodic cap, meaning they can only adjust X percent yearly.

Indices for Loans

Your loan can be based on lots of different indices. At any given time, you can go to mortgageprofessor.com or bankrate.com and look up the current rate of that index, as well as its volatility—which will give you an idea of what your rate and payment might do.

Some commonly used indices are:

- 11th district cost of funds index (COFI)
- Treasury bill (T-Bill)
- London Inter Bank Offering Rates (LIBOR)
- CD indexes

- Bank prime loan (prime rate)
- Fannie Mae's required net yield (RNY)
- Cost of savings index (COSI)
- Constant maturity treasury (CMT)

There are others, but these are the most common.

The charts at Mortgage-X.com can give you an idea on what the indexes have been from December of 2001 through December of 2007. The words *Mortgage (ARM) Indexes* can be found at www.mortgage-x.com/general/mortgage_indexes.asp.

Among other things, they document which index is better to select if you have a choice, including the amount in add-on margins for COFI/MTA loans, LIBOR loans, Prime Rate loans, and so on. You can even select various years and months and compare them historically.

Each adjustable rate has an index and a margin. The index is depicted in the graphs above. The margin is based on your negotiations with the bank, your credit report, FICO score, and loan program. Your interest rate is determined by the margin plus the index.

> One reason I am not a big fan of mortgage brokers, among many, is that some are compensated based on how large of a margin they can get for the bank. They are paid more if they can get higher yield spreads. You can see in the simple equation in the chart how much that can affect your payment.

Note that the margin won't change the whole time you have the loan. You are impacted by the index, not the margin.

Negative Amortization or Pay Option ARMs

Neg Am or pay option ARMs got a lot of people into trouble in the early 2000s. These caps are much like the yearly or lifetime cap but are based on payment caps. Your loan still accrues interest at the full rate, but your payment stays lower.

Even if the rate adjusts substantially higher, the payment cannot exceed X percent over last year.

As an example, assume you have a loan with a 5 percent rate at the start and a $100,000 principle. This equals $500 per month in interest. The following year, the new rate is 7 percent. This means your payment would go up to $700. But, if you have a 9 percent payment adjustment cap, it means the payment cannot go up more than 9 percent over the last year. So, 9 percent of $500 is $45, so your new payment would be $545. Watch closely for these payment caps because they are essential to keeping yourself out of hot water.

A very important and relevant portion to option ARMs is that they often have no lifetime cap but do have payment caps. That means that even though your payments might stay low for awhile, the interest can go up to the fully indexed plus margin rate you agreed on, which is often steep on these loans. If you don't pay the full interest payment, you begin adding to your principle, which is commonly referred to as a *negative amortization loan*.

Borrowers with negatively amortizing loans can always pay the interest amount and keep themselves from going upside down on their loan compared with their original balance. When might it be a good idea to pay the minimum and go upside down? Well, assume your rate is 7 percent and you can invest that money into other property and earn 10 percent yearly in appreciation plus cash flow. In this case, it might be wise, if you can stomach it, to leverage yourself and pay less than the interest.

One major upside to this loan type is if your income fluctuates. You can pay the fully amortized payment one month and then the negative amount the next if you have a rough month. You are also paying back money you borrowed today at a depreciated value years from now due to natural inflation. These loans can be extremely valuable if you know how to use them.

Most adjustable loans vary in rate every month, three months, six months, once a year, three years, five years, seven years, and so on. Interest rates on Neg Am loans can adjust monthly. A loan with a six-month adjustment period is called a six-month ARM. One-month ARMs mean that the rate is adjusting monthly. If interest rates go up and you continue paying your minimum, you are adding more each month than the first month to your balance. The opposite is true if rates head south.

Some lenders are in trouble for offering what consumer advocates call *teaser rates*, which is that initial six-month or one-year rate that is incredibly low. The lower rate is far lower than the fully indexed rate (index plus margin). This type of loan is available in fifteen-, thirty-, and forty-year types, with the longer terms holding bigger margins. Also, they carry a risk premium and have a maximum loan-to-value cap.

Loan-to-Value Cap

Loan-to-value caps are getting a lot of homeowners in trouble these days. What this essentially means is that the loan cannot exceed X percent of its original balance. If the max loan-to-value ratio is 110 percent and you borrow $100,000, then when the balance becomes $110,000, you *must* pay the full interest on the loan. This rapid adjustment got a lot of homeowners in trouble in 2007 and 2008 because the loan simply cannot hold a balance higher than the loan-to-value cap. If you have a lot of equity, hitting that cap won't necessarily hurt you. But, if you owe more than your house is worth come time to refi, you could be in trouble.

Option ARMs allow you to make multiple payment types each month. You can pay the fifteen-year fully amortized payment, the interest-only payment, the thirty-year amortized payment, or a minimum that allows you to add that deferred interest to the balance.

> Still yet, if you take out a second mortgage or a HELOC on this type of loan, the bank assumes you will go to full value even if you are paying your fully amortized payment, so it drastically reduces from the equity you can borrow from in your home.

Prepayment Penalties

Option ARMs often come with steep prepayment penalties, meaning you cannot refinance for one, two, or three years or longer. If you do, often you have to pay the bank the entire amount you would have paid had you kept the loan. This is to keep people from enjoying teaser rates and then refinancing after the first year, causing the bank to make little to no money on the loan.

Hybrid Loans

Hybrid loans are far less common than the loans discussed so far. These are combinations of fixed- and adjustable-rate loans.

A fixed-period ARM is a period of time, generally two to ten years, of fixed payments before the initial rate changes. At the end of this period, interest rates adjust annually. These are known as 30/3/1, 30/5/1, and so forth loans. This means they are thirty-year loans, three years fixed, one year adjustments; thirty-year loans, five years fixed, one year adjustments. Generally you are given one adjustment cap, often the first one, but it varies greatly by loan type.

A two-step mortgage is a loan that has a fixed rate for a period of time (three, five, seven years); then the rate changes to whatever the current market rate is. After that, the adjustment maintains the new fixed rate for the remaining twenty-three years, twenty-five years, twenty-seven years, and so on. This can be risky—especially if rates are on the rise. Many banks don't offer these hybrid loans.

A convertible adjustable-rate mortgage is an ARM that allows you to convert it to a fixed-rate mortgage at designated, specific times. This is generally within the first five years of the adjustment rate. If rates begin to rise, it might be time to lock the rate.

Usually the conversion charge is low, and there are options to reduce rates usually by buying down the loan with cash or prepayment penalties. The new converted rate is typically slightly higher than market rate at that time.

Graduated mortgage payments are loans that start low and gradually increase at predetermined times. These can be great if you know you can afford the home in five years but need the lower payment and have a lot of self-discipline. Your eventual higher payments will be higher to catch you up from the lower payments. On large mortgages, this can equate to a lot of money. Be very careful of these loans because the acceleration pace in later years can be really high.

Buying Down Your Mortgage

You can buy down your rate or even buy out the prepayment requirement by paying points. Ask your lender, after you receive your GFE, what your options are. Then, calculate the cost (1 point is 1 percent of the loan amount, 2 points is 2 percent, and so on) of the buy-down versus the additional money you will spend in interest or prepayment penalties, and you can make an educated decision as to whether it's worth buying down the loan. This does require cash, so it isn't an option for many people.

You can also do rate buy-downs. For instance, a 2-1 buy-down means that if your interest rate is 9 percent, your first year would be 7 percent, the second year 8 percent, and the third year 9 percent. 3-2-1 and 1-0 buy-downs are also available. You do pay back the difference, though, between these rates in the second and third year, respectively.

Final Decisions

The final decisions on the type of mortgage you go with will really depend on how long you intend to keep the house, how high your payments are, and your cash flow situation. If you are going to keep the house for seven years or less, you can pay a lot less interest on an adjustable-rate mortgage. If you're going to keep the home for more than fifteen or thirty years, consider a fixed-rate mortgage or an ARM and pay more each month so you are reducing principle also. In addition, you need to decide whether your goal is appreciation or to own your home. If you don't care about owning it and can live on the appreciation in thirty years when you retire, you might want to pay only interest and let the house appreciate, take the cash out in a HELOC or second mortgage, and live off of that equity when you retire.

Glossary

Some terms as defined in the LPA Glossary. Thanks to the Land-lord Protection Agency!

abandon/abandonment Vacating or giving up use of or rights in real property. Also a tenant vacating premises before a lease expires without consent of the landlord.

abstract of title Digest of conveyances, transfers, wills, and other legal proceedings pertinent to title of a property, such as liens, charges, or encumbrances.

acceleration clause A common provision of a mortgage or note providing the holder with the right to demand that the entire outstanding balance is immediately due and usually payable in the event of default.

accrued interest Interest earned but not yet paid.

acknowledgement Formal declaration by a person executing an instrument that such act is intended as a free and voluntary act made before a duly authorized officer.

Adjustable-Rate Mortgage Loans (ARM)   Loans with interest rates that are adjusted periodically based on changes in a preselected index. As a result, the interest rate on your loan and the monthly payment will rise and fall with increases and decreases in overall interest rates. These mortgage loans must specify how their interest rate changes, usually in terms of a relation to a national index such as (but not always) Treasury bill rates. If interest rates rise, your monthly payments will rise. An interest rate cap limits the amount by which the interest rate can change; look for this feature when you consider an ARM loan.

adjustment interval   On an ARM loan, the time between changes in the interest rate or monthly payment.

administrator   The person appointed by a probate court to settle the estate of a dead person.

adverse possession   Right of an occupant of land to acquire title against the real owner, under color of title, where possession has been actual, continuous, hostile, visible, and distinct for the statutory period.

agent   A person who represents another (a principal) by the principal's authority.

agreement of sale   Contract signed by buyer and seller stating the terms and conditions under which a property will be sold.

alternative documentation   A method of documenting a loan file that relies on information the borrower is likely to be able to provide instead of waiting on verification sent to third parties for confirmation of statements made in the application.

amortization   Repayment of a loan with periodic payments of both principal and interest calculated to pay off the loan at the end of a fixed period of time.

amount of advance notice   The number of days' notice that must be given before a change in the tenancy can take effect. Usually, the amount of advance notice is the same as the number of days between rent payments. For example, in a month-to-month tenancy, the landlord usually must give the tenant thirty days advance written notice that the landlord is increasing the amount of the security deposit.

Annual Percentage Rate (APR)   The cost of credit expressed as a yearly rate. The annual percentage rate is often not the same as the interest rate. It is a percentage that results from an equation considering the amount financed, the finance charges, and the term of the loan.

appeal   A request to a higher court to review a lower court's decision in a lawsuit.

application fee   Fee charged by a lender to cover the initial costs of processing a loan application. The fee can include the cost of obtaining a property appraisal, a credit report, and a lock-in fee or other closing costs incurred during the process, or the fee might be in addition to these charges.

application   An initial statement of personal and financial information required to apply for a loan.

appraisal fee   A fee charged by a licensed, certified appraiser to render an opinion of market value as of a specific date.

appraisal   A written estimate of a property's current market value completed by an impartial party with knowledge of real estate markets.

arbitration   Using a neutral third person to resolve a dispute instead of going to court. Unless the parties have agreed otherwise, the parties must follow the arbitrator's decision.

arbitrator   A neutral third person, agreed to by the parties of a dispute, who hears and decides a dispute. An arbitrator is not a judge, but the parties must follow the arbitrator's decision (the decision is said to be *binding* on the parties). See *arbitration*.

assignment   The transfer of ownership, rights, or interests in property by one person (the assignor) to another (the assignee).

assumption   A method of selling real estate in which the buyer of the property agrees to become responsible for the repayment of an existing loan on the property.

balloon mortgage   Balloon mortgage loans are short-term fixed-rate loans with fixed monthly payments for a set number of years followed by one large final balloon payment (the *balloon*) for all of the remainder of the principal. Typically, the balloon payment is due at the end of five, seven, or ten years. Borrowers with balloon loans might have the right to refinance the loan when the balloon payment is due, but the right to refinance is not guaranteed.

bankruptcy　A proceeding in a federal court to relieve certain debts of a person or a business unable to pay its debts.

bearer　The legal owner of a piece of property.

bequest　A gift of personal property by will.

blanket mortgage　A mortgage that covers more than one parcel of real estate.

bona fide　In good faith.

borrower (mortgagor)　An individual who applies for and receives funds in the form of a loan and is obligated to repay the loan in full under the terms of the loan.

broker　An individual who brings buyers and sellers together and assists in negotiating contracts for a client.

buy-down mortgage　A mortgage loan with a below-market rate for a period of time.

buyer's market　Market conditions that favor buyers. With more sellers than buyers in the market, sellers might be forced to make substantial price concessions.

caps (interest)　Consumer safeguards that limit the amount the interest rate on an adjustable-rate mortgage can change in an adjustment interval and/or over the life of the loan. For example, if your per-period cap is 1 percent and your current rate is 7 percent, your newly adjusted rate must fall between 6 percent and 8 percent regardless of actual changes in the index.

caps (payment)　Consumer safeguards that limit the amount monthly payments on an adjustable-rate mortgage can change. Because they do not limit the amount of interest the lender is earning, these consumer safeguards can cause negative amortization.

cash out   Any cash received when you get a new loan that is larger than the remaining balance of your current mortgage, based on the equity you have already built up in the house. The cash out amount is calculated by subtracting the sum of the old loan and fees from the new mortgage loan. For example, if your existing loan is $100,000, you might refinance it with a loan of $120,000. After you pay off your current loan ($100,000) and any loan-origination costs for the new loan (for example, $2,000 in points), you would be left with $18,000 cash out. Cash-out loans might not be available for all types of property.

cashier's check (or bank check)   A check whose payment is guaranteed because it was paid for in advance and is drawn on the bank's account instead of the customer's.

ceiling   The maximum allowable interest rate of an adjustable-rate mortgage.

Certificate of Eligibility   Document issued by the Veterans Administration (VA) to qualified veterans that verifies a veteran's eligibility for a VA Loan. It's obtainable through local VA offices by submitting form DD-214 (Separation Paper) and VA form 1880 (request for Certificate of Eligibility).

certificate of title   Written opinion of the status of title to a property, given by an attorney or a title company. This certificate does not offer the protection given by title insurance.

Certificate of Veteran Status   FHA form filled out by the VA to establish a borrower's eligibility for an FHA Vet loan. It's obtainable through local VA offices by submitting form DD 214 (Separation Paper) with form 26-8261a (request for Certificate of Veteran Status).

claim of right to possession   A form that the occupants of a rental unit can fill out to temporarily stop their eviction by the sheriff after the landlord has won an unlawful detainer (eviction) lawsuit. The occupants can use this form only if the landlord did not serve a Prejudgment Claim of Right to Possession form with the summons and complaint, the occupants were not named in the writ of possession, and the occupants have lived in the rental unit since before the unlawful detainer lawsuit was filed.

closing (or settlement) The settlement or closing is the conclusion of your real estate transaction. It includes the delivery of your security instrument, the signing of your legal documents, and the disbursement of the funds necessary for the sale of your home or loan transaction (refinance).

closing costs Costs for services that must be performed before your loan can be initiated. Examples include title fees, recording fees, appraisal fees, credit report fees, pest inspection fees, attorney's fees, and surveying fees.

collateral Assets (such as your home) pledged as security for a debt.

commission Money paid to a real estate agent or broker for negotiating a real estate or loan transaction.

commitment A promise to lend and a statement by the lender of the terms and conditions under which a loan is made.

condominium A form of property ownership in which the homeowner holds title to an individual dwelling unit and a proportionate interest in common areas and facilities of a multiunit project.

conforming loan A mortgage loan that meets all the requirements to be eligible for purchase by federal agencies such as Fannie Mae and Freddie Mac. The maximum conforming loan amount is $240,000 for a one-unit property.

contingency A condition that must be satisfied before a contract is legally binding.

contract of sale The agreement between the buyer and seller on the purchase price, terms, and conditions of a sale.

conventional loan Loans that are not made under any government housing program; they are not subject to the restrictions of government housing programs, such as loan size limits.

conversion clause A provision in some loans that allows you to change an ARM to a fixed-rate loan, usually after the first adjustment period. The new fixed rate will be set at current rates, and there might be a charge for the conversion feature.

convertible ARMs   A type of ARM loan with the option to convert to a fixed-rate loan during a given time period.

conveyance   The document used to effect a transfer, such as a deed or mortgage.

Cost of Funds Index (COFI)   An index of the weighted-average interest rate paid by savings institutions for sources of funds, usually by members of the 11th Federal Home Loan Bank District.

credit report   A report detailing the credit history of a prospective borrower that's used to help determine borrower creditworthiness.

credit reporting agency   A business that keeps records of people's credit histories and that reports credit history information to prospective creditors (including landlords).

deed of trust   A legal document that conveys title to real property to a third party. The third party holds title until the owner of the property has repaid the debt in full.

deed   Legal document by which title to real property is transferred from one owner to another. The deed contains a description of the property and is signed, witnessed, and delivered to the buyer at closing.

default judgment   A judgment issued by the court, without a hearing, after the tenant has failed to file a response to the landlord's complaint.

default   Failure to meet legal obligations in a contract, including failure to make payments on a loan.

delinquency   Failure to make payments as agreed in the loan agreement.

demurrer   A legal response that a tenant can file in an unlawful detainer lawsuit to test the legal sufficiency of the charges made in the landlord's complaint.

Department of Fair Housing   The state agency that investigates complaints of unlawful discrimination in housing and employment.

discount points (or points)   Points are an up-front fee paid to the lender at the time you get your loan. Each point equals 1 percent of your total loan amount. Points and interest rates are inherently connected—in general, the more points you pay, the lower the interest rate you get. However, the more points you pay, the more cash you need up front because points are paid in cash at closing.

discrimination (in renting)   Denying a person housing, telling a person that housing is not available (when the housing is actually available at that time), providing housing under inferior terms, harassing a person in connection with housing accommodations, or providing segregated housing because of a person's race, color, religion, gender, sexual orientation, national origin, ancestry, source of income, age, disability, marital status, or whether there are children under the age of 18 in the person's household. Discrimination also can be a refusal to make reasonable accommodation for a person with a disability.

down payment   The amount of your home's purchase price you need to supply up front in cash to get your loan. For conventional loans, you should strive for a down payment that's at least 20 percent of your home's value because lenders generally do not require private mortgage insurance with a down payment of at least 20 percent of your home's purchase price. (Note, however, that FHA and VA loans have different policies regarding insurance.)

due-on-sale clause   Provision in a mortgage or deed of trust allowing the lender to demand immediate payment of the loan balance on the sale of the property.

earnest money   Deposit made by a buyer toward the down payment in evidence of good faith when the purchase agreement is signed.

effective rate   The effective rate is a consumer-oriented rate that takes into account the projected amount of time you tell us you will actually have the loan, as well as the specific costs, fees, and potential rate changes associated with it. The fees and costs are distributed over the time you plan to be in the house, allowing you to do an apples-to-apples comparison of a variety of loan types. The effective rate is not the APR. It is similar in that it factors in interest, mortgage insurance, and other fees (including points); however, the APR assumes that you keep your loan for the entire term, while the effective rate takes into account how long you tell us you plan to be in your house.

Equal Credit Opportunity Act (ECOA)   Federal law requiring creditors to make credit equally available without discrimination based on race, color, religion, national origin, age, gender, marital status, or receipt of income from public assistance programs.

equity   The difference between the current market value of a property and the total debt obligations against the property. On a new mortgage loan, the down payment represents the equity in the property.

escrow account   An account held by the lender to which the borrower pays monthly installments, collected as part of the monthly mortgage payment, for annual expenses such as taxes and insurance. The lender disburses escrow account funds on behalf of the borrower when they become due. Also known as *impound account*.

escrow   A transaction in which a third party acts as the agent for seller and buyer, or for borrower and lender, in handling legal documents and disbursement of funds.

eviction notice (or three-day notice)   A three-day notice the landlord serves on the tenant when the tenant has violated the lease or rental agreement. The three-day notice usually instructs the tenant to either leave the rental unit or comply with the lease or rental agreement (for example, by paying past-due rent) within the three-day period.

eviction   A court-administered proceeding for removing a tenant from a rental unit because the tenant has violated the rental agreement or did not comply with a notice ending the tenancy (also called an *unlawful detainer* lawsuit or *summary proceedings*).

fair housing organizations   City or county organizations that help renters resolve housing discrimination problems.

Fannie Mae   A common nickname for the Federal National Mortgage Association.

FDIC   See *Federal Deposit Insurance Corporation*.

Federal Deposit Insurance Corporation (FDIC) Independent deposit insurance agency created by Congress to maintain stability and public confidence in the nation's banking system.

Federal Home Loan Mortgage Corporation (FHLMC, or Freddie Mac) This agency buys loans that are underwritten to its specific guidelines. These guidelines are an industry standard for residential conventional lending.

Federal Housing Administration (FHA) A federal agency within the Department of Housing and Urban Development (HUD), which insures residential mortgage loans made by private lenders and sets standards for underwriting mortgage loans.

Federal National Mortgage Association (FNMA, or Fannie Mae) This agency buys loans that are underwritten to its specific guidelines. These guidelines are an industry standard for residential conventional lending.

federal stay An order of a federal bankruptcy court that temporarily stops proceedings in a state court, including an eviction proceeding.

fee simple Absolute ownership of real property.

FHA loans Fixed- or adjustable-rate loans insured by the U.S. Department of Housing and Urban Development. FHA loans are designed to make housing more affordable, particularly for first-time homebuyers. FHA loans typically permit borrowers to buy a home with a lower down payment than conventional loans. With FHA insurance, eligible buyers can purchase a home with a down payment as little as 3 percent of the appraised value or the purchase price, whichever is lower. FHA borrowers typically are required to participate in a face-to-face meeting with their lender or a government-approved mortgage counselor prior to closing on a new mortgage loan. The current FHA loan limits vary depending on home type and home location.

first mortgage A mortgage that is in first lien position, taking priority over all other liens. In the case of a foreclosure, the first mortgage will be repaid before any other mortgages.

fixed rate An interest rate that is fixed for the term of the loan.

fixed-rate loans   Fixed-rate loans have interest rates that do not change over the life of the loan. As a result, monthly payments for principal and interest are also fixed for the life of the loan. Fixed-rate loans typically have fifteen-year or thirty-year terms. With a fixed-rate loan, you will have predictable monthly mortgage payments for as long as you have the loan.

flood insurance   Insurance that compensates for physical damage to a property by flood. It's typically not covered under standard hazard insurance.

forbearance   The act by the lender of refraining from taking legal action on a mortgage loan that is delinquent.

foreclosure (or repossession)   Legal process by which a mortgaged property can be sold to pay off a mortgage loan that is in default.

Freddie Mac   A common nickname for the Federal Home Loan Mortgage Corporation.

good faith estimate (GFE)   Written estimate of the settlement costs the borrower will likely have to pay at closing. Under the Real Estate Settlement Procedures Act (RESPA), the lender is required to provide this disclosure to the borrower within three days of receiving a loan application.

grace period   Period of time during which a loan payment can be made after its due date without incurring a late penalty. The grace period is specified as part of the terms of the loan in the note.

gross income   Total income before taxes or expenses are deducted.

guest   A person who does not have the rights of a tenant, such as a person who stays in a transient hotel for fewer than seven days.

habitable   A rental unit that is fit for human beings to live in. A rental unit that substantially complies with building and safety code standards that materially affect tenants' health and safety is said to be *habitable*. See *implied warranty of habitability* and *uninhabitable*.

hazard insurance   Protects the insured against loss due to fire or other natural disasters in exchange for a premium paid to the insurer.

holding deposit   A deposit that a tenant gives to a landlord to hold a rental unit until the tenant pays the first month's rent and the security deposit.

HUD (Housing and Urban Development)   A U.S. government agency established to implement federal housing and community development programs; it oversees the Federal Housing Administration.

HUD-1 Uniform Settlement Statement   A standard form that itemizes the closing costs associated with purchasing a home or refinancing a loan.

implied warranty of habitability   A legal rule that requires landlords to maintain their rental units in a condition fit for human beings to live in. A rental unit must substantially comply with building and housing code standards that materially affect tenants' health and safety.

impound account   An account held by the lender to which the borrower pays monthly installments, collected as part of the monthly mortgage payment, for annual expenses such as taxes and insurance. The lender disburses impound account funds on behalf of the borrower when they become due. (Also known as *escrow account*.)

index   A published rate used by lenders that serves as the basis for determining interest rate changes on ARM loans.

initial inspection   An inspection by the landlord before the tenancy ends to identify defective conditions that justify deductions from the security deposit. The landlord must perform an initial inspection if the tenant requests it.

initial rate   The rate charged during the first interval of an ARM loan.

interest rate cap   Consumer safeguards that limit the amount the interest rate on an ARM loan can change in an adjustment interval and/or over the life of the loan. For example, if your per-period cap is 1 percent and your current rate is 7 percent, your newly adjusted rate must fall between 6 percent and 8 percent regardless of actual changes in the index.

interest rate   The annual rate of interest on the loan, expressed as a percentage of 100.

interest   Charge paid for borrowing money, calculated as a percentage of the remaining balance of the amount borrowed.

item of information   Information in a credit report that causes a creditor to deny credit or take other adverse action against an applicant (such as refusing to rent a rental unit to the applicant).

joint liability   Liability shared among two or more people, each of whom is liable for the full debt.

joint tenancy   A form of ownership of property giving each person equal interest in the property, including rights of survivorship.

jumbo loan   A mortgage larger than the $240,000 limit set by the Federal National Mortgage Association and the Federal Home Loan Mortgage Corporation.

junior mortgage   A mortgage subordinate to the claim of a prior lien or mortgage. In the case of a foreclosure, a senior mortgage or lien is paid first.

landlord   A business or person who owns a rental unit and who rents or leases the rental unit to another person, called a tenant.

late charge   Penalty paid by a borrower when a payment is made after the due date.

lease   A rental agreement, usually in writing, that establishes all the terms of the agreement and that lasts for a predetermined length of time (for example, six months or one year).

legal aid organizations   Organizations that provide free legal advice, representation, and other legal services in noncriminal cases to economically disadvantaged persons.

lender   The bank, mortgage company, or mortgage broker offering the loan.

LIBOR (London Inter Bank Offered Rate)   The interest rate charged among banks in the foreign market for short-term loans to one another. A common index for ARM loans.

lien   A legal claim by one person on the property of another for security for payment of a debt.

loan application fee   Fee charged by a lender to cover the initial costs of processing a loan application. The fee may include the cost of obtaining a property appraisal, a credit report, and a lock-in fee or other closing costs incurred during the process or the fee may be in addition to these charges.

loan application   An initial statement of personal and financial information required to apply for a loan.

loan origination fee   Fee charged by a lender to cover administrative costs of processing a loan.

loan-to-value ratio (LTV)   The percentage of the loan amount to the appraised value (or the sales price, whichever is less) of the property.

lock or lock-in   A lender's guarantee of an interest rate for a set period of time. The time period is usually that between loan application approval and loan closing. The lock-in protects you against rate increases during that time.

lockout   When a landlord locks a tenant out of the rental unit with the intent of terminating the tenancy. Lockouts, and all other self-help eviction remedies, are illegal. (Also, when tenants lock themselves out of the rental unit and require the landlord or a locksmith to allow them back into the unit.)

margin   A specified percentage added to your chosen financial index to determine your new interest rate at the time of adjustment for ARM loans.

mortgage banker   An individual or a company that originates and/or services mortgage loans.

mortgage broker   An individual or a company that arranges financing for borrowers.

mortgage insurance Insurance to protect the lender in case you default on your loan. With conventional loans, mortgage insurance is generally not required if you make a down payment of at least 20 percent of the home's appraised value. (Note, however, that FHA and VA loans have different insurance guidelines.)

mortgage loan A loan for which real estate serves as collateral to provide for repayment in case of default.

mortgage note Legal document obligating a borrower to repay a loan at a stated interest rate during a specified period of time. The agreement is secured by a mortgage or deed of trust or other security instrument.

mortgage A legal document by which real property is pledged as security for the repayment of a loan.

mortgagee The lender in a mortgage loan transaction.

mortgagor The borrower in a mortgage loan transaction.

motion to quash service of summons or motion to show cause A legal response that a tenant can file in an unlawful detainer lawsuit if the tenant believes that the landlord did not properly serve the summons and complaint.

negative amortization A loan payment schedule in which the outstanding principal balance of a loan goes up rather than down because the payments do not cover the full amount of interest due. The monthly shortfall in payment is added to the unpaid principal balance of the loan.

negligence/negligently A person's carelessness (that is, failure to use ordinary or reasonable care) that results in injury to another person or damage to another person's property.

nonassumption clause A statement in a mortgage contract forbidding the assumption of the mortgage by another borrower without the prior approval of the lender.

note Legal document obligating a borrower to repay a loan at a stated interest rate during a specified period of time. The agreement is secured by a mortgage or deed of trust or other security instrument.

notice of default   Written notice to a borrower that a default has occurred and that legal action may be taken.

novation   In an assignment situation, a novation is an agreement by the landlord, the original tenant, and the new tenant that makes the new tenant (rather than the original tenant) solely responsible to the landlord.

origination fee   Fee charged by a lender to cover administrative costs of processing a loan.

payment cap   Consumer safeguards that limit the amount monthly payments on an adjustable-rate mortgage can change. Because they do not limit the amount of interest the lender is earning, they can cause negative amortization.

per diem interest   Interest calculated per day. (Depending on the day of the month on which closing takes place, you will have to pay interest from the date of closing to the end of the month. Your first mortgage payment will probably be due the first day of the following month.)

periodic rental agreement   An oral or written rental agreement that states the length of time between rent payments—for example, a week or a month—but not the total number of weeks or months that the agreement will be in effect.

PITI (Principal, Interest, Taxes, and Insurance)   The components of a monthly mortgage payment.

points (or discount points)   Points are an up-front fee paid to the lender at the time you get your loan. Each point equals 1 percent of your total loan amount. Points and interest rates are inherently connected—in general, the more points you pay, the lower the interest rate you get. However, the more points you pay, the more cash you need up front because points are paid in cash at closing.

power of attorney   Legal document authorizing one person to act on behalf of another.

preapproval   The process of determining how much money a prospective homebuyer or refinancer will be eligible to borrow prior to application for a loan. A preapproval includes a preliminary screening of a borrower's credit history. Information submitted during preapproval is subject to verification at application.

prejudgment claim of right to possession   A form a landlord in an unlawful detainer (eviction) lawsuit can have served along with the summons and complaint on all persons living in the rental unit who might claim to be tenants but whose names the landlord does not know. Occupants who are not named in the unlawful detainer complaint but who claim a right to possess the rental unit can fill out and file this form to become parties to the unlawful detainer action.

prepaid expenses   Taxes, insurance, and assessments paid in advance of their due dates. These expenses are included at closing.

prepaid interest   Interest paid in advance of when it is due. Typically charged to a borrower at closing to cover interest on the loan between the closing date and the first payment date.

prepayment penalty   Fee charged by a lender for a loan paid off in advance of the contractual due date.

prepayment   Full or partial repayment of the principal before the contractual due date.

prequalification   The process of determining how much money a prospective homebuyer will be eligible to borrow prior to application for a loan. Information submitted during prequalification is subject to verification at application.

principal   The amount of debt, not counting interest, left on a loan.

Private Mortgage Insurance (PMI)   Insurance to protect the lender in case you default on your loan. With conventional loans, mortgage insurance is generally not required if you make a down payment of at least 20 percent of the home's purchase price. (Note, however, that FHA and VA loans have different insurance guidelines.)

purchase agreement   Contract signed by the buyer and the seller stating the terms and conditions under which a property will be sold.

real property   Land and any improvements permanently affixed to it, such as buildings.

reconveyance   The transfer of property back to the owner when a mortgage loan is fully repaid.

recording fee   Money paid to an agent for entering the sale of a property into the public records.

recording   The act of entering documents concerning title to a property into the public records.

refinancing   The process of paying off one loan with the proceeds from a new loan secured by the same property.

relief from forfeiture   An order by a court in an unlawful detainer (eviction) lawsuit that allows the losing tenant to remain in the rental unit, based on the tenant's convincing the court that the eviction would cause the tenant severe hardship and that the tenant can pay all of the rent that is due, or to otherwise fully comply with the lease.

rent control ordinances   Laws in some communities that limit or prohibit rent increases or that limit the circumstances in which a tenant can be evicted.

rent withholding   The tenant's remedy of not paying some or all of the rent if the landlord does not fix defects that make the rental unit uninhabitable within a reasonable time after the landlord receives notice of the defects from the tenant. (More often than not, this is a lease violation because the rental unit is not always uninhabitable.)

rental agreement   An oral or written agreement between a tenant and a landlord made before the tenant moves in that establishes the terms of the tenancy, such as the amount of the rent and when it is due. See also *lease* and *periodic rental agreement*.

rental application form   A form that a landlord can ask a tenant to fill out prior to renting that requests information about the tenant, such as the tenant's address, telephone number, employment history, credit references, and the like.

rental period or rent period   The length of time between rental payments; for example, a week or a month.

rental unit   An apartment, a house, a duplex, or a condominium that a landlord rents to a tenant to live in.

renter's insurance   Insurance protecting the tenant against property losses, such as losses from theft or fire. This insurance usually also protects the tenant against liability (legal responsibility) for claims or lawsuits filed by the landlord or by others alleging that the tenant negligently injured another person or property.

repair and deduct remedy   The tenant's remedy of deducting from future rent the amount necessary to repair defects covered by the implied warranty of habitability. The amount deducted cannot be more than one month's rent. (When the implied warranty of habitability is misinterpreted, this is often construed as *withholding of rent*, a lease violation in many cases.)

RESPA (Real Estate Settlement Procedures Act)   RESPA is a federal law that gives consumers the right to review information about loan settlement costs. The law gives you the right to review this information after you apply for a loan and again at loan settlement. The law only obliges lenders to provide these settlement costs after application.

retaliatory eviction or action   An act by a landlord, such as raising a tenant's rent, seeking to evict a tenant, or otherwise punishing a tenant, because the tenant has used the repair and deduct remedy or the rent withholding remedy or has asserted other tenant rights.

sales agreement   Contract signed by buyer and seller stating the terms and conditions under which a property will be sold.

second mortgage   An additional mortgage placed on a property that has rights that are subordinate to the first mortgage.

security deposit   A deposit or a fee that the landlord requires the tenant to pay at the beginning of the tenancy. The landlord can use the security deposit, for example, if the tenant moves out owing rent or leaves the unit damaged or less clean than when the tenant moved in.

security settlement challenge crusher   A letter designed to quickly squash any unfounded tenant arguments about deductions made from the security deposit refund.

security settlement statement An essential landlord form that allows the landlord to make valid, itemized and explained deductions from security deposits.

serve/service Legal requirements and procedures that seek to ensure that the person to whom a legal notice is directed actually receives it.

settlement (or closing) The settlement or closing is the conclusion of your real estate transaction. It includes the delivery of your security instrument, the signing of your legal documents, and the disbursement of the funds necessary for the sale of your home or loan transaction (refinance).

settlement cost (HUD guide) HUD-published booklet that provides an overview of the lending process and that is given to consumers after completing a loan application.

settlement costs Also known as *closing costs*, these costs are for services that must be performed before your loan can be initiated. Examples include title fees, recording fees, appraisal fees, credit report fees, pest inspection fees, attorney's fees, taxes, and surveying fees.

sixty-day notice A written notice from a landlord to a tenant telling the tenant that the tenancy will end in sixty days. A sixty-day notice usually does not have to state the landlord's reason for ending the tenancy.

sublease A separate rental agreement between the original tenant and a new tenant to whom the original tenant rents all or part of the rental unit. The new tenant is called a *subtenant*. The agreement between the original tenant and the landlord remains in force, and the original tenant continues to be responsible for paying the rent to the landlord and for other tenant obligations. (Compare to assignment.)

subpoena An order from the court that requires the recipient to appear as a witness or provide evidence in a court proceeding.

survey A measurement of land, prepared by a licensed surveyor, showing a property's boundaries, elevations, improvements, and relationship to surrounding tracts.

sweat equity   Value added to a property in the form of labor or services of the owner rather than cash.

tax impound   Money paid to and held by a lender for annual tax payments.

tax lien   Claim against a property for unpaid taxes.

tax sale   Public sale of property by a government authority as a result of non-payment of taxes.

tenancy   The tenant's exclusive right, created by a rental agreement between the landlord and the tenant, to use and possess the landlord's rental unit.

tenant screening service   A business that collects and sells information on tenants, such as whether they pay their rent on time and whether they have been defendants in unlawful detainer lawsuits.

tenant   A person who rents or leases a rental unit from a landlord. The tenant obtains the right to the exclusive use and possession of the rental unit during the lease or rental period.

term   The period of time between the beginning loan date on the legal documents and the date the entire balance of the loan is due.

thirty-day notice   A written notice from a landlord to a tenant telling the tenant that the tenancy will end in thirty days. A thirty-day notice usually does not have to state the landlord's reason for ending the tenancy.

title company   A company that insures title to property.

title insurance   Insurance that protects the lender (lender's policy) or the buyer (owner's policy) against loss due to disputes over ownership of a property.

title search   Examination of municipal records to ensure that the seller is the legal owner of a property and that there are no liens or other claims against the property.

title   Document that gives evidence of ownership of a property. Also indicates the rights of ownership and possession of the property.

transfer tax   Tax paid when title passes from one owner to another.

Truth-in-Lending Act   Federal law requiring written disclosure of the terms of a mortgage (including the APR and other charges) by a lender to a borrower after application. Also requires the right to rescission period.

U.S. Department of Housing and Urban Development   Also called HUD, it's the federal agency that enforces the federal fair housing law, which prohibits discrimination based on gender, race, religion, national or ethnic origin, familial status, or mental handicap.

underwriting   In mortgage lending, the process of determining the risks involved in a particular loan and establishing suitable terms and conditions for the loan.

uninhabitable   The condition of a rental unit that has such serious problems or defects that the tenant's health or safety is affected. A rental unit might be uninhabitable if it is not fit for human beings to live in, or if it fails to substantially comply with building and safety code standards that materially affect tenants' health and safety. (Compare to *habitable*.)

unlawful detainer lawsuit   A lawsuit that a landlord must file and win before he can evict a tenant (also called an *eviction* lawsuit).

usury   Interest charged in excess of the legal rate established by law.

VA loans   Fixed-rate loans guaranteed by the U.S. Department of Veterans Affairs. They are designed to make housing affordable for eligible U.S. veterans. VA loans are available to veterans, reservists, active-duty personnel, and surviving spouses of veterans with 100 percent entitlement. Eligible veterans might be able to purchase a home with no down payment, no cash reserve, no application fee, and lower closing costs than other financing options. The maximum VA loan amount is currently $203,000.

variable rate   Interest rate that changes periodically in relation to an index.

Verification of Deposit (VOD)   Document signed by the borrower's bank or other financial institution verifying the borrower's account balance and history.

Verification of Employment (VOE)   Document signed by the borrower's employer verifying the borrower's position and salary.

waive   To give up a right, claim, privilege, and so on for a waiver to be effective, the person giving the waiver must do so knowingly and must know the right, claim, privilege, and so on that she is giving up. In some states, a waiver can unknowingly be given merely by the actions or inactions of the individual.

waiver   Voluntary relinquishment or surrender of some right or privilege.

walk-through   A final inspection of a home to check for problems that might need to be corrected before closing.

writ of possession   A document issued by the court after the landlord wins an *unlawful detainer (eviction) lawsuit.* The writ of possession is served on the tenant by the sheriff. The writ informs the tenant that the tenant must leave the rental unit by the end of five days; otherwise, the sheriff will forcibly remove the tenant.

zoning ordinances (or zoning regulations)   Local law establishing building codes and usage regulations for properties in a specified area.

Fast Forms

When you need well-designed and legally binding forms quickly, consider using the Landlord LPA for your forms, which as noted earlier you can access through my website at www. accidentallandlordbook.com or through the LPA directly.

In this book the LPA and I have teamed up to provide you with numerous forms you can scan and use or download from the LPA's website. Many are free! Any of the forms in this book may be freely reproduced; but definitely check out the hundreds of forms they have on their website. The downloadable version (some for a small fee) will allow you to type into the document and save it for future use. You can access their site and other sources quickly from www.drdaniellebabb.com

The Application Forms

This is perhaps the single most important document next to the lease or rental agreement. You will want to compare all the information listed on the application to what you discover through the criminal background check and the credit history. Here is a sample from the LPA. You can find more details on this form by going to www.thelpa.com/lpa/forms/ef-rental.html.

FORM PF3A RENTAL APPLICATION

© 1996 – 2007 BY The Landlord Protection Agency, Inc.
Publisher, East Meadow, NY 11554

APPLICATION TO RENT

TENANT'S PERSONAL AND CREDIT INFORMATION

MUST BE FILLED OUT *COMPLETELY* TO BE PROCESSED

PERSONAL DATA:

NAME_____ BIRTHDATE_____ SOCIAL SECURITY #_____

DRIVERS LIC. #_____

NAME OF CO-TENANT_____ BIRTHDATE_____ SOCIAL SECURITY #_____

DRIVERS LIC. #_____

MAIDEN NAME OR ALIAS/ IF DIVORCED, PREVIOUS NAME_____

PRESENT ADDRESS_____ ZIP_____ PHONE #_____

HOW LONG AT PRESENT ADDRESS_____ REASON FOR MOVING_____ CURRENT RENT: $_____

CURRENT LANDLORD NAME_____ PHONE #_____

PREVIOUS ADDRESS_____ ZIP_____ PREVIOUS RENT:$_____

PREVIOUS LANDLORD NAME_____ PREVIOUS LANDLORD PHONE #_____

NUMBER OF OCCUPANTS_____ RELATIONSHIPS TO SELF_____

NUMBER OF OCCUPANTS WHO SMOKE_____ AGES_____

LIST ANY PETS_____ NUMBER OF VEHICLES____

CAR MAKE_____ YEAR_____ MODEL_____ COLOR_____ LIC.PLATE #_____

CAR MAKE_____ YEAR_____ MODEL_____ COLOR_____ LIC.PLATE #_____

OCCUPATION:

	PRESENT OCCUPATION	PRIOR OCCUPATION	CO-TENANT'S OCCUPATION
EMPLOYER			
SELF-EMPLOYED, D.B.A.			
BUSINESS ADDRESS			
PHONE			
POSITION HELD			
HOW LONG			
NAME AND TITLE OF SUPERIOR			
TYPE OF BUSINESS			
MONTHLY GROSS INCOME			

REFERENCES   PLEASE LIST AND INDICATE ALL SAVINGS (S) AND CHECKING (CK) ACCOUNTS

BANK NAME & BRANCH	ACCOUNT#	BALANCE	DATE OPENED	BANK PHONE

CREDIT BALANCES & OUTSTANDING LOANS

CREDITOR	ACCOUNT #	BALANCE OWED	DATE OPENED

PLEASE ATTACH ADDITIONAL INFORMATION IF ANY TO SEPARATE PAGE

ADDRESS OF PREMISES OFFERED FOR RENT_____

I UNDERSTAND AND AGREE THAT SECURITY, FIRST MONTH'S RENT AND BROKER'S FEES MUST BE POSTED PRIOR TO THE EXECUTION OF A LEASE AGREEMENT IN CERTIFIED FUNDS, MONEY ORDER, OR CASH.

RENTAL PRICE:_____. SECURITY:_____. BROKER'S FEE:_____

I HEREBY DEPOSIT THE SUM OF $_____.00 WITH THE LANDLORD/AGENT TO SECURE THE ABOVE PREMISES TO RENT, PENDING EXECUTION OF A LEASE AGREEMENT. I UNDERSTAND THAT MY DEPOSIT MAY BE APPLIED TOWARD ANY RENT LOSS OR OTHER EXPENSES THE LANDLORD/AGENT MAY INCUR AS A RESULT OF MY FAILURE TO FULFILL MY PROMISE TO RENT THE ABOVE NAMED PREMISES BY SIGNING A LEASE AGREEMENT NO LATER THAN_____TO OCCUPY BY_____. LEASE TERM:_____.

LANDLORD/AGENT AGREES THAT THE DEPOSIT IS REFUNDABLE IF THE ABOVE APPLICANT IS NOT APPROVED, PROVIDING THAT THIS APPLICATION HAS BEEN FILLED OUT COMPLETELY AND TRUTHFULLY.

HAVE YOU OWNED A HOME IN THE PAST?_____. IF YES, HOW LONG?_____. HOW MANY?_____.

HAVE YOU EVER FILED A PETITION FOR BANKRUPTCY?_____ IF YES, WHEN?_____.

HAVE YOU EVER BEEN EVICTED FROM ANY TENANCY?_____

HAVE YOU EVER WILLFULLY AND INTENTIONALLY REFUSED TO PAY RENT WHEN DUE?_____

I HEREBY AUTHORIZE LANDLORD/AGENT TO VERIFY THE VALIDITY OF ALL THE ABOVE INFORMATION, AND TO INQUIRE NOW OR PERIODICALLY WITH MY EMPLOYERS, FINANCIAL INSTITUTIONS, AND ANY OF THE CREDIT REPORTING BUREAUS AVAILABLE TO HIM. I AGREE TO SUPPLY ANY ADDITIONAL INFORMATION NEEDED BY OWNER/AGENT TO PROCESS THIS APPLICATION AND I ACKNOWLEDGE

THAT MY DEPOSIT WILL BE FORFEIT IF I DO NOT COMPLY WITH ANY SUCH REQUEST. I AGREE THAT MY SCREENING FEE OF $_____per adult applicant IS NON-REFUNDABLE.

I HEREBY ACKNOWLEDGE RECEIPT OF A COPY OF THIS APPLICATION AGREEMENT. I AGREE THAT LANDLORD MAY TERMINATE ANY AGREEMENT ENTERED INTO IN RELIANCE ON ANY MISSTATEMENT MADE ABOVE. I DECLARE, UNDER PENALTY OF PERJURY, ALL OF THE ABOVE INFORMATION TO BE TRUE AND CORRECT, TO THE BEST OF MY KNOWLEDGE.

• APPLICANT_____ DATE_____

• APPLICANT_____ DATE_____

ATTENTION RENTAL AGENTS: SECURE YOUR TRANSACTION! Before submitting, be sure you have:

1. Full required deposit in cash, check, or money order made out to the owner or "cash."   2. Required screening fee.   3. Application completed in full.

This vital form will collect information on the applicant and help you verify information with data you collect online. The application will also be accompanied by the rental application fee. In addition, you should also have applicants fill out a form to request a full criminal background release.

CRIMINAL & CREDIT
FULL BACKGROUND CHECK
INQUIRY RELEASE FORM

Applicant: _____

Address: _____

_____

Social Security #: _____-_____-_____

Telephone #: _____

Rental applied for: _____

    I, _____ hereby authorize prospective Landlord or Agent to verify any past records or lack thereof concerning my background with the _____ Police Dept. and/or other law enforcement authorities.

    I authorize Police / law enforcement agency to release any records that may exist to my prospective landlord for the purpose of screening me as a tenant for the premises located at the above listed address.

I authorize Landlord or Agent to inquire with my employers, financial institutions and any of the credit reporting bureaus available to verify my financial and credit status.

    I understand that any false information I may have given may be grounds for denial of my application to rent. Furthermore, I hereby state that the information I have given on my application and verbally is true and correct under the penalty of perjury.

Applicant's Signature: _____

Date: _____

RENTAL AGREEMENT

The Tenant(s) known as _____, hereby agree to rent the dwelling located at
_____.
The premises are to be occupied by the above named tenants only. Tenant may not sublet premises.

TERM The term shall commence on _____, at $_____ per month payable on the _____ of each month in full.

LATE FEES In the event rent is not paid by the _____( ) day after due date, Tenant agrees to pay a late charge of $_____

UTILITIES Tenant shall be responsible for the payment of the following utilities: water, electric, gas, heating fuel, Telephone.

APPLIANCES Appliances provided in this rental are : stove, refrigerator, dishwasher, ____air conditioner(s), _____.
Repairs will be born by said Tenants if damage is due to negligence of Tenants.

SECURITY Amount of security deposit is $_____. Security shall be held by Landlord until the time said Tenants have vacated the premises and Landlord has inspected it for damages. Tenant shall <u>not</u> have the right to apply Security Deposit in payment of any rent. Security deposits must be raised proportionately with rent increases.

INSURANCE Tenant is responsible for liability/fire insurance coverage on premises. Tenant agrees to obtain a "Renter's Insurance" policy and to provide Owner or agent with a copy of policy within seven (7) days of lease execution.

NOTICES Should tenant decide to vacate the premises, a _30_ day written notice to the landlord is required. Should landlord decide to have tenants vacated, a _30_ day written notice is required. Tenant agrees to allow premises to be shown at any and all reasonable times for re-rental.

REAL ESTATE COMMISSION (If applicable) In the event a commission was earned by a real estate broker, Tenant shall not take possession of the premises unless all fees due broker are paid in full as agreed. Commission is payable when this lease is signed by the Tenant(s). It is solely for locating the rental for the Tenant and is not refundable under any circumstances regardless of any disputes or conditions between the Landlord and Tenant before or after occupancy is taken.

ACKNOWLEDGMENT Tenants hereby acknowledge that they have read, understand and agree to all parts of this document, and have received a copy.

	AMOUNT RECEIVED	**BALANCE DUE**
RENT :	_____	_____
SECURITY:	_____	_____
BROKER'S FEE:	_____	_____

_____
_____
_____
_____

THE UNDERSIGNED TENANT(S) ACKNOWLEDGES RECEIPT OF A COPY HEREOF.

DATE: _____

OWNER/AGENT_____   TENANT_____

ADDRESS_____   TENANT _____

PHONE_____   PHONE_____

Rental Agreement

The rental agreement is the agreement between you and the tenant, or if you are using a property manager, between the manager and the tenant. This outlines the rental amount, any deposit criteria, the state the home must be returned in, penalties for being late, lease cancellation or expiration notifications, the eviction process and who pays for fees, and whether pets are allowed. It also spells out details such as how many keys and garage door openers were issued to the tenant. This is the form that protects you; use it well and use it wisely. Note that this is the same form described in Chapter 4.

Month-to-Month Rental Agreement

Rental contracts are absolutely vital, even if you are using month-to-month contracts and not leasing. Here is one from the LPA for month-to-month arrangements.

LPA 02010- House / Apt Lease, plain English format, furnished or unfurnished, 11-00

RENTAL AGREEMENT

In consideration of the agreements stated herein, the Tenant(s), known as _____

and the Landlord, _____, hereby rents them the dwelling located at

_____

for the period commencing on the _____ day of _____, 20____, and monthly thereafter until the last day of landlord or tenants _____ day notice to vacate, at which time this agreement is terminated. Tenant(s), in consideration of Owner's permitting them to occupy the above premises, hereby agree(s) to the following terms:

Monthly Rent _____	$ _____
Security Deposit _____	$ _____
Key Deposit/Oil Co. Deposit _____	$ _____
Real Estate Commission _____	$ _____
TOTAL Due at Lease Signing _____	$ _____

1. TERM   The term hereof shall commence on _____, 20_____.
The term hereof is **month to month** until the last day of landlord or tenants _____ day notice to vacate, at which time this agreement is terminated.
Tenant agrees to cooperate with Owner in the showing of the premises for sale or re-rental and agrees to make premises accessible and in presentable condition once notice is given to vacate.

2. RENT   Rent shall be $_____ per month, payable in advance, upon the _____ day of each calendar month to Owner or his authorized agent, at the following address:
_____
or at such other places Owner may designate. Rent must be paid in full and no amount subtracted from it. Tenant may be required to pay other charges to Owner under the terms of this lease. They are to be called "added rent". Added rent charges can result when Owner or his agent must pay for any expenses, which are the tenant's responsibilities under the terms of the lease. This added rent is payable as rent, together with the next monthly rent due. If tenant fails to pay added rent on time, Owner shall have the same rights against tenant as if it were a failure to pay rent.

3. LATE FEES   In the event rent is not paid by the _____(_____) day after due date, Tenant agrees to pay a late charge of $_____. Tenant agrees to further pay $_____ for each dishonored bank check.

4. UTILITIES   Tenant shall be responsible for the payment of the following utilities and services:_____.

5. USE   The premises shall be used as a residence by the undersigned tenants with no more than _____ adults and ____ children, and for no other purpose, without written consent of the Owner. Occupancy by guests staying over ___ days will be a violation of this provision. In the event any other people occupy and live in this rental, in any capacity, without Owner's written consent, it will constitute a breach of this lease and it is agreed that the rent will be increased $_____ per person per month, and the Owner at his sole option may terminate this lease.

6. PETS   No pets shall be brought on the premises without prior written consent of the Owner.

7. HOUSE RULES   In the event that the premises are a portion of a building containing more than one unit, or a single family dwelling, Tenant agrees to abide by any and all house rules, whether initiated before or after the execution hereof, including but not limited to rules with respect to noise, odors, disposal of refuse, pets, parking, and use of common areas.

8. MAINTENANCE, REPAIRS OR ALTERATIONS   Tenant acknowledges that the premises are in good order and repair, unless otherwise indicated herein. Tenant shall at his own expense, and at all times, maintain the premises in a clean and sanitary manner including all equipment, appliances, furniture, and furnishings therein and shall surrender the same at termination hereof, in as good condition as received, normal wear and tear excepted. Tenant shall be responsible for damages caused by his negligence and that of his family, invitees, or guests.
- **PAINT**   Tenant shall not paint, paper, or otherwise redecorate without the prior written consent of the Owner. All paints and materials and work plans must be approved in writing by Owner or his authorized agent.
- **GROUNDS**   Tenant shall be required to maintain any surrounding grounds. Tenant is responsible for snow and ice removal from walks, driveways, steps, and any areas where safety should be observed.
- **ADDITIONAL ITEMS.** Should Tenant attach any fixtures, blinds, or any other objects to the real property by nails, screws, or glue, it is agreed that these objects will remain with the premises and be may be subject to cost of removal at Owner's discretion Tenant is responsible for minor repairs. Repairs resulting less than $_____ shall be deemed minor repairs. Should Tenant neglect maintenance responsibilities, Owner or agent may assume them on Tenant's behalf and any expenses incurred by Owner in connection therewith shall be additional rent (added rent), payable to Owner on demand.

9. ORDINANCES & STATUTES   Tenant shall comply with all statutes, ordinances, and requirements of all municipal, state, and federal authorities now in force, of which may hereafter be in force pertaining to the use of the premises.

10. SPACE "AS IS"   Tenant has inspected the premises. Tenant states that they are in good order and repair and takes premises "as is".

11. ASSIGNMENT AND SUBLETTING   Tenant shall not assign this agreement or sublet any portion of the premises.

12. APPLIANCES The appliances provided in the dwelling by the Owner are as follows:

_____

If Tenant does not agree to be responsible for the care and maintenance of the appliances, but rather use his own appliances, he may request that Owner's appliances be removed from the premises.

13. HEATING AND COOLING SYSTEMS It is the responsibility of the tenant to maintain a service contract with a fuel company, which is approved by Owner or his authorized agent, with regard to the heating system. Tenant agrees to provide Owner with a copy of said service contract within seven (7) days from the commencement of this lease. If the dwelling is equipped with central air conditioning or individual units, the air conditioning equipment care and maintenance shall be the tenant's responsibility, unless otherwise specified herein. Electric and kerosene heating units are prohibited without Owner's written permission.

14. RIGHT OF ENTRY FOR PERIODIC INSPECTION The Owner or his agent may enter the premises with prior consent of the tenant, or with 24 hours written notice to any tenant on the premises to be entered. The Owner may enter during reasonable hours and for the purpose of inspecting the premises, making necessary or agreed repairs, decorations, alterations, or improvements, supplying necessary or agreed services, or exhibiting the dwelling unit to prospective or actual purchasers, mortgagees, prospective tenants, workmen, contractors, or insurance inspectors. The Owner shall be deemed to have given 24 hours written notice by posting a notice in a noticeable place stating such intent to enter, at least 24 hours before the intended entry. However, in the event of an emergency constituting a danger to life, health, or property, the Owner or his agent may enter the property at any given time without the consent of or notice to the tenant.

15. INDEMNIFICATION Owner shall not be liable for any damage or injury to the tenant, or any other person or to any property, occurring on the premises or any part thereof, or in common areas thereof, unless such damage or injury is the proximate result of the negligence of the Owner, his agents, or employees. Tenant agrees to hold Owner harmless from any claims from damages, no matter how caused except for injury and damages for which Owner is legally responsible.

16. POSSESSION If Owner is unable to deliver possession of the premises at the commencement hereof, Owner shall not be liable for any damages caused thereby, nor shall this agreement be void, but Tenant shall not be liable for any rent until possession is delivered. Tenant may terminate this agreement if possession is not delivered within _____ days of the commencement of the term hereof.

17. SECURITY The security deposit set forth, shall secure the performance of the tenant's obligations herein. Owner may, but shall not be obligated to apply all or portions of said deposit on account of Tenant's obligations herein, including, if Tenant is in default of this lease, attorneys fees to recover the premises from the tenant. Any balance remaining upon termination shall be returned to the tenant. Tenant shall <u>not</u> have the right to apply Security Deposit in payment of any rent. Security deposits must be raised proportionately with rent increases.

18. WAIVER No failure of Owner to enforce any term hereof shall be deemed a waiver, nor shall any acceptance of partial payment be deemed a waiver of Owner's right to the full amount thereof. This lease supersedes any other lease on the premises during the term stated herein. No terms in this lease shall be deemed waived, regardless of any conflicting terms or rules in any governmental rent assistance programs.

19. DEFAULT If Tenant shall fail to pay rent when due, or perform any term hereof, after not less than three (3) days written notice of such default given in a manner required by law, the Owner, at his option, may terminate all rights of the tenant herein, unless Tenant within said time shall cure such default. If Tenant abandons or vacates the premises while in default of the payment of rent, Owner may consider any property left on the premises to be abandoned and may dispose of the same in any manner allowed by law. In a proceeding to get possession of the premises, Tenant agrees to make no motions to the court concerning issues such as habitability or delaying the legal process with requests for additional time. Tenant waives all rights to return to the premises after possession is returned to Owner by a court. Tenant agrees to waive rights to trial by a jury in any matter that comes up between the parties under or because of this lease. Tenant shall not have the right to make a counterclaim or set off.

20. ATTORNEY'S FEES In any legal action to enforce the terms hereof or relating to the premises, regardless of the outcome, the Owner or agent shall be entitled to all costs incurred in connection with such action, including a reasonable attorney's fee.

21. NOTICES Any notice which either party may or is required to give, may be given by mailing the same, by certified mail, to Tenant at the premises, or to Owner at the address shown below or at such other places as may be designated by the parties from time to time.
Tenant is required to notify Owner in writing of Intention to Vacate or Intention to Re-new at least _____ days before the expiration of this lease. Tenant agrees to follow instructions provided in the **Intention to Vacate form** and the **Intention to Re-new form.**
Tenant agrees to immediately notify Owner or Agent in writing by certified mail of any dangerous or hazardous conditions existing on the premises.

22. OPTION TO RENEW LEASE Tenant has the option, providing the terms and conditions of this lease have been complied with and satisfied, to renew this agreement for a period of __**1 year** __, at an annual increase of _____, subject to Owner's approval.

23. HOLDING OVER Any holding over after expiration hereof, with the consent of the Owner, shall be construed as a month-to-month tenancy in accordance with the terms hereof, as applicable. The terms and conditions of this lease will continue to apply.

24. TIME Time is of the essence of this agreement.

25. INSURANCE Tenant agrees to obtain a "Renter's Insurance" policy and to provide Owner or agent with a copy of policy within seven (7) days of lease execution.

26. SUCCESSORS This lease is binding on all parties who lawfully succeed to the rights or take the place of the Owner or Tenant.

27. TENANCY & SERVICE OF PROCESS Every tenant who signs this agreement agrees to be fully responsible jointly and severally for all items agreed herein, and furthermore agrees to be the agent of the other tenants and occupants of the premises and is both authorized and required to accept on behalf of the other tenants and occupants, service of summons and other notices relative to the tenancy.

28. BANKRUPTCY If (1) Tenant assigns property for the benefit of creditors, (2) Tenant files a voluntary petition or an involuntary petition is filed against Tenant under any bankruptcy or insolvency law, or (3) a trustee or receiver of Tenant or Tenant's property is appointed, Owner may give Tenant 30 days written notice of the cancellation of the term of this lease. If any of the above is not fully dismissed within the 30 days, the term shall end as of the date stated in the notice. Tenant must continue to pay rent, damages, losses, and expenses without offset.

29. SMOKE DETECTOR(S), FIRE EXTINGUISHER Tenant(s) acknowledge that the dwelling is equipped with smoke detector(s), and fire extinguisher(s). Tenant(s) agree to test the smoke detector(s) on a regular basis (2-3 times per month), and to report any problem with them immediately to owner in writing. Tenant agrees to replace the battery for the smoke detector as necessary with a new alkaline battery.

30. ILLEGALITY - SEVERABILITY If any part of this lease is not legal according to local laws, the rest of the lease will be unaffected. Illegal activity of Tenant(s), invitees, or guests on premises constitutes a breach of this lease.

31. ENTIRE AGREEMENT The foregoing constitutes the entire agreement between the parties and may be modified only an official change of terms notice issued by the owner/agent in writing, or a writing signed by both parties. The following exhibit has been made a part of this agreement before the parties' execution hereof:

_____
_____
_____

THE UNDERSIGNED TENANT(S) ACKNOWLEDGES RECEIPT OF A COPY HEREOF.

DATE: _____

OWNER/AGENT_____   TENANT_____

ADDRESS_____   TENANT _____

PHONE_____   PHONE_____

Agreement to Lease with Option to Purchase

I found this interesting agreement to lease with an option to purchase—that is, a purchase option for the tenant—on www.buyincomeproperties.com/html/ BuyerLeaseOption.html. I have included it here, but you can view it online, too. These are very serious details with serious ramifications and this is a very simple form, so be sure to have a real estate attorney review it if you decide to use it to seal a deal with a tenant.

Seller Option to Purchase Real Estate

You can use this form in conjunction with a separate lease agreement! Get the full form at www.buyincomeproperties.com/html/LeaseOptionOption2.html.

Seller Option to Purchase Real Estate

THIS AGREEMENT made by and between _____ (hereinafter called "Optionor") and _____, (hereinafter called "Optionee"). The masculine singular pronoun shall be used throughout this Agreement, regardless of the sex or number of parties.

1. OPTIONED PROPERTY: Optionor, in consideration of the payment of an option fee under this Option Agreement, and rents paid and faithful performance of Optionee under a Rental Agreement entered into between the parties on this date, hereby grants to Optionee the right and option to purchase the premises below at the termination of the Rental Agreement entered into this date for the terms and subject to the covenants and conditions hereinafter set forth, the following described property: _____ _____. Together with all improvements thereon, all privileges, appurtenances, easements and all fixtures, presently situated in said building except the following: _____

2. TERM: The term of this Agreement shall be _____ months beginning on the first day of _____ and ending on the last day of _____, 20___.

3. OPTION FEE: Optionee agrees to pay $_____ as a NON-REFUNDABLE FEE, as consideration for the Optionor to grant the Option to Optionee to purchase the above premises. Simultaneous with the execution of this Option Agreement the Optionee shall deposit the sum of $_____ with Optionor and agrees to pay _____ on _____, 20___ until the total option fee has been paid in full. If the Optionee maintains the premises in accordance with the rental agreement and pays the monthly rent on or before the first day of each month they receive a $_____ discount, which discount shall be applied to the non-refundable option fee.

4. OPTION PRICE: The option price of the Property shall be determined as follows: The base price shall be $_____.
    The base price shall increase by the percent change in the Consumer Price Index (CPI-U) of the U.S. Department of Labor from the beginning of the term of this option..The amount obtained in (a) and (b) above shall be the purchase price.
    The Option Fee as provided in Paragraph 3 above shall be refunded to the Optionee to be used only as a down payment upon the purchase of the Property, as said Option Fee is NON-REFUNDABLE in the event that Optionee does not exercise the Option and purchase the Property.

5. REPAIRS AND MAINTENANCE: Optionee agrees to maintain the lawn, remove snow, repair and /or replace any and all facilities related to the premises, to provide ordinary and customary preventive maintenance, and to maintain the building in good to excellent condition throughout the Term of this Agreement. This includes all walks, drives, electrical, plumbing, bath and kitchen fixtures, appliances, roofing, painting, lawn, landscaping and all exterior and interior items or work required. The costs of such maintenance and repairs shall be allocated as follows:
    The costs of repairs, maintenance and improvements, which are less than or equal to $500.00 per repair shall be paid by Optionee. Optionor agrees to pay for fixing any roof leak, if Optionee immediately notifies Optionor of the roof leak. If Optionee does not

notify Optionor immediately of the roof leak, the Optionee shall pay for fixing the roof and all resulting damage to the building, regardless of cost.

The cost of repairs and maintenance in excess of $500.00 shall be shared equally by Optionor and Optionee, provided that Owner has approved of each expenditure in writing prior to the commencement of any work on the premises, and provided that the work is performed by a reputable contractor.

Notwithstanding the above, the cost of all repairs required as a result of negligence by Optionee or his or her guests shall be paid in full by the Optionee.

Optionee may only make improvements or modifications to the property upon written approval of the Optionor. Any unapproved improvement or modifications to the property must be removed at Optionee expense within seven (7) days of written notice to Optionee by Optionor.

6. TERMS OF THE OPTION: Provided the Optionee has fully paid all the sums due and has performed all other covenants under the Rental Agreement of the same date, and has paid the full Option Price in Paragraph 2, the Optionee may exercise the option to purchase after one year by giving the Optionor sixty (60) days written notice of their intention to exercise the Option. Upon exercise the Optionee agrees to cooperate with the Optionor in affecting a Internal Revenue Code Section 1031 exchange, at no cost to the Optionee. Optionee will arrange their own financing and pay all closing costs connected with the transfer of the property and obtaining the loan, so that the sale or exchange can be completed in sixty (60) days of the exercise of the option. Optionor agrees to deliver a good and sufficient General Warranty Deed conveying a marketable title to said property to the Optionee.

7. BINDING EFFECT: This Option and the agreements contained herein shall be binding upon inure to the benefit of heirs, executors, administrators, successors and assigns of the respective parties.

8. DISCLOSURES: Optionee acknowledges receipt of the "Residential Property Disclosure" statement, the EPA "Disclosure of Information on Lead-Based Paint and Lead-Based Paint Hazards" statement, and the EPA "Protect Your Family From Lead In Your Home" booklet. and understands their contents.

9. MISCELLANEOUS: Optionee agrees that they have examined the title to the Property and found no errors in the title and hereby accepts all assessments and encumbrances upon the property.

10. APPLICABLE LAW: This agreement shall be interpreted according to the Laws of the State of _____.

IN WITNESS WHEREOF, Optionor and Optionee have executed this agreement on the _____ day of _____, 20____.

_____   _____
Optionor   Optionee

Real Estate Sublease

In general, I don't recommend you allow subleases, but if you do, you might want to provide your tenant with a binding form that will help her protect herself and your property! You can download one at www.buyincomeproperties.com/html/Real_Estate_Sublease.html or you can use the one here from the LPA.

LPA 02099- Sub-Lease, plain English format,
simple, 11-04

© 2004 BY The Landlord Protection Agency, Inc.
Publisher, E. Meadow, NY 11554

SUBLEASE AGREEMENT

Made between _____, Lessor and

_____ Lessee, now

occupying _____ under a lease

dated _____, 20_____.

Lessor hereby agrees and consents to the subletting of the above specified premises with the understanding that the Sub-tenant

accepts the premises subject to all conditions as set forth in the said lease of _____, 20 _____, and which he

agrees to perform and fulfill as if he were the Lessee and that any breach of the lease made by the Sub-tenant shall constitute a

breach as if made by the Lessee.

It is further understood and agreed that in granting this privilege to the Lessee, the Lessor does not waive any of his rights under

the existing lease nor does he abrogate any of his rights for the recovery of the premises or for distress or otherwise, for rent, or for

other charges which may become due.

Unless otherwise approved, the Lessee shall sublet the above listed premises specifically to

_____

for the period commencing on the _____ day of _____, 20_____, and monthly thereafter until
the last day of _____, 20_____, at which time this agreement is terminated.

_____
_____
_____
_____
_____
_____

THE UNDERSIGNED PARTIES ACKNOWLEDGES RECEIPT OF A COPY HEREOF.

DATE: _____

OWNER/LESSOR _____   LESSEE _____

ADDRESS_____   SUB-TENANT _____

PHONE_____   PHONE _____

Pet Addendum

The pet addendum spells out the type of pet, any added insurance the tenant
must carry, the additional deposit required by the tenant, and possibly any

additional cleaning fees you will require. You also can specify the rules here—for instance, dogs can only be in the dog run and not in the garden and must be on a leash at all times. The following is a sample pet agreement from the LPA.

© 2000 By The Landlord Protection Agency, Inc.

PET AGREEMENT

Premises: _____

This Pet Agreement addendum is made this _____ day of _____, 20____, and is added to and amends that certain agreement by and between _____ as Tenant(s) and _____ as Landlord(s), which agreement is dated _____ day of _____, 20____. This is a conditional privilege granted to the tenant in exchange for guaranteeing that the rules in this Pet Agreement are strictly followed. This privilege may be terminated if any of the Pet Agreement rules are violated. This privilege may also be terminated if tenant should violate or place Lease Rental Agreement for the premises in default.

Tenants shall be permitted to keep a pet _____ named _____.

# of pets _____ Breed _____ Color_____ Weight _____
        Breed _____ Color_____ Weight _____

The Pet Agreement Rules are as follows:
- Only a pet described and named in this Pet Agreement shall be permitted on the premises. Any others shall be a violation of the agreement.
- Tenants agree to be fully responsible and liable, and pay for any damages or injury caused by or as a result of their pet. Pet damages can apply to floors, carpeting, walls, windows, screens, moldings, furniture, and landscaping, etc.
- Tenants agree that they will not allow their pet to disturb or annoy neighbors in any way, whether the pet is inside the dwelling or outside.
- Tenant will keep control over the pet at all times, whether inside the dwelling or outside.
- Tenants agree that pet will not be left unattended over any unreasonable periods of time.
- Tenants agree that no pet=s offspring are allowed on premises.
- Tenants promise not to leave food for the pet outside the dwelling, which can attract other animals and bugs.
- Tenants agree to keep their pet clean at all times, and keep the premises in a clean and sanitary manner, properly disposing of pet droppings as quickly as possible.
- Tenant shall post a Pet Security deposit in the amount of $_____, which is to be held by owner until such time the premises are returned. The deposit will then be refunded to tenant as long as the premises are returned as agreed.
- Tenant shall pay a one time only Pet Fee in the amount of $_____.

The parties have entered into this Agreement on the date first above stated, and acknowledge receipt of a copy hereof.

LANDLORD: **TENANT:**

_____   _____

_____   _____

Agreement to Terminate Lease

If you and the tenant agree to terminate the tenancy, here is a sample form you can use (www.buyincomeproperties.com/realestateforms/AGREEMENT_TO_ TERMINATE_LEASE.htm).

TERMINATION OF TENANCY

Tenant   ss#: 000-00-0000
Tenant   ss#: 000-00-0000

Premises: _____
_____

   This letter is notification that you are hereby required within __**30**___ days, **or at the end of your next monthly rent period**, to remove from and deliver up possession of the above-described premises, which you currently hold and occupy.

If you do not, legal proceedings will be instituted against you to recover possession of said premises; to declare the forfeiture of the Lease-Rental Agreement under which you occupy said premises; and to recover rents, damages, court costs and attorney's fees, according to the terms of your Lease or Rental Agreement.

Please be advised that any of the above legal actions may be detrimental to your credit rating.

> This area can be used for an explanation if needed.
> Such as:
> **We have decided to terminate your tenancy rather than renew the lease because your payment record has not met our minimum standards.**

Occupancy in the premises after _____
shall constitute agreement to pay a holdover penalty of $200.00 per day and subject you to legal action to recover the premises and any monies due.

Dated this _____ day of _____.   Owner/Manager

_____

PROOF OF SERVICE

I, the undersigned, being at least 18 years of age, declare under the penalty of perjury that I served the Notice to Pay Rent or Quit, of which this is a true copy, on the above mentioned Tenant in Possession, in the manner indicated below.

[ ] On _____, 20___, I handed the Notice to Tenant.

[ ] I handed the Notice to a person of suitable age and discretion at the Tenant's residence / business on _____, 20___.

[ ] I posted the Notice in a conspicuous place at the premises named above, of which the Tenant has possession.

[ ] I sent by Certified mail or First Class mail a true copy of the Notice to the Tenant at his/her place of residence on _____, 20___.

_____

Notice to Pay Rent or Quit—Demand for Payment

This notice serves to let your tenant know that he is late on paying rent. This is a strong warning letter and is written as such. It also warns the tenant that his credit is in jeopardy. If you want to download the form, you can do so at www.thelpa.com/d/369707578.401179/payorquit.doc. Or, you can alternatively use the one here and duplicate it. It is recommended you use the one online and print it in color because it's designed to get your tenant's attention!

NOTICE TO PAY RENT OR QUIT
DEMAND FOR PAYMENT

Date: _____

To: _____ Social Security number: _____

_____ Social Security number: _____

RE:
Address: _____

You are hereby notified that rent is now overdue and payable on the above referenced premises in the amount of $_____ plus applicable late charges and attorney's fees for the period between _____ and _____.

You are hereby required to pay said rent within ____,____ days (by _____, 20_____) or to remove from and deliver up possession of the above mentioned premises. If you do not, legal proceedings will be instituted against you to recover possession of said premises; to declare the forfeiture of the Lease-Rental Agreement under which you occupy said premises; and to recover rents, damages, court costs, and attorney's fees, according to the terms of your Lease or Rental Agreement.

_____
Owner/Manager

WARNING! YOUR CREDIT IS IN JEOPARDY!

PROOF OF SERVICE

I, the undersigned, being at least 18 years of age, declare under the penalty of perjury that I served the Notice to Pay Rent or Quit, of which this is a true copy, on the above mentioned Tenant in Possession, in the manner indicated below.

[ ] On _____, 20___, I handed the Notice to Tenant.

[ ] I handed the Notice to a person of suitable age and discretion at the Tenant's residence/business on _____, 20___.

[ ] I posted the Notice in a conspicuous place at the premises named above, of which the Tenant has possession.

[ ] I sent by Certified mail or First Class mail a true copy of the Notice to the Tenant at his/her place of residence on _____, 20___.

PROTECT YOUR CREDIT

Evictions Ramifications Notice

Sometimes your tenant won't understand the consequences of eviction, which can devastate her credit and make it nearly impossible for her to rent another home. The eviction ramification letter explains what happens immediately and in the future if your tenant is evicted. You can download the form at www.thelpa.com/free/eviction-letter.pdf.

Notice of Eviction Ramifications, LPA Form F 20   © 2006 By The Landlord Protection Agency, Inc.

Eviction and How it Affects You

Dear Tenant,

As you know, your account is now or soon will be in "Eviction Status". It's possible that you may not know about or understand the ramifications of what it means to be the subject of an eviction proceeding. Below is a list of easy to understand consequences a person will face as a result of a legal eviction:

1. Eviction Court. This can be a humiliating experience and also matter of permanent public record.

2. Dispossession. You will be forcibly removed from the premises. This can be a humiliating experience and also matter of permanent public record.

3. Judgment (s). Your credit rating will be severely damaged. This may also result in

   - A collection process until your debt is paid in full

   - Possible seizure of assets you may own, including bank accounts

   - Garnishment of wages

   - Notification of credit bureaus causing inability to qualify for lines of credit, including credit cards, car loans, and mortgages.

   - Notification of National Tenant Reporting Services causing inability to qualify for rental housing (Most quality rentals require credit and tenant screening.)

We understand that you are having difficulties paying your rent or complying with your lease agreement. We sincerely hope you will be able to resolve any problems you are currently experiencing and bring your account out of eviction status.

Sincerely.

Owner/Manager

An evictions ramifications notice lets the tenant know what happens if she is evicted and how it can be detrimental to her. Many tenants think that because you are a one-person shop, you don't have the resources or the know-how to report them.

Make it very clear that this is not true. If you decide to become a member of the LPA, you will have its forms (with its logo on them) to let tenants know you mean business.

The Tenant's Notice of Intention to Vacate

This form allows the tenant to give you proper notice with ease when he is vacating. This encourages the tenant to allow you to show the property for rerental or sale. It includes a place for the tenant to provide a forwarding address in order to receive security refunds, which helps encourage tenants to follow the move-out procedures because they will want their money back. The LPA suggests that you copy this notice and provide it in the back of the tenant's lease, and it is my suggestion you provide it again when you send the lease renewal or move-out notice.

The Landlord Protection
LPA
AGENCY ™

TENANT'S NOTICE TO VACATE

To: _____   Date: _____

Please take notice of our intention to vacate our residence located at
_____ on or
before _____ .

The reason we are moving is:
_____

We understand that our deposit will be refunded as agreed, less past due unpaid charges, if any, after we have moved out completely and returned possession of the premises to the management, as long as we leave the residence in clean and undamaged condition.

We understand that our Lease/Rental Agreement states that we have agreed to a _____ day written notice to vacate. We understand that we are responsible for paying rent through the end of the term agreed to in the Lease/Rental Agreement or until another tenant is approved by the management and has taken occupancy, whichever happens first. As we have agreed in our Lease/Rental Agreement, we will make the premises accessible to show to prospective tenants or purchasers at any and all reasonable times, whether we are present or not.

Please Return Deposits to our new address at:
_____

☐ We would like to request a reference from you.   ☐ Thank you, but we do not need a reference.

Tenant: _____

Tenant: _____

Settlement Charges Guide

The settlement charges guide gives your tenants a heads-up on the type of move-out charges they can expect for damages, cleaning, or neglect as a result of their tenancy. You can mail this along with the Security Deposit Settlement form to show how deductions were calculated. What some tenants consider wear and tear really are damages, and they need to pay for them. This is also from the LPA, and it is noted that you should modify these for your actual expenses, which can vary dramatically. It does give you an idea, though, on what you should be looking at because first-time (or even seasoned) landlords can overlook a lot! Take a look at www.thelpa.com/free/charges.doc for the full document.

Early Payment Discount Voucher

Although your tenants probably won't pay early, you can certainly encourage them to. You can use this once or for any number of rental periods you choose. The lease should contain an early payment discount clause if you want to offer one, but you can include these vouchers as reminders. The goal is to make it as easy as possible for tenants to take advantage of paying rent early and to make the incentive very obvious! You can use the one here, but I recommend you download it at www.thelpa.com/d/571296531.31506/earlydiscount.doc because it offers a great color printout you can use with a modifiable coupon amount!

Lead Paint Disclosure

We discussed the lead paint disclosure earlier in the book. This form is required by HUD on all housing structures built before 1978; real estate agents must also disclose whether they have knowledge of any lead-based paint hazards. You must include this with your lease. The full link is www.thelpa.com/free/lead.pdf. You should include this form with the lead-based paint handout. You can get this free at www.thelpa.com/free/leadpaint.pdf. Print it and provide one to your tenants.

SETTLEMENT CHARGES GUIDE

Below is a list of estimated charges of assorted items or jobs that may sometimes be required after a residence is vacated. All charges are including labor and any parts or materials required. Tenants are not responsible for normal wear and tear, although excessive wear and tear and neglect may incur charges.

CLEANING

Clean refrigerator	50.00
Clean stovetop	30.00
Replace stove drip-bowls	28.00
Clean oven	50.00
Clean stove hood	30.00
Clean kitchen cabinets	45.00
Clean kitchen floor	50.00
Clean tub/shower and surround	30.00
Clean toilet and sink (per bath)	20.00
Clean bathroom. Cabinets and floor	25.00
Clean carpets (per room)	75.00
Vacuum throughout dwelling	40.00
Window cleaning (per unit)	11.00
Clean greasy parking spaces	25.00
Clean fireplace	35.00

GENERAL REPAIRS

Replace refrigerator shelf	25.00
Replace stove/oven knob	16.00
Repair ceramic tile	150.00
Replace countertop	275.00
Replace cutting board	40.00
Replace kit/bath cabinet knobs	10.00
Replace mirror	45.00
Replace medicine cabinet	85.00
Replace towel bar	22.00
Replace tub/shower enclosure	195.00
Re grout bath/shower tiles	165.00
Repair porcelain	135.00
Replace thermostat	75.00
Replace fire extinguisher	35.00
Remove junk and debris	250.00
Replace doorbell button	5.00
Replace doorbell unit	50.00
Replace Garage door (each)	525.00

FLOORING

Remove carpet stains	80.00
Deodorize carpet	80.00
Repair carpet	150.00
Repair hardwood floor	95.00
Refinish hardwood floor	380.00
Repair linoleum	85.00
Replace bathroom linoleum	385.00
Replace kitchen linoleum	385.00
Replace floor tile	75.00
Replace ceramic tile	150.00

WALLS

Remove mildew and treat surface	25.00
Cover crayon/marker/pen marks	35.00
Repair hole in wall	55.00
Remove wallpaper	145.00
Repaint (per wall/ceiling)	20.00

DOORS

Repair hole in hollow core door	55.00
Repair forced door damage	75.00
Replace door (inside)	155.00
Replace door (outside)	285.00
Replace sliding glass door	475.00
Replace sliding door screen	55.00

WINDOWS & TREATMENTS

Replace window pane	75.00
Replace Venetian blind	75.00
Replace window shade	15.00
Replace window screen	20.00

LOCKS

Replace key	5.00
Replace door lock	37.00
Replace passage doorlock	18.00
Replace deadbolt lock	18.00

PLUMBING

Replace kitchen faucet	95.00
Replace bathroom faucet	85.00
Replace shower head	24.00
Replace toilet tank lid	25.00
Replace toilet seat	12.00
Replace toilet	165.00
Replace garbage disposer	125.00
Snake toilet	25.00
Clear sewer/cesspool line	85.00

ELECTRICAL

Replace light bulb	2.50
Replace light fixture globe	12.00
Replace light fixture	55.00
Replace electrical outlet/switch	5.00
Replace electrical cover plate	1.50

GROUNDS / EXTERIOR

Major yard Cleanup	425.00
Minor yard Cleanup	225.00
Mow lawn front and back	50.00
Clean gutters	185.00
Trim bushes	20.00

EXTERMINATING

Exterminate for cockroaches	450.00
Exterminate for fleas	275.00

www.theLPA.com

Dear Tenant,

As an excellent tenant, your landlord has selected you to receive a special rent reduction opportunity:

$ Early Payment Voucher $

$50.00

This voucher entitles

_____

to $_____ off the rent payment on the rental located at

_____

in exchange for early payment of rent. (See details below)

A discount is offered to the tenant as an incentive to pay rent before it's due date. If rent is received by 5:00 P.M. _____ days <u>before</u> it's due date or sooner, the tenant may deduct $_____ making the payment $_____. Payment shall only be deemed made as of the date <u>received by the Owner or his agent,</u> and not by the postmark on the envelope.

This special offer is granted to the tenant for the months of

_____20 ___ to _____20 ___

Authorized by _____ Date _____

PF37 Early Payment Discount Voucher

Disclosure of Information on Lead-Based Paint and Lead-Based Paint Hazards

Lead Warning Statement

Housing built before 1978 may contain lead-based paint. Lead from paint, paint chips, and dust can pose health hazards if not taken care of properly. Lead exposure is especially harmful to young children and pregnant women. Before renting pre-1978 housing, landlords must disclose the presence of known lead-based paint and lead-based paint hazards in the dwelling. Tenants must also receive a Federally approved pamphlet on lead poisoning prevention.

Lessor's Disclosure (initial)

    (a) Presence of lead-based paint or lead-based paint hazards (check one below):

        Known lead-based paint and/or lead-based paint hazards are present in the housing (explain).

_____

_____

        Lessor has no knowledge of lead-based paint and/or lead-based paint hazards in the housing.

    (b) Records and reports available to the lessor (check one below):

        Lessor has provided the lessee with all available records and reports pertaining to lead-based paint and/or lead-based paint hazards in the housing (list documents below).

_____

        Lessor has no reports or records pertaining to lead-based paint and/or lead-based paint hazards in the housing.

Lessee's Acknowledgment (initial)

_____ (c) Lessee has received copies of all information listed above.

_____ (d) Lessee has received the pamphlet *Protect Your Family from Lead in Your Home.*

Agent's Acknowledgment (initial)

    (e) Agent has informed the lessor of the lessors obligations under 42 U.S.C. 4582(d) and is aware of his/her responsibility to ensure compliance.

Certification of Accuracy

The following parties have reviewed the information above and certify, to the best of their knowledge, that the information provided by the signatory is true and accurate.

Lessor	Date	Lessor	Date
Lessee	Date	Lessee	Date
Agent	Date	Agent	Date

Credit Reporting Disclosure Notice to Tenant

The credit reporting disclosure notice informs your tenants that you will report both positive and negative credit histories to the credit and tenant reporting bureaus, which you can do on the LPA's site. This tells tenants that their record will be impacted by rent payments, cleanliness, and their overall performance. This not only helps you in the event that the tenants fail to perform, but it also encourages tenants from day one that you mean business and they cannot take advantage of you. The earlier this is established, the better. Take a look at the list of essential forms available online at the LPA at www.thelpa.com/lpa/forms.html.

PF 57 Credit Reporting Disclosure to Tenant   © 2007 By The Landlord Protection Agency, Inc.

The Landlord Protection
LPA
AGENCY ™

Disclosure Notice:
Credit Reporting and Tenant Performance

Applicant: _____   Applicant: _____

Social Security #: _____ - ___ - _____   Social Security #: _____ - ___ - _____

Rental applied for: _____

Lessor/Agent: _____

Credit and Tenant Reporting Statement
Landlords engaged in the rental of housing and collection of rent may report and share positive and negative payment information with credit bureaus, tenant reporting agencies, other landlords, and financial institutions.

The prospective Tenant understands that the above named prospective Landlord may report various tenant and credit information to national tenant and credit reporting bureaus including but not limited to Experian, TransUnion, Equifax, and The National Tenant Rating Bureau.

Positive or negative rental history will be determined by the following factors:

- Rent payment record
- Cleanliness and upkeep of rental unit
- Overall tenant performance and cooperation

Furthermore, I declare under the penalty of perjury that the information I have given on my application and verbally is true and correct.

_____   _____
Applicant   Date

_____   _____
Applicant   Date

Denial Letter and Adverse Action Letter

Here are two forms that will help protect you from pushy renters. Also, you need to protect yourself if the renter feels illegitimately discriminated against. The Denial Letter lets the tenant know why you have denied her application, and the Adverse Action Letter is required for you to reject an applicant due to credit issues to comply with the Fair Credit Reporting Act (FCRA) regulation. Be sure to include the Adverse Action Letter if you are turning someone down due to credit, and include the Denial Letter regardless of the reason you are turning her down. This also takes some of the difficulty out of telling someone "no" even when you really need to. Take a look at the list of essential forms available online at the LPA at www.thelpa.com/lpa/forms.html.

© 2000 By The Landlord Protection Agency, Inc.

DEAR APPLICANT,

WE REGRET TO INFORM YOU, THAT YOUR RENTAL APPLICATION WAS DECLINED FOR THE FOLLOWING REASON(S):

[ ] Applicant's price offer not accepted.

[ ] Rent/Income ratio does not meet minimum standards.

[ ] Lack of credit history, or derogatory information contained in credit report. See enclosed Adverse Action letter

[ ] Unable to obtain favorable current or past landlord reference.

[ ] Unable to verify current or past employment.

[ ] Applicant unable to comply with security deposit requirement.

[ ] Application was not accompanied by required screening fee.

[ ] Application contained false information. (False information on an application constitutes intent to defraud and perjury. Any deposits may be forfeit. Legal remedies may be pursued.)

[ ] Residence allows NO PETS.

[ ] Residence requires NO SMOKING.

[ ] Application submitted incomplete.

[ ] Intended occupancy date or lease term unacceptable.

We would like to thank you for the opportunity to review your rental application and hope that we may be of service some time in the future.

RESPECTFULLY

Manager

Dear Applicant: Date: _____

Thank you for the opportunity to consider your application to rent. We regret we are unable to approve your application due to one or more of the following reasons.

According to the Fair Credit Reporting Act, you are entitled to know when adverse action was taken in whole or in part based on information received from a consumer reporting agency. Credit information having an adverse impact on your application was received from:

✍ One or more of the following consumer credit reporting agencies:

    ✍ Equifax Information Services
      PO Box 105873
      Atlanta, GA 30348-5873
      1-800-685-1111

    ✍ Experian (TRW)
      PO Box 2104
      Allen, TX 75013-2014
      1-888-397-3742

    ✍ Trans Union
      PO Box 1000
      Chester, PA 19022
      1-800-888-4213
      www.transunion.com\direct

The consumer credit reporting agencies only role was to provide credit information and cannot give the reason why your application was not approved.

Under the Fair Credit Reporting Act you have a right to receive a free copy of your credit report if one is requested within 60 days of this notice. You have a right to dispute the accuracy or completeness of any information in your credit file.

References and or information having an adverse impact on your application was received from:

✍ The following consumer reporting agency:

_____
_____
_____
Ph. #: _____

The Information Source's only role was to provide consumer report information and cannot give the reason why your application was not approved.

Under the Fair Credit Reporting Act you have a right to dispute the accuracy or completeness of any information in your consumer file. To do so you must contact the above consumer-reporting agency within sixty (60) days of receiving this notice.

✍ This adverse action was taken due to incomplete, inaccurate, or false information contained within the rental application.

Sincerely,

_____

Mold Addendum

The mold addendum makes the tenant responsible for keeping the property free of mold and mildew through proper maintenance and makes him responsible for cleaning and repair expenses from mold damage he causes. This is important because it can cost you a lot of money later, and some landlords have been sued for allowing mold in their properties. Take a look at the list of essential forms available online at the LPA at www.thelpa.com/lpa/forms.html. Some tenants will say that the mold was there beforehand. One thing you can do to mitigate this concern is to have an inspection done, and provide a mold inspection report to the tenant.

© 2006 By The Landlord Protection Agency, Inc.

MOLD ADDENDUM

This addendum is made this _____ day of _____, 20____, and is added to and amends that certain agreement by and between _____ as Tenant(s) and _____as Landlord(s), which agreement is dated _____ day of _____, 20____. Failure to comply with the terms of this addendum is a violation of said agreement constituting grounds for eviction and tenant's liability for any damages as a result of tenant's failure to comply.

1) **Acknowledgement** Tenant acknowledges that the rental is free of mold and agrees to take responsibility for preventing mold growth that can become a health hazard to occupants of the rental.

2) **Liability** Tenant agrees to be responsible for any defects or damages concerning mold during or as a result of the tenant's occupancy, and agrees to check for mold on a regular basis. Tenant accepts full liability for the entire amount of cleaning expenses and damage reparations caused by mold or mildew during or as a result of tenant's occupancy.

3) **Maintenance Care** Tenant agrees to take full responsibility for keeping the residence clean and dry and free from moisture accumulations where mold could be allowed to grow. (The kitchen and bathroom(s) are the most common places mold is known to form.)

4) **Climate Control** Tenant agrees to keep the temperature and humidity within reasonable levels as to prevent the growth of mold.

5) **Violation of Agreement** Violation of any of the provisions in this Mold Addendum shall constitute a material default of the terms of the Lease Agreement and subject to the remedies and/or penalties concerning lease violations stated in the Lease Agreement.

6) **Contract** The parties acknowledge and agree that this addendum once signed shall be a part of the above mentioned lease, and that no other agreements concerning mold shall be valid unless such agreement(s) are written and signed by the parties.

Tenants have read and acknowledge this addendum and agree to carry out the responsibilities described above.

Owner/Agent_____   Tenant_____ Date_____

Tenant Finder Pre-Screening Telephone Worksheet

If you placed a yard sign, then obviously the potential tenant knows the address of the property you are renting. But if you placed an ad elsewhere before committing time to an unqualified renter, use this telephone worksheet to evaluate prospects, provided by LPA!

This chart helps you score each applicant so you can spend your time and resources on those most likely to qualify—and rent! This particular worksheet is essential in that not only does it score and help you find the tenants, but it also tells you the reason you're doing it so you can learn! To download the complete file and enter your information into it directly, go to www.thelpa.com/lpa/forms. html.

Rental Applicant Checkpoints List

Different organizations have their own lists of checkpoints you might consider. One that has some interesting information and a different calculation method is the applicant checkpoints list at www.buyincomeproperties.com/html/ RentalAppChkPoints1.html.

The tenant qualifying chart shown here can be accessed on the LPA website. It is another essential tool for finding a great tenant and qualifying her.

Inspection Failure Report

Sometimes your tenants will fail inspection, whether it is a drive-by or a walk-in review. It can give you an idea of the type of letter to send to your tenants, although you might choose to send it with a more stern warning about what the consequences are by not taking care of these issues—or by letting them occur again. This is an example that can be modified. You can get the form and then modify it at www.buyincomeproperties.com/html/Inspection_Failure_Report. html. Another option is the form from the LPA called the Periodic Inspection Report.

The Landlord Protection

LPA

AGENCY ™

Tenant-Finder™
Pre-Screening Telephone Worksheet

1. Name(s) _____

_____

4. How many adults _____
Why am I asking this? Need to know. All adults go on lease.

6. # of children _____
Why am I asking this? Need to know. Safety reasons.

8. # of Pets _____ 9. What Kind(s) _____
Need to know if a pet agreement is needed. (If you do not accept pets, this interview is over.)

10. Smoking _____
If you do not accept smoking, this interview is over.

12. Reason for moving _____
Need to know. Is tenant being evicted? Problems with landlord?

13. Landlord Reference ? ____
Did present landlord have a good or bad experience?

15. Area Searching In _____
If this rental doesn't work out, you may be able to offer the applicant an alternative.

16. Length of Lease _____
For how long is this applicant willing to commit ?

17. Meets Security Deposit Requirement? _____
Can this applicant afford to move in to your rental ?

18. Was applicant cooperative on this interview ? _____
*The level of cooperation on the first telephone contact is an indication of how cooperative this person will be as **your** tenant.*

2. Phone _____
Why am I asking this? To schedule appointments.

3. Work # _____
Why am I asking this? To schedule appointments.

5. Cell # _____
Why am I asking this? To schedule appointments.

7. Occupancy Date _____
Why am I asking this? To confirm rental availability.

11. # Vehicles _____
Does the property accommodate their parking needs?

14. Credit_____
Anything to hide? Pays bills and rent on time?

M O N E Y 0 2 3

P E O P L E 1 2 3

C R E D I T 0 2 3

T E N A N T 0 2 3

T I M I N G 1 2 3

TOTAL SCORE = _____

Score your Tenant-Finder™ Worksheet to help you evaluate the prospective applicant. Before making an appointment to show your property to an applicant, examine your findings. **The LPA Tenant-Finder™ Prospect Qualifying Chart** will help you determine a more accurate score for each applicant.

The Landlord Protection
LPA ™
AGENCY ™

© 2006 By The Landlord Protection Agency, Inc.

TENANT-FINDER™ PROSPECT?QUALIFYING?CHART

Screening Category	NOT GOOD	AVERAGE	EXCELLENT
MONEY Notes:	**NEVER 0 Points** Does not have the money needed to cover all move in expenses. (First month's rent, security deposit, and/or charges.) Income is not sufficient to pay the rent, utilities, plus the living expenses. Unable to raise a deposit until the previous landlord returns the security deposit.	**2 Points** Income is marginal. Has the deposit, to put down in advance but may have to wait until just before the occupancy date to raise the balance. Negotiates the price by nickel and diming you on defects on the property. Offers to exchange improvement work for rent.	**3 Points** Income easily covers the monthly rent. Giving you the deposit and the first month rent is not an issue. May negotiate or require certain items be fixed, but not worried about making a reasonable investment in the property to make it home.
PEOPLE	**0-1 Point** Excessive # of people. Unacceptable pets. Poor attitude. Uncooperative answering questions. Appearance. Excessive vehicles or truck(s). Smoking. Car is an eyesore.	**2 Points** Seem OK but not volunteering information. # of people at the limit. Their pet worries you. Smoking. Borderline manners & attitude. Makes demands you are uncomfortable with.	**3 Points** Totally cooperative and pleasant. Neat and clean appearance. No smoking. No pets. Respectful.
CREDIT	**0-1 Point** Judgments. Eviction. Bankruptcy. Collection accounts. Not willing to fill out application and allow credit report. Poor credit score.	**2 Points** Some accounts have been late, some small accounts currently late. No bankruptcies. May have a paid judgment. Average credit score.	**3 Points** Well established credit. All accounts current. Low amount of debt. No records of any derogatory credit. High credit score.
TENANT	**NEVER 0 Points** Complains about current landlord. Been in court with landlord(s). Knows all about landlord tenant law. Already complaining and challenging rules. Changes subject to distract you from your screening questions.	**2 Points** Problems in the past, but is open and answers questions truthfully. No real problems. Slightly defensive and on guard. May ask why you are asking these questions, but still cooperative.	**3 Points** Happy to provide references from employer and past landlord(s), or have you look at their current home. Organized people. Former homeowner. Willing to take on responsibilities.
TIMING	**0-1 Point** In a rush. Needs rental before you can deliver. Or: Has no set moving date. Just shopping. May move in the next few months.	**2 Points** Lease date causes loss of ½ - 1 month rent. Early Lease date makes it difficult to do planned work on rental.	**3 Points** Dates work for both parties. Tenant willing to pay for any financial overlaps between rentals.

Evaluate each category as it relates to your prospect and assign a point value. If in doubt, about a point, pick the lower number. Add up the points to get a total score.

- Any score below 9 is not acceptable.
- Prospects scoring in the range of 9 – 11 are the tenants that can occupy most of your property management time.
- The most successful landlords always rent to prospects in the 12 – 15 range.

TOTAL SCORE:

© 2003 THE LANDLORD PROTECTION AGENCY Form PF34

PERIODIC INSPECTION REPORT

TENANT(S)	PREMISES	
MOVE- IN DATE	MOVE-IN PHOTOS Y OR N	MOVE-IN VIDEO Y OR N
MOVE-OUT DATE	MOVE-OUT PHOTOS Y OR N	MOVE-OUT VIDEO Y OR N

The premises are being delivered in clean, sanitary, good operating condition, with no spots, stains, or damages, unless otherwise noted below in the "Move In Condition" box. If indicated above, the condition of the premises has been fully documented, dated, witnessed, and verified on video tape and photographs.

AREA OR ITEM	√ = O.K. LIST CONDITION AND DATE OF INSPECTION

LIVING ROOM, DINING & HALLS
Walls/Ceiling......................................
Floor/Carpet.......................................
Closets/Doors/Locks...........................
Lights/Mirrors.....................................
Window Treatments...........................
Windows/Screens...............................
Fireplace(s)...

KITCHEN
Walls/Ceiling/Floor............................
Countertops/Tile................................
Cabinets/Closets................................
Oven/Stove..
Hood/Fan/Lights................................
Refrigerator.......................................
Dishwasher..
Sink/Faucet/Disposal.........................
Windows/doors/screens....................

BEDROOMS   (Specify BR # 1-4)
Walls/Ceiling.....................................
Floor/Carpet......................................
Lights/Mirrors....................................
Window Treatments..........................
Windows/Screens..............................
Closets/Doors/Shelves.......................

BATHROOMS (Specify # 1-4)
Walls/Ceiling.....................................
Floor..
Cabinets/ Mirrors..............................
Sink(s)...
Tub/Shower.......................................
Tiles/Grout..
Lights/Vent/Fan.................................
Toilets..
Windows/Doors ....
Towel Bars/Accessories.....................

WASHER/DRYER...............................
HEATING/AIR CONDITIONING..........
BALCONY/DECK/PATIO....................
GARAGE(S)/STORAGE......................
GARAGE DOOR(S)............................
PARKING AREA.:...............................
GARDEN/PLANTS/GRASS..............
SMOKE DETECTOR..........................
NUMBER OF KEYS (SETS).............
FENCES/GATES................................

INSPECTION COMMENTS

Tenant acknowledges this report as part of the lease with the Owner for the above premises. Tenant agrees to return the premises in like condition upon termination of tenancy, normal wear and tear excepted.

Tenant Acknowledgement   Date   Tenant Acknowledgement   Date

Property Condition Report

You will want to get more information on the condition report, and here is a link to use at www.thelpa.com/lpa/forms/ef-property.html?mv_pc=1566.

This report is a move-in and move-out checklist that is signed by the tenant upon move-in and that notifies her that the condition has been fully documented. Notify the tenant that this protects her and you—it's mutually beneficial. When you do the move-out checklist, do it alone so you aren't distracted by the tenant or more likely to go easy on her when she should rightfully pay for a repair. To charge a tenant for the items in the charge sheet, you'll also need to be sure you documented it was working to begin with, so this form is important. The form will also help you make calculations for charges.

Settlement Statement

This is a crucial form for the security deposit that allows you to itemize, validate, and explain any deductions from the security deposit. Security deposits are arguably one of the most stressful components of landlording when tenants complain about deductions. Make your tenant aware that his refund, if applicable, of any security deposits will be sent to his forwarding address so there is no reason for him to meet you at the property. If you need to collect keys, you can do so at the property, but inform the tenant ahead of time that the walk-through will be done at a later time and documentation will be sent to him in the mail. To download the complete file and enter your information into it directly, go to www.thelpa.com/lpa/forms.html.

Rent Receipt

The rent receipt should be given or mailed to the tenant each time she pays rent. This is good for your recordkeeping and also gives the tenant a sense of security and fairness. The web page for this is www.thelpa.com/free/rent-receipt.pdf.

CONDITION INSPECTION REPORT

The Landlord Protection LPA AGENCY ™

TENANT(S)	PREMISES	
MOVE- IN DATE	MOVE-IN PHOTOS Y OR N	MOVE-IN VIDEO Y OR N
MOVE-OUT DATE	MOVE-OUT PHOTOS Y OR N	MOVE-OUT VIDEO Y OR N

The premises are being delivered in clean, sanitary, and good operating condition, with no spots, stains or damages, unless otherwise noted below in the "Move In Condition" box. If indicated above, the condition of the premises has been fully documented, dated, witnessed, and verified on video tape and photographs.

AREA OR ITEM	CONDITION AT MOVE IN	CONDITION AFTER MOVE OUT	CHARGES
	√ = O.K.	√ = O.K.	

LIVING ROOM, DINING & HALLS
Walls/Ceiling...........................
Floor/Carpet............................
Closets/Doors/Locks...................
Lights/Mirrors..........................
Window Treatments.....................
Windows/Screens.......................

KITCHEN
Walls/Ceiling/Floor.....................
Countertops/Tile........................
Cabinets/Closets.......................
Oven/Stove.............................
Hood/Fan/Lights........................
Refrigerator............................
Dishwasher.............................
Sink/Faucet/Disposal...................

BEDROOMS (Specify BR # 1-4)
Walls/Ceiling...........................
Floor/Carpet............................
Lights/Mirrors..........................
Window Treatments.....................
Windows/Screens.......................

BATHROOMS (Specify # 1-4)
Walls/Ceiling...........................
Floor...................................
Cabinets/ Mirrors......................
Sink(s).................................
Tub/Shower............................
Tiles/Grout.............................
Lights/Vent/Fan........................
Toilets.................................
Windows/Doors ....
Towel Bars/Accessories................

WASHER/DRYER.......................
HEATING/AIR CONDITIONING..........
BALCONY/DECK/PATIO..................
GARAGE(S)/STORAGE...................
GARAGE DOOR(S)........................
PARKING AREA..........................
GARDEN/PLANTS/GRASS...............
SMOKE DETECTOR.......................
NUMBER OF KEYS (SETS)...............
FENCES/GATES..........................

MOVE IN COMMENTS

Tenant has inspected the above premises prior to occupancy and accepts it with the conditions and/or exceptions noted above. Tenant acknowledges this report as part of the lease with the Owner for the above premises. Tenant agrees to return the premises in like condition upon termination of tenancy, normal wear and tear excepted.

Tenant	Date	Tenant	Date

MOVE OUT COMMENTS

CLEANING & OTHER CHGS	SECURITY SETTLEMENT	FORWARDING ADDRESS & PHONE #
GENERAL $_____ WINDOWS $_____ CARPET $_____ APPLIANCES $_____ GROUNDS $_____ GUTTERS $_____ DEBRIS $_____ PAINTING $_____ REPAIRS $_____ LATE FEES $_____ UNPAID RENT $_____ TOTAL $_____	TOTAL SECURITY DEPOSIT .... $_____ TOTAL CREDITS .... $_____ TOTAL CHARGES .... - $_____ **BALANCE DUE FROM TENANT..** $_____ OR **BALANCE DUE TO TENANT...** $_____	 *NEW PHONE #* REPORT PREPARED BY: DATE:_____

SECURITY SETTLEMENT STATEMENT

Tenant Name(s) _____ DATE _____

Address of Premises _____

Below is a detailed statement concerning your Security Deposit Settlement. Any deductions from your deposit (if any) shall be itemized with a complete explanation.

ADMINISTRATIVE INFORMATION

Rent Paid Through _____   Lease expiration Date _____

Date Notice of Intention to Vacate was Given _____   Actual Move-Out Date _____

Reason for Vacating _____   All Keys Returned? _____

Forwarding Address _____

Has a Move in Condition Report been filed?	Y or N
Has a Move out Condition Report been filed?	Y or N
Have the premises been video taped prior to occupancy?	Y or N
Were the premises video taped after being returned?	Y or N
Photographs In	Y or N
Photographs Out	Y or N

Comments _____

DEPOSITS

Security Deposit $ _____

Pet Deposit _____

Other Deposits _____

TOTAL DEPOSITS $ _____

ADJUSTMENTS TO DEPOSIT

1. Repairs $ _____

2. Cleaning

3. Missing Items

4. Keys

5. Lease Violation

6. Insufficient Notice

7. Unpaid Rent

8. Unpaid Charges

9. Miscellaneous

TOTAL DEDUCTIONS $ _____

SETTLEMENT DUE

☐ Pay to Lessee   ☐ Pay to Management   **BALANCE DUE** $ _____

Paid By Check # _____   Date Paid _____   Approved By: _____

LPA **Rent Receipt**

Date: _____

To: _____ Address: _____

Received from _____ the sum of $_____, as rent for the period of _____ for the premises described above.

Landlord/Agent: _____

Balance Due: $_____

Paid By: Cash   Check   Money Order
(Circle one)

LPA **Rent Receipt**

Date: _____

To: _____ Address: _____

Received from _____ the sum of $_____, as rent for the period of _____ for the premises described above.

Landlord/Agent: _____

Balance Due: $_____

Paid By: Cash   Check   Money Order
(Circle one)

LPA **Rent Receipt**

Date: _____

To: _____ Address: _____

Received from _____ the sum of $_____, as rent for the period of _____ for the premises described above.

Landlord/Agent: _____

Balance Due: $_____

Paid By: Cash   Check   Money Order
(Circle one)

Lease Addendum

Any lease addendum form is where you make additional clauses or add information to the lease. This is given to the tenant at the time of leasing. There can be many types of addendums.

Anytime you make a change to the lease, the lease addendum should be used if the change isn't made in the lease itself. Here is a copy of what one should look like (you can download the file for free at www.thelpa.com/free/lease-addendum.doc).

The Landlord Protection
LPA
AGENCY ™

ADDENDUM

This addendum is made this _____ day of _____, 20____, and is added to and amends that certain agreement by and between _____ as Tenant(s) and _____ as Landlord(s), which agreement is dated _____ day of _____, 20____.

Said agreement is amended as follows:

_____
_____
_____
_____
_____
_____
_____
_____
_____
_____
_____
_____
_____
_____
_____
_____
_____
_____
_____
_____
_____
_____

Signed:

_____   _____

_____   _____

Notice to Vacate or Renew Lease

A notice to renew the lease or vacate is another valuable form. This form generally preserves and extends all previous terms and states any potential new ones. You need to send this at least one to two months before the lease expiration to give the tenant time to supply notice that she will be leaving or signing a new lease. Be sure you send this early enough that your tenant can comply with the lease requirements! About one to two months before the tenant's lease is up you should send the notice to vacate or renew lease form. You might want to include a copy with the initial lease, too. A sample is shown here, but you can download it from the LPA at www.thelpa.com/free/intention-vacate.pdf.

Move-Out Instructions Reminder Letter

You should send a move-out reminder letter about two weeks before a tenant is to vacate. This form should remind him of tasks he must do to get a full security deposit back, including how to secure the property again and how to return the keys. This form is helpful in keeping tenants organized so they know what they need to do and when they need to do it. If you want to provide specifics, you can include a letter telling the tenant to remove all garbage and debris (see the next section) because not doing so will result in some of his security deposit being forfeited for the removal of trash.

If your tenant does want to move out (whether you are choosing for the tenant to leave or the tenant has chosen to break tenancy), you will want to send this letter because it helps ensure a smoother transition with less difficulty from the tenant, and it provides a clear road map on what to do from this point. A sample of the form can be downloaded at www.thelpa.com/free/moveout.pdf.

The form will also help you to show the property to other interested parties or sell the home if you want. It also spells out the cooperation the tenant is expected to provide under the terms of the lease agreement.

www.theLPA.com

YOUR LETTERHEAD
HERE

NOTICE TO VACATE OR RENEW LEASE

Date of notice: _____

TENANT(S):_____

PREMISES: _____

_____

LEASE EXPIRATION DATE: _____

RENT INCREASE: _____

Instructions:
1. **Please indicate if you wish to renew your lease, or if you intend to vacate by the expiration of your current lease by circling either "renew" or "vacate".**
2. **Be sure to sign and date this notice.**
3. **Return this completed notice to your landlord or his agent in the envelope provided by _____ so that we may process your request .**

Please circle whether you wish to re-new or vacate

RENEW LEASE   **or**   **VACATE**

Notice to Owner, _____,
I agree to renew our lease for a term of _____ at the rent of $_____
beginning _____ and ending on _____. I understand that the terms,
rights, and conditions in our original lease will still apply as agreed.

or

I intend to vacate the premises on _____, leaving the property in good condition as agreed
in my lease, no later than the expiration of the term of our lease.

_____   Date:_____
Tenant's signature

_____   Date:_____
Tenant's signature

LETTER TO TENANT
MOVE-OUT REMINDER

Dear Tenant,

Thank you for giving us advanced notice that you are moving. Now that you are moving out, your lease/rental agreement requires that you leave your unit in a clean and undamaged condition. We have every intention of returning all of your security as long as you have fulfilled your agreement with us.

Specifically, you should:

- **Cooperate with the showing of the residence for sale or re-rental, keeping it in presentable condition.**

- **Begin to put out all unwanted items for trash or special pick-up. (Avoid piles of debris in front of your home on moving day.)**

- **Remove <u>all</u> food, debris, and other personal belongings.**

- **Clean (and defrost if necessary) refrigerator.**

- **Clean stovetop, oven, and any other appliances.**

- **Replace any burned out light bulbs.**

- **Clean all floors and/or carpeting.**

- **Be sure grounds and lawn are trim and clean, free of weeds, leaves, etc.**

- **Report any and all damage in writing.**

- **Upon leaving, please be sure to fully secure the rental by locking all windows and doors. The designated place to leave all keys to your unit is _____.**

After you have vacated the rental, it will be inspected and re-video taped for compliance with your lease/rental agreement and the expense of cleaning or repairing damage, if any, will be charged against your security deposit. You will be notified of any charges. Good luck in your new home.

Sincerely,

Move-Out, Clean-Up, and Debris Letter

The move-out, clean-up, and debris letter informs the tenant of her responsibility to not leave trash or other debris behind and states that not doing so will result in the costs of removing such trash being deducted from her deposit. This usually causes the tenant to think about move-out day and cleaning out trash herself, saving you a lot of time and headache in rerenting or selling the home. Take a look at www.thelpa.com/free/debris.pdf to see this form.

Your
Letterhead
Here

Clean-up and Large Item Removal Reminder

Date: _____

Dear _____,

     Now that you have given us notice of your Intention to Vacate, you will be in the process of packing your belongings. Please use this time before vacating to discard any of your personal property that you will not be taking with you. Large items may require special arrangements for their removal, such as scheduling "Special Pick Up" from the Department of Sanitation, etc.

     Please keep in mind that these arrangements need to be made as soon as possible to avoid leaving the premises with accumulations of materials and debris.

     In the event that you vacate, abandoning personal property or junk on the premises or in front of the property, you may be held responsible for the cost of removal for those materials. It is our intention to have a clean livable rental inside and out, to present to the new tenants on their move-in day.

     We know how difficult it can be to be moving, so please accept our best wishes and thanks for all your cooperation.

Sincerely,

Manager

Move-In Information Sheet and Phone Numbers

Providing the following information sheet with phone numbers for your new tenants is a nice touch to beginning their tenancy on a positive note. Here is a sample form for you to fill out from LPA (downloadable at www.thelpa.com/free/movein.pdf).

The Landlord Protection Agency
LPA
AGENCY ™

Your
Letterhead
Here

Important Information for New Residence

Welcome! We wish you health and happiness in your new home. Listed below please find helpful information relating to your new residence.

Management	_____	Oil Co.	_____
Police	_____	Water Co.	_____
Ambulance	_____	Telephone	_____
Fire Dept.	_____	Cable TV	_____
Electric Co.	_____	Landscaper	_____
Gas Co.	_____	Sanitation Dept.	_____

Other Helpful Numbers

Plumber	_____	Sewer/Cesspool	_____
Carpet Cleaner	_____	Cleaning Service	_____

Household Safety Information

Location of fire extinguisher(s) _____

Location of Smoke Detector(s) _____

Location of Circuit Breaker Panel _____

Location of Water Shut Off Valve _____

Location of Oil Tank _____

Days of Garbage Pick-up _____

Days of Recycle _____

Painting Instruction

In most cases you should not allow your tenants to paint! However, some tenants do want to paint, particularly if they intend to live in the home for awhile or have signed a long lease. If you allow them to do so, here is a painting instruction sheet you should provide at the time of lease or rental signing. They will need to submit this to you for approval, listing the rooms they intend to paint. Take a look at www.thelpa.com/free/paint.pdf.

Rental Increase Reminder

A rental increase letter is a form you send to the tenant about any rent increases. Remind him that the increase is either already agreed to or that the rent will be increasing. Then, he can either choose to leave or choose to renew, using the appropriate form for renewing or vacating mentioned previously.

Sometimes you will want to increase rent—whether annually in smaller increments or in larger increments because you don't want a tenant living there any longer. Here is a rental increase reminder you should send several weeks before the increase to remind the tenant of the increase. Again, at the very least keep track of the dates and times these are sent; better yet, send them via return receipt requested or by some traceable method. The early payment discounts note is included in the rent increase reminder. Only use this if you intend to offer this moving forward (along with a letter of explanation) or have offered it in the past and want to continue doing so. Check out this link for the full file: www.thelpa. com/free/increase-reminder.doc.

PAINTING INSTRUCTIONS

Steps to follow:

Materials for Job:

Paint (latex is recommended), brushes *(1 ½ - 2" for trim and 3 " on flat surfaces like walls and doors)*, rollers, the correct roller pads, masking tape, moist rag, drop cloths, spackle, putty knife, screw drivers, extension pole for roller, roller pan, caulking gun ,caulking.

PREPARATION

Clear the room or area to be painted.
Lay down drop clothes, overlap and secure them with duct tape if possible. Remove all hooks & nails.
Clean all walls & ceilings. Wipe them down of any substances, such as tape, stickers, cobwebs, dust, etc.
Patch holes with spackle. Allow to dry. Sand if necessary.

Remove all light switch and outlet plates, light fixtures if possible, etc. so they do not accidentally get painted. Cover light switches and outlets with masking tape.

Caulk gaps.

List Rooms to be painted

Living room, Dining room, kitchen,
Stairwell to basement, Hallways, Bathrooms
_____
_____
_____

PAINTING

1.Pour paint into about half the roller pan.

2. Use 2" brush to paint all corners and areas around window and door trim.

3. Use roller to paint ceiling first and then wall surfaces. Make sure you use enough paint, but don't overload your roller so much that it will drip. Also, don't roll out your roller so much that it pull the wet paint off the wall again. Frequently reload your roller with the right amount of paint. Use extension pole whenever possible. You can make longer, smoother strokes using the roller extension pole.

- Have your damp rag ready to wipe any mistakes or drips.
- Apply paint as evenly as you can.
- Apply second coat if necessary by repeating the steps of painting.

Clean brushes before changing paint if using semi-gloss or gloss paint on trim and doors. When painting doors, remove doorknobs and lock hardware to avoid painting whenever possible.

CLEAN-UP

Wash rollers and paint brushes in water. Roller pads should be removed from the rollers. Squeeze and work the nap and brush bristles in the water and then wash thoroughly with soap and rinse well. Clean out the roller and roller pan too, along with any other equipment that may have gotten paint on it.

Fold up drop cloths, take them outside and shake them out. Fold them up neatly for the next time they'll be needed.

Replace all light switch and outlet plates, doorknobs, etc.

Any questions, please call your landlord or property manager.

Thank you,
The Management

http://www.thelpa.com/lpa/index.html

Your
Letterhead
Here

ANNUAL RENT INCREASE REMINDER

Date: _____

Dear _____,

Address:_____

_____

Your rent is due to increase as agreed in your lease. As of _____ your new rent amount will be $_____ per month. Early payment discounts as agreed will remain in effect.

The Oil Adjustment Verification

This form shows a measured reading of fuel so you can charge the new tenant for any oil she uses. In some states where heating oil is used, the landlord pays, but bills the tenant. The file can be found at www.thelpa.com/free/oil.pdf.

Your
Letterhead
Here

OIL ADJUSTMENT STATEMENT

DATE: _____

PREMISES: _____
_____

FUEL OIL ADJUSTMENT
The fuel tank on the premises as of _____ contains _____ gallons of oil. A fuel adjustment in the amount of _____ must be paid by Tenant prior to Tenant's occupancy.

Check one: Owner ☐ will ☐ will not be responsible to reimburse tenants for fuel upon vacating.

_____
Manager

Waterbed Addendum

Although it might sound silly, waterbeds can be a source of problems in homes. If they leak, they can cause major damage to the home! Some landlords refuse to allow them, but you can use this form if it's okay with you that the tenant has a waterbed. Download the file at www.thelpa.com/free/waterbed.doc.

WATERBED ADDENDUM

This addendum is made this _____ day of _____, 20_____, and is added to and amends that certain agreement by and between _____ as Tenant(s) and _____as Landlord(s), which agreement is dated _____ day of _____, 20_____.

It is the tenant's intention to keep a waterbed in the residence named in the attached Lease/Rental Agreement. This shall be a conditional privilege granted to the tenant in exchange for guaranteeing that the rules in this waterbed addendum are strictly followed. The Owner/Agent reserves the right to revoke this privilege if the tenant violates any of the agreements herein.

The permission is granted to keep a waterbed under the following terms and conditions:

1) Tenant agrees to keep a waterbed located on the _____ floor of the dwelling.

2) Tenant agrees to be responsible for any defects or damages concerning the premises in relation to the waterbed during or as a result of having the waterbed in the dwelling.

3) Tenant agrees to obtain liability insurance to include coverage concerning the waterbed.

4) Tenant agrees to post $_____additional security deposit which will be returned after tenant vacates, providing the premises are returned as agreed.

5) In the event the Tenant gets rid of the waterbed, it is agreed that it will not be replaced with another waterbed without the owner/agent's expressed written permission. It is also agreed that removal will be done in a proper professional manner, not to cause any hardship on the dwelling or landlord.

Owner/Agent_____   Tenant_____ Date_____

Tenant_____ Date_____

Tenant Recommendation Letter

If you have had an outstanding tenant and want to recommend this tenant to others without fielding phone calls five years down the road, consider offering this form to tenants. Letting tenants know that paying rent and leaving the home in the condition it was rented in will result in one of these letters can sometimes encourage renters to do the right thing, too. You can download the file at www.thelpa.com/free/recommendation.pdf.

The Landlord Protection Agency™ — LPA

```
Your
Letterhead
Here
```

Attention: _____
Date: _____

Tenant Recommendation Letter

To whom it may concern,

   Let it be known that _____ has been a tenant in our rental unit located at _____ from _____ to _____. The rent was $_____ per month and has always been paid promptly. This tenant has proven to be an upstanding individual.

Sincerely,

Manager

_____
_____
_____
_____

www.theLPA.com

Security Deposit Refund Receipt

If you return any portion of a security deposit to a tenant, be sure to give him this receipt and ask him to sign. This will help if the tenant makes any disputes later. You can even ask him to take this letter along with the itemized list of charges to his own counsel, which often stops unruly tenants from continuing to pester you about damages they caused to the property. Check out the entire file at www. thelpa.com/free/security-receipt.doc.

| Your |
| Letterhead |
| Here |

SECURITY DEPOSIT SETTLEMENT REFUND RECEIPT & RELEASE FORM

I hereby accept _____ as my security deposit refund in full from my

rental of

_____.

I have no further claims whatsoever in regard to my rental of this property.

Tenant: _____

Tenant: _____

Key Receipt

This is used when the tenant returns keys to you. This is also an indication of a transfer of tenancy. The file is downloadable at www.thelpa.com/free/key.pdf.

KEY RECEIPT

I have vacated my residence at _____. This key receipt is my acknowledgement that I have returned the keys and possession of the premises. I understand I shall no longer have access to my former residence.

Date: _____

Keys received by: _____

Tenant: _____

Lease Cosigner Agreement

The lease cosigner agreement might be required if the tenant's references or credit is not satisfactory to you. If you feel there are no better alternatives, you can hold an additional party responsible for the tenant's performance on the rental. To do this, you should fully check out and credit-qualify the cosigner as though she is a full applicant—after all, this is the person securing the lease for you! Download the full file at www.thelpa.com/free/cosigners.pdf.

CO-SIGNER AGREEMENT
(ADDENDUM TO LEASE / RENTAL AGREEMENT)

This agreement is attached to and forms a part of the Rental Agreement dated _____ between
_____as Owner/Agent and

_____as Tenant.

I/We, the co-signers_____, residing at

_____ _____ have

completed a Rental Application for the express purpose of enabling the Owners to check my credit. I have read the Rental

Agreement, and I promise to guarantee the Tenants' compliance with the financial obligations of this Agreement. I

understand that I may be required to pay for rent, cleaning charges, or damage assessments. I/We agree to comply with and

uphold all of the terms of the lease agreement.

I also understand that this Co-Signer Agreement will remain in force throughout the entire term of the tenant's tenancy, even

if their tenancy is extended and/or changed in its terms.

Co-Signer :_____

Social Security #: _____

Co-Signer: _____

Social Security #: _____

Accepted by Owner/Manager_____

Work Order Form

Another important form is the work order form. Although I have preferred that tenants fill these out on a website so the forms are then sent to me via email, you can choose to have the tenant fill out a form and mail or fax it to you. One important reason for this is that tenants sometimes will be upset when a handyman (or you, if you're doing your own maintenance) comes onto the property for a repair. This is a nice reminder that the tenant asked for the repair to be done. It also shows a history that you properly attended to tenant requests and are providing a property with excellent living conditions.

This is a form that many professional management companies use when they perform repairs on either occupied or unoccupied rentals. When it is an occupied rental, it is preferred that you have the tenant sign the work order to acknowledge work is being done and to document work that is agreed to when you hire a handyman or other expert to work on the rentals. Download the file at www.thelpa.com/free/work.doc.

Appliance Agreement

The appliance agreement form should be given along with the lease to indicate which appliances are and are not included. You can state it in the lease, but in cases where there are extra appliances you may wish to use a separate form. Examples include additional refrigerators, dual ovens, and so on.

MAINTENANCE REQUEST & WORK ORDER

UNIT: _____   DATE: _____

WORK REQUESTED (JOB DESCRIPTION):

_____
_____
_____
_____
_____
_____
_____
_____

CHARGE TO: (CIRCLE ONE)   TENANT   OWNER   MANAGEMENT

ASSIGNED TO: _____

WORK COMPLETED:

_____
_____
_____
_____
_____
_____

DATE COMPLETED: _____

APPROVED BY: _____

IF INCOMPLETE, EXPLAIN:

_____
_____
_____

APPLIANCE AGREEMENT

Premises: _____

This Appliance Agreement addendum is made this _____ day of _____,
20_____, and is added to and amends that certain agreement by and between
_____ as Tenant(s) and
_____ as Landlord(s), which
agreement is dated _____ day of _____, 20____.

The dwelling may contain various appliances, such as:
(Included = ? or New)

# INCLUDED		# INCUDED	
Stove	_____	Washer	_____
Refrigerator	_____	Dryer	_____
Dishwasher	_____	Air Conditioner	_____
Wall Oven	_____	Pool Filter	_____
Microwave	_____	Auto Garage Door Opener	_____
Garbage disposal	_____	Trash Compactor	_____
Dehumidifier	_____	Ceiling Fan	_____

These appliances are not included in the rent, but the use of them may be allowed for the tenant's
convenience only. If Tenant wishes to use these appliances, Tenant shall assume responsibility
for care, repairs, and maintenance. If appliances are equipped with manuals and/or warrantee
papers, Tenant shall not lose or discard these documents, and will be responsible for their return.

If Tenant does not agree to be responsible for the appliances, but rather use his own, he may
request that Owner's appliances be removed from the premises. All washer/dryer installations must
be approved and authorized by Owner in writing. Tenant agrees to replace all water supply hoses
to washing machine that show any signs of wear every year. Tenant also agrees to turn off water
supply to washing machine when it is not in use.

The parties have entered into this Agreement on the date first above stated, and acknowledge
receipt of a copy hereof.

LANDLORD: TENANT:

_____   _____

_____   _____

No Smoking

If you require your tenants to not smoke, use this form. The effects of smoking can be extremely expensive to clean and nearly impossible to get out of the home. It also devalues the property—who wants to move into a house that smells like an ashtray? When you do property checks, do a sniff check, too.

PF 54 No Smoking Notice

© 2007 By The Landlord Protection Agency, Inc.

The Landlord Protection
LPA
AGENCY ™

No Smoking Notice & Reminder

To _____   Date

_____

Address

_____

_____

In the event your lease agreement does not contain a No Smoking clause, this notice informs you that the terms under which you occupy the above described premises are to be changed to include the following:

Lease Agreement   *(Please check all that apply)*

_____ Smoking **is not** allowed in the rental unit.
_____ Smoking **is not** allowed anywhere on the rental property.

PLEASE DO NOT SMOKE IN OUR RENTAL PROPERTY.
Tenant agrees not to smoke on the rental premises and further agrees not to allow visitors or guests to smoke in the above described premises.

Violation of Agreement   Violation of any of the provisions in your No Smoking clause shall constitute a material default of the terms of the Lease Agreement and subject to the remedies and/or penalties concerning lease violations stated in the Lease Agreement. Tenant is responsible for the payment of all charges resulting from a smoking violation including, but not limited to smoke damage or the removal of smoke residue including painting, cleaning, carpet replacement.

Please contact your Manager _____ if you can not comply with this notice or your lease agreement.

Your continued occupancy of the premises after _____, **shall constitute full agreement** with all of the above in addition to and as part of your lease. (Please keep this notice with your lease document.)

Owner/Agent_____ Date_____

Want to get a great deal at the LPA? Readers of this book get a special discount at the LPA! You can access its website directly at www.thelpa.com/lpa/member-1.html or through my website at www.drdaniellebabb.com. Use coupon code REBOOK08 for a great deal!

Resources

In this appendix, you will find lots of useful tools, sites, and other options to manage your property. This is a compilation of resources I use to manage my own homes, and those that come highly recommended by trusted experts.

www.thelpa.com   The Landlord Protection Agency can help you screen tenants, run background checks, and get all the electronic forms you need to protect yourself and your home.

www.craigslist.com   Craig's List is a national site where a lot of people look for rooms for rent and homes for rent and post listings of roommates or rentals wanted.

www.thelpa.com/lpa/ntr_index.html   The National Tenant Register allows you to register tenants wanted in ads.

www.rent-o-meter.com   You can check out what others are paying with rental comparatives for free!

www.zillow.com   At Zillow, you can get comparative analyses for sale prices and post listings!

Earth.google.com   Google Earth allows you to take a look at your properties using satellite imaging.

www.hud.gov   Check out the Housing and Urban Development website to review rules and regulations regarding renting your property.

www.domania.com   Domania allows you to look for homes for sale and to do sales comparative analyses.

www.thelpa.com/lpa/lllaw.html   Landlord tenant laws vary by state and locale. Be sure to check this site to find out what you can charge in deposits, how evictions work, and more!

www.epa.gov   The Environmental Protection Agency site allows you to find out the rules and regulations where you are renting your home; you can search by state.

www.firstgov.gov   FirstGov is the U.S. government's official portal for most agencies or offices managed by the government.

www.epa.gov/lawsregs/index.html   Check out the EPA's regulations for your specific area, and find out how the EPA creates the laws and rules we all have to live by.

www.meganslaw.com   You can use the Megan's Law Sex Offender Registry List to know who you are renting to.

www.thelpa.com/lpa/carbon_monoxide.html   This site lists carbon-monoxide laws and information.

www.thelpa.com/lpa/forms/state-lease   Determine which specific clauses your leases can, cannot, or must contain, with lease agreements organized by the state!

www.clearscreening.com/index.php?refid=10009   Screen your tenants before you let them in.

www.thelpa.com/lpa/credit-reports-tvs.html   Verify your tenants and know who they are.

Index

M

N

O

P–Q

U

V

W-X-Y-Z